South Korea's Middle Power Diplomacy in the Middle East

This book examines the theoretical and empirical approaches to the study of middle powers with reference to South Korea's bilateral relations with Iran, Saudi Arabia, the UAE, and Iraq.

It maps the development, political, and diplomatic trajectories between South Korea and Iran, Saudi Arabia, the UAE, and Iraq against the historical backdrop of ROK–U.S. alliance and the rise of China. Jeong provides a nuanced analysis of the intersectionality of political economy and foreign policy analysis contextualizing the state-building processes in ROK and the Middle Eastern countries.

This accessible book is intended for students and scholars in area studies and international affairs, career diplomats, and South Korean businesses in the Middle East. It should also prove of practical value for journalists and policy makers who are interested in studying the nexus of domestic, regional, and international factors that have configured South Korea's Middle East policy.

Hae Won Jeong is Assistant Professor at Abu Dhabi University. She specializes in international politics of the Middle East and has published on Gulf–Asia relations, foreign policy, and public diplomacy of the Middle East and nation-building in the Gulf.

Changing Dynamics in Asia-Middle East Relations
Series editor: Jonathan Fulton

A number of political and economic initiatives in recent years underscore the surge in relations across Eurasia and the Indian Ocean region. The USA's Indo-Pacific strategy, China's Belt and Road Initiative, India's Look East and Look West strategies, and several less formal but no less important state-to-state relationships all indicate that ties across Eurasia are growing. Economic relations between Persian Gulf states and various Asian energy markets have diversified to the point that trade, investment and finance are complemented with diplomatic and security cooperation. Soft power initiatives are building relations across non-elite levels, creating familiarity in language, culture, and religion. At the same time, increased interactions present potential for tensions as competition between Asian states plays out in the Middle East, and Middle Eastern rivalries affect the trajectory of Asian states' regional involvement.

This series publishes monographs and edited collections on the political, economic, strategic, and diplomatic interactions between Middle East and Asian states. Contributions from a diverse range of perspectives and all regions are welcome on International Relations, International Political Economy, Foreign Policy and issue-specific topics such as security cooperation, politics of sport, politics of religion, energy politics, Belt and Road Initiative and Eurasian development.

For more information, please visit the series webpage:

South Korea's Middle Power Diplomacy in the Middle East
Development, Political and Diplomatic Trajectories
Hae Won Jeong

South Korea's Middle Power Diplomacy in the Middle East

Development, Political and Diplomatic Trajectories

Hae Won Jeong

LONDON AND NEW YORK

First published 2022
by Routledge
2 Park Square, Milton Park, Abingdon, Oxon OX14 4RN

and by Routledge
605 Third Avenue, New York, NY 10158

Routledge is an imprint of the Taylor & Francis Group, an informa business

© 2022 Hae Won Jeong

The right of Hae Won Jeong to be identified as author of this work has been asserted in accordance with sections 77 and 78 of the Copyright, Designs and Patents Act 1988.

All rights reserved. No part of this book may be reprinted or reproduced or utilised in any form or by any electronic, mechanical, or other means, now known or hereafter invented, including photocopying and recording, or in any information storage or retrieval system, without permission in writing from the publishers.

Trademark notice: Product or corporate names may be trademarks or registered trademarks, and are used only for identification and explanation without intent to infringe.

British Library Cataloguing-in-Publication Data
A catalogue record for this book is available from the British Library

Library of Congress Cataloging-in-Publication Data
Names: Jeong, Hae Won, author. Title: South Korea's middle power diplomacy in the Middle East: development, political and diplomatic trajectories / Hae Won Jeong.
Description: Abingdon, Oxon; New York, NY: Routledge, 2022. |
Series: Changing dynamics in Asia-Middle East relations |
Includes bibliographical references and index.
Identifiers: LCCN 2021043921 (print) | LCCN 2021043922 (ebook) |
ISBN 9780367551315 (hardback) | ISBN 9780367551322 (paperback) |
ISBN 9781003092100 (ebook)
Subjects: LCSH: Korea (South)–Foreign relations–2002– |
Korea (South)–Foreign relations–Middle East. |
Middle East–Foreign relations–Korea (South) | Middle powers.
Classification: LCC DS923.27.J46 2022 (print) |
LCC DS923.27 (ebook) | DDC 327.519505609/05–dc23/eng/20211013
LC record available at https://lccn.loc.gov/2021043921
LC ebook record available at https://lccn.loc.gov/2021043922

ISBN: 978-0-367-55131-5 (hbk)
ISBN: 978-0-367-55132-2 (pbk)
ISBN: 978-1-003-09210-0 (ebk)

DOI: 10.4324/9781003092100

Typeset in Times New Roman
by Newgen Publishing UK

To Abba

Contents

Acknowledgments viii

1 State-building processes in South Korea and the Middle East 1

2 From Tehran boulevard to post-JCPOA Iran 26

3 Oil, business diplomacy and Saudi–Korea Vision 2030 63

4 Nuclear energy and security cooperation with the UAE 104

5 Business and security implications after the Gulf wars and post-ISIS Iraq 137

6 Conclusion 175

Index 193

Acknowledgments

I am grateful for the past and present encounters I had with Korean expatriate communities in the Gulf and the inspiration they gave me in writing different sections of this book.

I have had the privilege of gaining exposure to the Middle East since my teenage years through my dedicated parents, Jae Seop Jeong and Jin Kyoung Son. This book would not have been completed without their moral and spiritual support.

I would like to thank the librarians in Abu Dhabi and Seoul for their kind assistance in helping access electronic and archival sources and print sources both remotely and physically during the pandemic.

I would also like to take this opportunity to express my gratitude to the two anonymous reviewers for their constructive feedback on the manuscript and the editorial team and staff at Routledge for their assistance in various stages of this project.

1 State-building processes in South Korea and the Middle East

South Korea's foreign policy priorities since the Cold War

The importance of American alliance in South Korea's Middle East policy is conspicuous in the historical legacies of the Cold War. The partition of the Korean Peninsula emerged as a direct result of the Soviet Union and the U.S. dividing it into two spheres of influence after the WWII. The U.S. proposed the 38th parallel as the line of demarcation between the two Koreas in August 1945 while Imperial Japan was defeated in August 1945. Korea was placed in the four-power United Nations (UN) trusteeship which was presided over by the U.S., Britain, Soviet Union, and China. After the U.S.–USSR Joint Commission was adjourned twice from March to October 1946, Korea's future status was entrusted to the UN, and the UN Temporary Commission on Korea held elections in South Korea, in February 1948. Six months later, Rhee Syngman became the founding president of Republic of Korea (ROK) on August 15, 1948, and subsequently, North Korea was established a month later on September 9 headed by premier Kim Il-sung.[1]

After the Korean War ended in July 1953, the post-Korean War security alignment and the subsequent Cold War competition with North Korea, a communist bloc, set the tone for ROK's foreign policy imperatives in the Middle East from the 1960s to 1970s. ROK's diplomatic relations with the Middle East were largely dictated by Cold War divisions in the Middle East, as South Korea supported the U.S. allies in the region. Turkey was the first country in the Middle East and North Africa (MENA) region to establish diplomatic relations with South Korea in the 1950s; the Turkish Brigade served in the Korean War with the UN coalition led by the U.S. In the next decade, South Korea established diplomatic relations with Iran, Israel, Jordan, Oman, Saudi Arabia, and Tunisia, whereas Pyongyang has had formal diplomatic ties with Egypt, Iraq, Sudan, Syria, North Yemen, and South Yemen during the same decade. In the 1970s and 1980s, South Korea expanded its diplomatic relations with Sudan and the remaining GCC states, namely Bahrain, Qatar, Kuwait, and the UAE, followed by Lebanon and Libya in the following decade.[2]

DOI: 10.4324/9781003092100-1

2 *State-building processes*

Among the MENA countries, Egypt, Iran, Jordan, Tunisia, Sudan, and Kuwait had diplomatic ties with both Koreas. Under Gamal Abdel Nasser, Egypt's relationship with the U.S. was fraught with tensions as the latter later refused to fund the construction of the Aswan High Dam. Nasser's Egypt also antagonized the U.S. by receiving military and economic aid from the Soviet Union. North Korea was on friendly terms with Egypt and gave political support in nationalizing the Suez Canal and showed political affinity as a founding member of the non-aligned movement (NAM). ROK opened a Consulate General in Cairo in 1962 but official bilateral relations were only established in 1995. While Iran (under the Shah), Jordan, and Tunisia were U.S. allies in the Cold War region, these countries also opened diplomatic ties with North Korea based on military and economic interests. Iran's relations with North Korea were mainly based on arms trade and military aid as were the case with Libya. While North Korea and Iran have collaborated in ballistic missile development and there were conventional arms and Scud missile sales during the Iran–Iraq War, there is no clear evidence to suggest that there is nuclear cooperation between the two countries.[3]

Although Jordan and Kuwait hosted the North Korean Embassy in the past, they cut ties with North Korea between 2017 and 2018 in response to the pressure by the Trump administration to isolate North Korea following the launch of an intercontinental ballistic missile test. In 2018, the Jordanian authorities commented that the bilateral ties with Pyongyang were "never very strong" and that their decision was "aligned with the policies of their [Jordan's] allies."[4] As a traditional U.S. ally and a recipient of the U.S. economic and military aid since the 1950s, Jordan's diplomatic ties with North Korea were also terminated on the aforementioned grounds in February 2018. The Gulf states, including Kuwait, the UAE, and Qatar, also downgraded their diplomatic ties with Pyongyang between September and October 2017 for the identical reasons cited earlier. As of 2017, there is an estimate of between 1,000 and 3,000 North Koreans in the Gulf countries,[5] and the North Korean laborers and companies in these countries have been supplying hard currency for the North Korean regime. Very little is known about Sudan's relations with Pyongyang. However, by June 2018, Sudan admitted that it has had military and security ties with North Korea and expressed its intention to cut all defense ties with North Korea. As a country that was embroiled in decades of civil war and listed on the U.S. state sponsors of terrorism list since 1993,[6] Sudan has been barred from engaging in arms trade and receiving economic aid from the U.S. and as a result continues to reel from an economic crisis. North Korea entered into a diplomatic relationship with South Sudan soon after its independence in November 2011.

Since the post-Cold War era, ideological competition with North Korea no longer dictates South Korea's foreign policy decisions in the Middle East. Instead, South Korea's Middle East policy has intersected with its strategic imperatives, namely the North Korean issue and economic and energy security. Given these ramifications, as this book argues, South

Korea's Middle East policy is closely intertwined with U.S. foreign policy in the Middle East.

The Korean War armistice agreement signed on July 27, 1953 that seemingly brought peace and stability to ROK for over 65 years is precarious as no peace treaty was officially signed. Cold War legacies have configured the Asia-Pacific (APAC) regional security theater with China recurrently being pitted against the U.S. and their allies in political disputes in the APAC. The proposition of declining U.S. influence gained momentum with Barack Obama's strategy of retrenchment and accelerated under the Trump administration's conservative foreign policy outlook. This is further exemplified by the U.S. troops drawdown and withdrawal from Afghanistan, Syria, and Iraq since the Obama administration. The U.S. spent nearly $6 tn while involved in futile wars in Afghanistan, Iraq, Syria, Libya, and Somalia.[7] According to Brown University's Costs of War project, the U.S. allies have borne significant human and budgetary costs in the post-9/11 wars measured in terms of the number of troops, military spending, and human fatalities in Iraq and Afghanistan. South Korea supplied the third-largest troops in the 2003 Iraq War after the U.S. and Britain and was the sixth country with the highest number of casualties.[8] Despite the increasing pressures by the U.S. for South Korea to raise its defense burden sharing since the 1970s, the strategic importance of the U.S. military presence on the Korean Peninsula cannot be overlooked.[9] This is particularly true considering that the U.S. as a global hegemon has maintained over 60 years of security alliance with ROK as well as Japan, NATO member states, and Australia under the nuclear umbrella in a form of security guarantee to non-NWS.

The importance of the ROK–U.S. alliance cannot be understated considering that should the U.S. hegemonic influence diminish further in the foreseeable future, this would also have a direct impact on the Middle East security policy of the East Asian allies. As it is argued throughout this book, geopolitics in the APAC and ROK's corollary status as a longstanding U.S. ally have been pivotal for understanding the trajectory of South Korea's foreign policy. This is illustrated through the symbolic significance attached to the joint ROK–U.S. military exercises that have provoked North Korea, including the naval exercise after the ROKS Cheonan Sinking in March 2010. Despite falling short of expectations for any major breakthroughs, the 2018 Singapore Summit and the 2019 Hanoi Summit also illustrate the significance of the U.S. role in diplomatically engaging North Korea. A combination of factors, including political and ideological legacies of the Cold War, the shifting U.S. foreign policy trajectories toward Asia and the Middle East are factored into the analysis of this book.

The shifts in political and geopolitical landscapes have been more acute and salient since Barack Obama's foreign policy legacy of pivot to Asia. The rebalancing act of America's foreign policy from the Middle East to Asia was borne out of geostrategic calculations and the economic significance accorded to Asia. However, as a result of this, the critics contend that U.S. retrenchment from the Middle East and Europe has exacerbated security tensions elsewhere by creating a security vacuum all the while reallocating military resources to Asia have produced the reverse of the desired effect, which is forging closer political and economic partnerships and bringing stability and prosperity to the APAC region.[10]

The Trump administration had effectively rolled back on Obama's policies through America First policy and maximum pressure campaign, which undermined the confidence of U.S. allies. In addition, Trump administration's defense cuts and security vacuum in the Middle East, Asia, and Europe have raised the concern that the decision would endanger its allies and undercut counterterrorism efforts in the Middle East all the while increasing the prospect for an empowered China in Northeast Asia. Despite launching the Terrorist Financing Targeting Center and the Global Center for Combating Extremist Ideology following the 2017 Riyadh Summit, the launch of the Arab NATO had failed, and the U.S. has been unable to contain Iran's regional ambitions through Trump's maximum pressure campaign.[11] As discussed in this book, the institutional challenges stemming from the absence of a long-term vision and coherence in U.S. foreign policy have posed economic and geopolitical challenges to U.S. allies in the APAC, Euro-Atlantic, and the Middle East regions. The future trajectory of South Korea's Middle East security policy is largely contingent upon the final outcome of Iran nuclear talks and the Biden administration's determination to mend fences and reinvigorate security cooperation with its allies and reinstate multilateralism.

The miracle on the Han River and the emergence of East Asian newly industrialized countries (NICs)

South Korea's economic industrialization and institutional capacity are key factors that have undergirded the country's bilateral relations with the Middle East.[12] Economic competitiveness is a major determinant that accounts for how South Korea was lifted from decades of poverty and colonial rule. Economic development is closely integrated into South Korea's state-building process. A phenomenon known as "the Miracle on the Han River" refers to South Korea's rapid economic growth in the post-Korean War period. The East Asian late industrializers are clustered as NICs and the which includes Hong Kong, Singapore, South Korea, and Taiwan. The South Korean developmental model, which is in parallel with the Japanese developmental model, underscores the role of the state bureaucracy for driving the industrialization process.

Analogous to "Miracle on the Han River," the "Japanese miracle" that emerged in the post-war economy Japan (post-1962) is documented in Chalmers Johnson's seminal work on the Japanese Ministry of International Trade and Industry (MITI) (present-day Ministry of Economy, Trade and Industry, METI). According to Johnson, Japanese miracle defied the odds of a late development, deficiency of natural resources, large population, and international balance of payments deficits; instead, it is characterized by a rise in demands, high productivity, good industrialization relations, and a high savings rate.[13] While Johnson advises against blindly emulating the Japanese model in other contexts, he makes a distinction between a developmental economy and a regulatory economy and suggests that the former should precede the latter.[14] This also explains the "Japanese miracle" as it represents the developmental state (DS), a state-led industrialization model which is centered on the relationship between the state bureaucracy and privately owned businesses.

The DS (otherwise referred to as capitalist DS), as alluded to above, is an alternative developmental pathway to a regulatory state (i.e. "liberalism") and a socialist state and is midway between the two extremes modes of development. On the one hand, regulatory state espouses neoliberalism as a normative practice since the early 1990s. It calls for maximum global economic integration and recognizes the state as a facilitator for privatization and ushering in the market economy. On the other hand, a socialist state is rooted in the economic practices of the former Soviet Union during the Cold War and is extricated from neoliberalism and market-oriented industrialization. As an alternative developmental paradigm to both extremes, the DS approach posits that the state assumes a gatekeeper role for promoting and preserving economic nationalism.

The process of industrialization is then necessarily *political* as the institutional practices and decision-making are inextricably tied to economic growth. As is the case with neopatrimonial and clientelistic states in Asia and Africa, the politics of economic development in these continents is then shaped by a marginalized private sector, blurred public and private domains, authoritarianism, and economic nationalism. In elucidating the features of the DS, Linda Weiss identifies three cross-cutting features in East Asian DS, which loosely includes Japan, Taiwan, and South Korea. The first defining characteristic of a DS lies in their developmental priorities, that is, in enhancing the productivity through generating investible surplus and by closing the technological gap; second, they adopt an elitist-meritocratic Weberian style bureaucratic agency with clearheaded organizational objectives that enjoys political support; third, DSs encourage cooperative links (rather than an arms-length relationship) in state-business relations.[15]

In the African colonial context, historian Frederick Cooper suggests that while the weak state capacities of the African states constrained them from exercising control over the societies they ruled, the gatekeeping role of these states played out as intermediaries between the colonies and the outside world, regulating the internal and external sources of revenues and prescribing the rules by which commerce was to be governed. In spite of a growing body of civil societies, their attempts to circumvent official channels of commercial control were also limited, and the colonial rule ensured that the growth and industrialization processes of African economies were sufficiently undermined to reinforce the colonies' dependence on external economies.[16]

6 State-building processes

The gatekeeping roles assumed by the East Asian new industrializers were shed in a different (and positive) light. What is striking about the Miracle on the Han River metaphor is that it symbolizes South Korea's rapid economic development that overcame poverty. To put things into perspective, South Korea and Ghana, which was the wealthiest country in sub-Saharan Africa (SSA), had a near-identical per capita GDP of $490 and $491 in 1957. However, in 30 years, South Korea's GDP per capita surpassed that of Ghana by ten times, while the latter was staggering from economic setbacks such as hyperinflation, overregulation, low production rate, institutional demoralization, and a weak human capital.[17] Moreover, according to the World Bank, there was a 10.6% growth in East Asia as opposed to a 6.3% growth rate in the developing countries between 1960 and 1988.[18]

This prompts the question as to what explains the stark contrast in a tale of two nations if Ghana and a host of other developing countries have also implemented protectionism (i.e. "distorted prices" mechanism)? A corpus of literature that addresses this concern is the "middle income trap thesis." Among the major premises of this thesis is that the Weberian-style bureaucracy is more prevalent in East Asian tiger economies. Moreover, a few advanced countries in Latin America, such as Mexico, Brazil, and Argentina, have abandoned import substitution in favor of export-oriented industrialization (EOI)-led growth, but have shown mixed results. Chile has successfully transitioned from basic neoliberalism to "pragmatic neoliberalism" whereby the state intervenes in support of the growth and export of its priority sectors ("industrial bias"), whereas Bolivia, Peru, and Venezuela have adopted a statist-populist developmental pathway. Other explanation includes the hard authoritarianism vs. soft authoritarianism dichotomy, in which the latter, as opposed to the former, operates under basic democratic principles all the while retaining a statist economic outlook.

The tale of South Korean developmental success is then attributed to developing an EOI strategy since the 1960s[19] and a state-led growth underpinned by a strong bureaucratic capability. The proponents of neoliberalism and globalization suggest that free trade is the engine to global prosperity by privileging free movements of capitals, goods, services, and labor. As an advocate of free trade and comparative advantage, Paul Krugman also insinuated that interventionist trade policies are susceptible to political abuse.[20] Nevertheless, some degree of protectionist policies and economic nationalism is defended on the grounds that developing countries are not prepared to enter free market competition at the infancy stage. By reviewing the history of capitalism of the industrialized economies, namely Britain and the U.S., Ha-Joon Chang argued that even the capitalist economies today did not build their economy upon the neoliberal policies as they profess but have imposed them on the developing countries. Instead, they themselves used interventionist policies in industrial, trade, and technology to promote infant industries at the embryonic stages of development.[21]

Echoing on the aforementioned points, Robert Wade dispels the myth that Taiwan and South Korea are liberal trade regimes. While Taiwan and South Korea underwent economic liberalization in 1958–1962 and 1962–1965, respectively, Wade argues that the state has actively been intervening in both economies but in a way that benefits their industrial growth and productivity. On the outset, although it appears that South Korea (13%) and Taiwan (14%) had lower tariffs relative to Colombia (35%), Israel (76%), and Argentina (112%) in 1969, the tariffs were applied at uneven rates across the industries, displaying industry bias and trade bias (in terms of the markets they sell).[22] In fact, as "late industrializers,"[23] the East Asian NICs were very much like the developing countries elsewhere that were not ready to compete in free market economy. South Korea and Taiwan, the two countries that emulated the Japanese model, also found themselves in a similar position in the textile industry during the incipient stages of their development. The gatekeeping role of these states, in allocating subsidies and distorting prices, was considered necessary in order to catch up with Japan's productivity rate for which an abundance of human capital, U.S. aid, and modern infrastructure were not enough to help these countries to compete on a level playing field.[24]

But what set the East Asian economies apart from other developing economies was that subsidies they introduced were not based on giveaways but followed a more principled approach based on performance levels in output, exports, and R&D.[25] As Amsden notes, "innovators also borrow technology from their competitors, but late industrializers are entirely dependent on 'learning' in order to compete."[26] The "learning process" referred to in this context implies that the catching up processes of the late industrializers that raised their productivity and per capita GDP in the absence of technology are distinct from the industrialization processes of Britain, Germany, and the U.S.[27] As will be briefly discussed below and expounded on in the following chapters, this learning curve, which is an integral part of state-building process especially for late industrializers in the 20th century onward, is shaped by historical and institutional processes.

South Korea's industrialization process dates back to the 1870s, closer to the period when the Joseon Dynasty (1392–1910) was entering a period of decline as a result of the Japanese incursion. This was followed by a period of industrialization lag for about 90 years. The inception of the catching up process and rapid economic growth was underway in the 1960s, but even by the 1980s, South Korea's R&D activity was minimal.[28] The rapid economic growth in South Korea from the 1960s to 1980s was a catching up period and a gamechanger in the state-building narrative but does not necessarily denote the optimal output in South Korea's economic history. The impulses that ushered in a period of "the Miracle on the Han River" are an interventionist state, conglomerates, meritocratic system and an abundance of low-cost and highly qualified human capital.[29] The structural characteristics of East Asian NICs, which are characterized by natural resources deficit but with abundant

8   State-building processes

sources of low-cost, skilled laborers are just as important as the institutional drivers that explain a high productivity rate.

For late industrializers, the role of political leadership is just as important as institutional capacity. The latter also needs political support to facilitate modernization and high productivity. As such, South Korea's state-building narrative is centered on the political leadership of a militaristic personality, Park Chung-hee. Park was not any less corrupt or clientelist than his predecessor, Rhee Syngman, but he is commended for launching a hybridized bureaucracy that was able to fulfill the dual objectives of meeting patronage needs while promoting industrialization.[30] After Park rose to power in 1963 following the coup on May 16, 1961, he assumed political leadership during the pinnacle of South Korea's industrialization leap until his popularity started to wane due to his heavy-handed rule after the Yushin Constitution was promulgated during the Fourth Republic (1972–1981). Park was also faced with fresh challenges such as the diminishing U.S. military commitment to ROK and North Korean threats. The extent to which the state intervenes in the economy is best illustrated through the role of the Korea Central Intelligence Agency in creating the nation's key economic institutions including the Economic Planning Board, Ministry of Finance, and the Ministry of Commerce and Industry.[31] Thereafter, Park actively intervened in economic policy reforms by strengthening the bureaucratic capacity of the Blue House Secretariat in 1969 economic recession. New positions were created in Second and Third Secretaries on Economic Affairs. Under the guise of democracy, Park was involved in vote-buying and he mobilized political support through the state-run political entities, namely People's Movement for National Reconstruction (*Kukto konsol-tan*) and personal vote (*Huwonhoe*) system and raised political funds from the chaebol.[32] Authoritarian-militaristic rule in ROK continued until Chun doo-hwan's presidency in the Fifth Republic. As the state democratized under the Sixth Republic, the state's ability to regulate the chaebol had declined,[33] and toward the 1990s, interdependent state-business relations gradually dissolved in favor of neoliberalism.

Another defining feature of the South Korean economy is the rise of the *chaebol* (conglomerates) in the post-Korean war period. While chaebols are categorically identified as "diversified business groups," the sheer scale and the role of these conglomerates have been critical for sustaining innovation, growth, and the overall national competitiveness. The emphasis is on raising a cadre of high-skilled workers, especially in managerial and engineering positions – these white-collar professionals served as gatekeepers of foreign technological transfers. While an abundance of well-educated workforces is a defining feature of the South Korean model, another striking feature is that its real wage growth rate exceeds that of other industrial revolutions past or present, including Japan. This synergizes growth prospects as it incentivizes and mobilizes the work force to acquire cutting-edge skills and technological capability.[34] As a consequence, *chaebols* have been at the backbone of the

South Korean economy and were among the top five Korean applicants for the European patent applications in 2018.[35]

Following a state-interventionist model meant that development under this paradigm was centered on state-business relations. As a result of "embedded autonomy," the state enjoys a degree of autonomy from society, yet maintains close relations with entrepreneurial groups while ensuring corporate coherence in meritocratic bureaucracy.[36] While encouraging public–private partnerships (PPPs), corruption and cronyism were also rampant in these societies. Nevertheless, what distinguishes the Korean case from other countries where "money politics" is prevalent is that while bribery and corruption were commonplace and politics drove business interests, strong institution and state-business relations characterized as "mutual hostages" facilitated long-term arrangements that were mutually beneficial in state-business relations.[37] The extent to which state cronyism was pervasive in Korea is evidenced in election campaigns, patronage, economic policies, and matrimony.[38]

Behind the glamor of the East Asian success stories, Asian economies dealt a major blow with the 1997 Asian-Pacific Financial Crisis. In the preceding year, South Korea acceded to the Organisation for Economic Co-operation and Development (OECD), and in 1995, it reached $10,000 per capita income.[39] However, the 1997 APAC Financial Crisis exposed the vulnerabilities of a state-interventionist model emanating from structural weaknesses and policy distortions such as state cronyism, moral hazard ("overlending"), weak capital inflows, and balance of payments crisis. The $57bn International Monetary Fund (IMF) package for South Korea was the largest in the history of IMF's economic bailout comparable to Argentina's loan in September 2018. The onset of the crisis was in Thailand in July 1997 when there were speculative attacks on the Thai baht which led to currency devaluations and massive capital flights, setting off a chain reaction in the Asian economy – Indonesia, Malaysia, and South Korea were among the hardest hit. As for South Korea, 62 companies became bankrupt and the share of nonperforming loans and debt-financed was on a rise in the pre-crisis economy.[40] Overseen by the Korea Tripartite Commission, which is an amalgamation of the government, business, and labor, South Korea weathered the storm through gold-collecting campaigns which helped them pay off the last of its $19.5bn debt by August 23, 2001. The moral of this crisis is that it is critical to preclude future crisis by taking adequate preemptive measures by enhancing fiscal and corporate disciplines, maintaining high levels of foreign currency reserves, and implementing sound financial practices.

In spite of the country's large pool of highly educated and skilled workers as the Asia's fourth-largest economy, population crisis, exacerbated by low birth rate and aging population, is a challenge for securing future prospects in a knowledge-based economy.[41] To compensate for this, developing innovation capabilities has been a chief strategy for enhancing future prospects for economic competitiveness. In the 2010s, the East Asian economies entered a pinnacle of innovation. Notably, South Korea ranked first place in the 2019

10 *State-building processes*

Bloomberg Innovation Index, which is attributed to its R&D performance and added manufacturing value. In relative terms, however, it was ranked 20th place in patent activity, implying a slowdown after a rapid increase over the two decades, from the mid-1990s to the mid-2010s. In the 2019 Global Innovation Index, South Korea ranked 11th place among the 50 high-income countries, with innovation inputs outperforming innovation outputs. In parallel with the Bloomberg Index, South Korea's strengths mainly lie in R&D intensity, especially in the business sector. It is also noted for its strong performances in patent applications by origin, Patent Cooperation Treaty by origin, industrial designs by origin, and high technology exports. While its performance in innovation activities generally exceeds the level of development, issues linked to external relations, such as R&D investments from abroad, foreign direct investment (FDI) inflows, information and communication technology services imports, and tertiary inbound mobility are areas for improvement.[42]

State-building and economic modernization in the Middle East

The MENA countries have exhibited institutional and structural challenges emanating from historical institutionalism, food and water insecurity, demography (i.e. "youth bulge"), and in Allison Amsden's terms, "unconventional" forms of economic modernization devoid of an agrarian-based industrialization. The interplay of state-building and the history of economic development in the MENA is in part rooted in the uneven colonial processes in the Levant, Maghreb, and the Arabian Peninsula. The occupied colonies and protected states of the modern Middle East reflected the colonial competition between the major colonizers of Britain, France, and Italy. Napoleon's unsuccessful campaign in Egypt (1798–1801), for example, was primarily driven by the interest in countering the British influence. The British protection in Egypt (1882–1922) established cotton production as cash crops for the British economy while it also held significant stakes in the Suez Canal in an imperial competition with the French. The French colonization and protection of the Maghreb, namely Algeria (1830–1962), Morocco (1912–1956), and Tunisia (1881–1956), were much more durable than elsewhere but especially in French Algeria where it was virtually treated as a province of France and a settler colony that imposed assimilationist policies and policies that privileged the settlers over the native-born Algerians.[43]

Britain's control of the region was arguably more transient. Violence was less egregious in the British mandates of Palestine (1920–1948), Transjordan (the present-day Jordan, 1921–1946), and Iraq (1920–1932) than the French mandates of Syria (1920–1943) and Lebanon (1920–1943) which were established following the Sykes–Picot Agreement (1916). Nevertheless, the institutional legacies of divide-and-rule politics, consociational politics in Lebanon, and the arbitrary drawing of boundaries during this period continued to engender conflicts and created geopolitical fault lines, as demonstrated through the emergence of Daesh, which adopted "the end of Sykes–Picot" as their central slogan.[44,45] By comparison, the British protection of the Gulf states was not only driven by their demand for crude oil and commercial interests for the British India, but, as James Onley argues, was voluntarily sought by the rulers in Oman, the Trucial States (the present-day UAE), Bahrain, Kuwait, and Qatar in the 19th and 20th centuries to defend their sheikhdoms from external attacks and to arbitrate peace settlements between rulers.[46] While the British protection in the Gulf Sheikhdoms and *Pax Britannica* illustrates a mutually interdependent relationship rather than a top-down relationship, the Gulf states were not immune to the ravages of the civil wars in the neighboring country, Yemen, which was historically occupied by the Ottomans in the 1500s and between mid-19th century and the first quarter of the 20th century, and colonized by Britain in the South (1937–1963) and the People's Democratic Republic of Yemen, which was later supported by Egyptian Republicans during the North Yemen Civil War (1962–1970).

While the colonial states and empires administered different sections of the MENA, Turkey, Iran, and Saudi Arabia were not under colonial rule. After the collapse of the Ottoman Empire, Turkey transitioned into a republic in 1923 under the one-party rule of Mustafa Kemal Atatürk (1923–1938). Monarchies that cemented their power through the political backings of the Ottoman, British, and French Empires were overthrown by the revolutionaries and displaced by republican governments in Libya (1969), Egypt (1952), Tunisia (1957), and Iraq (1958). Elsewhere in the Levant and Maghreb, the Hashemite Kingdom of Jordan and Morocco's Alaouite Dynasty since King Mohammed V (1957–1961) outlasted the political turmoil of the post-independence period. The Baathist Arab socialist regimes came to power in Syria (1966) and Iraq (1968), while the Marxist-oriented anticolonial and liberation movements were sweeping across the MENA. Caught in the crossfire of the antiimperialist and nationalist movements of Nasserism and Baathism, the Arab states were looking to establish their legitimacy on the newly founded nation-states but grounded on the linkage between *umma* and pan-Arabism. The Israeli declaration of independence (1948) was a death nail on the coffin for the Palestinian cause, while the United Arab Republic was formed and dissolved between 1958 and 1961. The military defeat in the Six Day War (1967) also marked the decline of Nasserism and undermined Pan-Arabism.

In the 1950s, economic nationalization was an integral part of nation-building narratives in Iran and Egypt. In Iran under the Shah, Mohammad Mosaddegh, the Prime Minister between 1951 and 1953 led the nationalization of the oil industry only to be overthrown in a CIA-led coup in August 1953. In Nasser's Egypt, the Suez Canal was nationalized in July 1956, but the Suez Crisis precipitated later in October, which invited external interventions from Israel, Britain, and France that stirred a public outcry. Later, the Shah's

12 *State-building processes*

institution of White Revolution, which was an extension of the Land Reform Law of 1962, was an economic modernization initiative that was preemptively introduced to stave off dissent by framing the initiative as a state-sponsored "revolution." The provisions of the state-initiated top-down "revolution," which entails land reform, privatization of state-owned enterprises, labor reforms, women's suffrage, among other things, continued well into the mid-1970s, but were considered a failure.[47] Land reforms backfired and social reforms faced staunch opposition from the clerical establishment, including Ayatollah Khomeini, who established mass popular support and mobilized the public through the 1963 demonstrations before going into exile between 1964 and 1979.

In parallel with the East Asian development pathway in the early stages, the statist policy of import substitution industrialization (ISI) strategies was prevalent across the MENA economies in the 1960s. The statist experimentations and an easy injection of oil revenues and strategic rents (e.g. foreign aid and arms transfers) engendered the bloated bureaucracies that were mostly inefficient. When the global economy was reoriented to a market economy after the 1982 Latin American debt crisis during the last decade of the 1980s ("la década perdida"), the MENA economies were unable to readapt their economies to EOI-led strategies like their East Asian and Latin American counterparts, as prescribed by the Washington Consensus. This led to a misallocation of capital and labor with a lack of total productivity growth.[48] Today, the MENA economies, especially Egypt, Iraq, and Syria, and to a lesser extent, Jordan, Morocco, Yemen, and Tunisia, have transitioned to market economies. Their economies continue to be characterized by protectionism of selected industries (including the banking sector) by "getting the prices wrong," and a heavily subsidized economy and state provision of social services and state-controlled trade unions.[49]

In the post-independence period, industrialization drives in the MENA were led by political personalities like Mustafa Kemal Atatürk (Turkey), Houari Boumediene (Algeria), and Gamal Abdel Nasser (Egypt), and state socialism had been the prevailing development pathway in the aforementioned countries and Iraq, Syria, and Tunisia.[50] The socialist regime in Iraq was more stable in the 1970s since the state-building process was financed by oil revenues. Between the 1960s and 1970s, Iraq had the second-highest state expenditure as a proportion of their GDP after Nasser's Egypt.[51] As centrally planned economies, Algeria, Egypt, Iraq, Syria, and Tunisia took rural land into public ownership for wealth redistribution while they were also partially reserved for state ownership. Although Iraq was one of the few countries in the region where oil revenues were directed toward the agricultural industry leading up to the 1958 revolution, the large agricultural industry became less productive after it was overtaken by the oil industry in 1950. The Iraqi economy was highly unbalanced and underdeveloped throughout the 1950s.[52]

On the eve of independence, the Middle East economies were awash with oil revenues generating a "rentier effect." At the turn of the century, oil was discovered in Persia (modern day Iran) (1908), Iraq (1923), Bahrain (1932), and Kuwait and Saudi Arabia (1938) followed by the UAE (1958). By 1928, oil cartels emerged from the Red Line Agreement, which bound the Iraqi Petroleum Company (IPC) (formerly Turkish Petroleum Company, TPC) consortium to hold 23.75% stakes of oil produced by TPC in the former Ottoman territory while Calouste Gulbenkian, an Armenian businessman and stakeholder, claimed a 5% share. While the colonial powers held geostrategic interests in the MENA, the significance of oil also accorded a greater economic and geopolitical importance to the region. Winston Churchill directed the British royal navy to convert the fleet from coal to oil on the eve of the first world war. Oil was a major pivot that lured the U.S. and European oil companies to the Middle East. Britain's Anglo-Persian Oil Company (APOC) was established after the oil was struck in Iran (1908), With the exception of the 5% stake held by Gulbenkian, the Iraq Petroleum Company was equally owned by four different oil companies including the Anglo-Iranian Oil Company (formerly APOC), Royal Dutch-Shell, Compagnie Française des Pétroles, and the Near East Development Corporation (an American consortium consisting of the Standard Oil of New Jersey and Socony-Vacuum). APOC and Gulf Oil Corporation founded the Kuwait Oil Company in a 50–50 joint venture for Kuwait concessions (1934) while Texaco joined Standard Oil of California and Standard Oil Company of New Jersey and Socony-Vacuum to find the Arab-American Oil Company (ARAMCO) (1936).[53] The Middle East policy was also at the backbone of the Truman, Eisenhower, and Carter doctrines. These doctrines were designed to impede communist expansion by providing military and economic aid in response to the Suez Crisis (1956) and the Soviet Invasion of Afghanistan (1979–1989). Given the strategic interest over the Middle East that contains more than two-thirds of world's proven oil reserves, Jimmy Carter in his State of the Union Address on January 23, 1980 declared, "An attempt by any outside force to gain control of the Persian Gulf region will be regarded as an assault on the vital interests of the United States of America."[54]

The inception of an oil-dependent economy which formed the social, political, and developmental basis for state-building across the MENA is grounded in the rentier state theory (RST) literature. Rentier state is defined as a state having more than 40% of the state income that accrues directly from an externally derived rent in which only a small fraction of the population (2%–3%) participates in rent-generating activities.[55] The central assumption of RST is succinctly summarized through Michael Ross' three-fold theory of "taxation effect," "spending effect," and "group-formation effect."[56] First, "taxation effect" is encapsulated in the slogan "no representation without taxation," which is inverted from the original form, "no taxation without representation." The former is an implicit reference to nondemocratic rentier economies that are in effect "allocation states," which renders them

14 *State-building processes*

autonomous from society, whereas the latter insinuates that taxation and political accountability go hand-in-hand. As for the latter, there is a historical reference to Britain's exaction of taxes to the 13 American colonies with the passage of the Stamp Act of 1765. This generated protests from the American colonies citing an absence of the colonial representation in the British parliament. Second, "spending effect" refers to the percentage of government expenditure to the total GDP. For rentier states, economic productivity is closely associated with public spending. Third, "group formation effect" assumes that the absence of civil societies in oil-dependent economies is an impediment to democratic transition. In Iraq, the post-1958 regime was short-lived and the Baath regime that succeeded in 1968 outlasted its predecessor by staying in power for 35 years. The soaring oil revenues became the basis for transforming Iraq into a rentier state following the nationalization of the oil industry in 1972. Thereafter, Saddam Hussein's Baath regime enjoyed considerable autonomy from society and exhibited the symptoms of the three properties outlined above. Group-formation effect was visible through the buying off of internal dissent by expanding the public sector with the help of an easy injection of oil largesse.

In a similar vein, the massive influx of oil royalty in the 1970s was a leverage to the state as it funded economic modernization and militarization programs under the Shah. Nevertheless, the rentier effect in the pre-revolution Iran was untenable as the inflationary pressure resulting from oil boom and economic recession in mid-1970s had an adverse effect. Politically, it was unable to contain the revolutionaries (e.g. the leftist nationalists, Marxist-liberal organizations, the clergy, and the bazaaris) which coalesced against the Pahlavi regime in the 1978–1979 revolution. Moreover, successful cooptation in group-formation effect does not always imply that the general public is socially and politically satisfied.

In Saudi Arabia, sources of revenue undergirded the state-building process, including the construction of the state bureaucracy and the military. Modern Saudi Arabia was founded in 1932 by Ibn Saud, in a religious-military alliance established between the Al Saud and the founder of the Wahhabi movement, Muhammad ibn Abd al-Wahhab. The first development plan (1970–1974) commenced on the onset of the oil boom and huge proceeds of the oil revenue that amassed to the state went toward infrastructure development during the first six development plans (1970–1999), especially from the second development plan (1975–1979) onward. By the third development plan (1980–1984), infrastructure development accounted for 40.4% of the total development expenditure.[57] The Saudi developmental paradigm deviates from the orthodoxy of Walt Rostow's Stages of Growth in the sense that despite having a sizeable agriculture industry relative to the GCC counterparts (as per stage one of Rostow's model), agriculture per se did not constitute the basis for industrialization. Rather, in the case of Saudi Arabia, stages two and three of the model are inverted – resource-based development preceded the growth of the agricultural sector, which was also financed by oil revenues. As Toby Craig Jones suggests, water was a form of political patronage that facilitated the subsidization and development of the agricultural industry, which in spite of a semi-arid climate later paved the way for Saudi Arabia to emerge as the sixth-largest wheat exporter in the world.[58] The oil boom inaugurated a centralized and hierarchical Saudi bureaucracy that replaced the diffused, noninstitutionalized associations, tribal, merchant, and agricultural communities that existed before the advent of the oil economy, and gave rise to a new class of Nejdi business elites and salaried civil servants of the Saudi bureaucracy.[59] By 1974, Saudi Arabia became a rentier state as the share of the oil sector was 78.35% of the total GDP.[60] While rentierism is a common denominator for many of the economies in the MENA, it has generated an uneven effect on the population.[61] Moreover, social, institutional, and political development is far from monolithic in these societies. As will be discussed in the following chapters, the magnitude and symptoms of rentierism are nuanced across different parts of the region.

Though Gulf states tend to be clustered together as a rentier subgroup, the Dubai Model is noted for its unique developmental pathway for transforming Dubai from a small fishing and pearling community to a key trading entrepot and more recently as a futuristic metropolis.[62] A combination of historical, institutional, and structural factors gave impetus to the Dubai model. Historically, it has developed as an outgrowth of a liberal immigration policy instituted since the early 20th century, creating an influx of an immigrant-based mercantile community. As a result, it has shown more liberal social, political, and business outlook. Institutionally, it is also considered as a distinct model as it is based on a federation system. The Emirate of Abu Dhabi has established itself as the political and administrative capital of the UAE based on the concentration of oil wealth and holds 94% of the UAE's oil reserves. In comparison, Dubai, though being the second-largest emirate with oil outputs, holds roughly 4% of the UAE oil reserves, which is equivalent to a quarter of Abu Dhabi's oil reserves. By having significantly less oil than Abu Dhabi, it has had an edge on innovating and diversifying its economy. Challenges and opportunities accorded to these factors will be examined in further detail in Chapter 4.

A comparison of the developmental pathways between the Middle Eastern countries and the East Asian NICs is centered on three points: neopatrimonialism, corruption, and human development. First, centralized state apparatus is a common feature in disparate developmental paradigms in East Asia and the Middle East. According to Hisham Sharabi, Arab societies are characterized by neopatriarchy, whereby patriarchy remains intact in the social fabric of these countries, and without showing signs of dissipating, it reinforces dependency and is rebranded in a modernized form as new patrimonialism or neo-patriarchy.[63] The allocation of state patronage and subsidies via a centralized state bureaucracy has fostered dependency while the state wields enormous social and political control in a hybrid militaristic-bureaucratic state apparatus in Arab republics. While authoritarianism in pre-1988 Korea and state dependency are common denominators for both regions, incentivized subsidies and state-business interdependency (or "mutual hostages") with a

16   *State-building processes*

purposive developmental outlook are conspicuously absent from the Middle Eastern development paradigm.

Second, although corruption and state cronyism are present in both Korea and Middle Eastern countries, they are manifested differently. The mainstream prescription of good governance and neoliberalism as per Washington Consensus is not universally applicable to the developing countries and the MENA. The control of the corruption indicator in the World Bank's Worldwide Governance Indicators (1996–2008)[64] reveals that the MENA as a whole performs considerably better than SSA and most of the emerging economies (i.e. BRICS) and is slightly above Latin America. Among the four case studies examined in this book, the UAE has the highest estimate (1.15) for the 2018 Index followed by Saudi Arabia (0.36), Iran (–0.96), and Iraq (–1.40).[65] While Gulf states tend to perform better in the index, there are considerable disparities between the UAE (1.15) and Bahrain (–0.15), as well as between the GCC countries and their non-GCC MENA counterparts (as shown above). A Weberian style meritocratic bureaucracy has not fully developed in these economies due to laxed pressure on the general population to contribute to economic productivity induced by the "rentier effect." By contrast, the East Asian NICs have effectively funneled corruption and state cronyism in state-led industrialization due to deficiencies in natural resources, Cold War vestiges, geopolitical pressures, and cultural factors (i.e. work ethics).

Third, even when the oil-poor rentier states in the Middle East are excluded from the sampling of case studies, there is a mismatch in qualitative and quantitative development among MENA countries. This is best captured through the performance of Middle Eastern countries in the Human Development Index (HDI). The paradox lies in economic and social incongruence. Despite the common denominators in demographic, geographical, and social factors, there is a disparity among the Gulf and Middle Eastern economies in social and human development. In the 2020 HDI, the UAE (31st), Saudi Arabia (40th), and Qatar (45th) were ranked as top-50 Middle Eastern countries.[66] Although small local populations work to the advantage when it comes to the allocation of rent and GDP per capita, conversely, a shortage of indigenous human capital explains the disparity between the input and output levels in innovation.

ROK's foreign policy identity as a middle power

South Korea was on the path of becoming a middle-power diplomacy since the Roh Moo-hyun's presidency (2003–2008). Thereafter, the Lee Myung-bak administration consolidated South Korea's role as a supporter of multilateralism by hosting high-profile international events including the G20 Summit, High-Level Forum for Development Effectiveness, and the 2012 Nuclear Summit. In these meetings, a number of global agendas including climate change, development assistance, and peacekeeping operations were brought to the foreground.[67] Despite being a latecomer to the ascendancy of middle-power diplomacy, it shares many of the core characteristics that define middle powers more generally: (1) mediating between great powers as a "diplomatic buffer" between the great powers and defusing political tensions; (2) thriving under multilateralism; and (3) promoting globalization initiatives. A middle power by operational definition does not function as a single entity but as a collective unit. Therefore, by definition, middle-power diplomacy cannot be represented and exercised by a single nation alone.[68] The collective nature of middle-power diplomacy is best reflected through the establishment of the middle-power network among Mexico, Indonesia, South Korea, Turkey, and Australia in 2013.

South Korea's ascendance to middle-power status is two-pronged and is attributed to: (1) the decline of U.S. hegemony and the rise of China, and (2) reorientation of the post-Cold War global order that privileges non-traditional security concerns, including human security and environmental security over traditional security issues and high politics. As this book argues, South Korea's foreign policy identity as a middle power which is reinforced by rapid industrialization and its economic narrative of "The Miracle on the Han River" since it surpassed the threshold level of state capacity has been vital for expanding its diplomatic and commercial engagements with the Middle East.

This book provides a timely contribution on South Korea's foreign policy in the Middle East and South Korea's foreign policy identity as a middle power considering ROK's engagement with global issues of nuclear proliferation, counterterrorism and counterpiracy, and climate change, which coincides with its recent ascendance to middle-power status. While ROK established diplomatic ties with 23 countries in the MENA in the last two decades of emerging as a middle power, this book focuses exclusively on its relationship with Iran, Iraq, Saudi Arabia, and the UAE. By focusing on these four case studies, this book aims to offer a nuanced analysis on the intersectionality of comparative political economy and foreign policy analysis by contextualizing the state-building processes and the shifting trajectories of strategic and diplomatic relations between South Korea and the Middle Eastern countries. These four countries are not only the top sources of crude suppliers for ROK in the Middle East but also the regional economic powerhouses or regional powers, past and present.

Marking South Korea's emergence as a middle power, this book is about mapping the history of South Korea's engagement with the Middle East against the wider backdrop of America's foreign policy in the Middle East and South Korea's national interests shaped by domestic, regional, and international imperatives. This book analyzes the history of South Korea's foreign policy in the Middle East through historical process-tracing methods. By mapping the institutional, economic, and political history of ROK and a select Middle Eastern countries, this book contends that South Korea's resource security should be a byproduct of deepening and broadening bilateral relations with the Middle East.

The aims and structure of the book

Against the wider backdrop of the historical and institutional processes of industrialization and economic productivity contoured in this chapter, the remainder of this book aims to map the nexus of political, institutional, and economic trajectories of South Korea's resource diplomacy and security policy in the Middle East at critical geopolitical junctures in the Middle East. The analysis of this book is situated at the intersectionality of comparative political economy and foreign policy analysis and employs historical process-tracing. The key questions this book aims to address are:

1 How has South Korea's quest for energy security shaped economic, political, and security policies in the Middle East since the post-Cold War era?
2 How do the histories of structural and institutional trajectories compare between South Korea and the Middle East?
3 What are the endogenous and exogenous factors that configure South Korea's foreign policy in the Middle East?

Chapter 1: This chapter provides a historical account of the state-building processes in South Korea and the Middle Eastern economies. It entails contextualizing South Korea's emergence as a middle-power diplomacy based on its own geopolitical challenges and discusses how the latter has informed South Korea's Middle East policy. The historical account of South Korea's state-building process is contextualized against the wider economic development of Japan and the NICs. This is contrasted with the state-building processes and the history of economic modernization and liberalization of the resource-based industrializations of the Middle Eastern economies. By shedding light on the role of the state bureaucracy embodied by the DS paradigm and the structural characteristics and challenges of the rentier states, this chapter sets out to explain how industrialization and the maturity of state capacities of South Korea and the Middle East strengthened interdependent relations.

Chapter 2: This chapter is prefaced by an analysis of South Korea's cultural and political engagements with Iran since the Cold War era. It discusses the pragmatic relationship that defines ROK–Iran relations in spite of the strategic partnership that have existed between Iran and North Korea since the Iran–Iraq War. The chapter goes into depth at how South Korea's bilateral relations with Iran has to a great extent been hamstrung by its longstanding alliance with the U.S. and continues to be subjected to the final outcome of Iran nuclear talks. Despite the significance of Park Geun-hye's historic visit to Tehran in May 2016, the chapter implies that there are difficult days ahead in ROK–Iran relations since it has been derailed by the tensions between the Iranian hardliners and America's Iran policy under the Trump administration.

State-building processes 19

Chapter 3: This chapter offers a historical survey of ROK–KSA relations centered on bilateral economic cooperation that dates back to the 1973 oil embargo. Of particular interest is the structural complementarity between the South Korean and Saudi economies that later laid the groundwork for introducing Saudi–Korea Vision 2030. Historically, Saudi Arabia has occupied strategic significance in South Korea's foreign policy calculus as the largest producer and supplier of crude oil. On the other hand, as an oil-deficit economy, South Korea's skilled manpower also offered the basis for strengthening economic cooperation since the nascent days of state-building. In addition to traditional diplomacy, this chapter also examines how government-to-business relations and state-business relations have synergized Saudi–ROK bilateral relations after the 1997 Asian Financial Crisis.

Chapter 4: This chapter focuses on the factors that paved the way for South Korea to elevate its diplomatic status with the UAE to a special strategic partnership – which is the only one of its kind in the Middle East. It maps how the maturation of South Korea and the UAE's state capacities facilitated multifaceted cooperation between the two countries, including in security, nuclear energy, and health cooperation. What distinguishes South Korea's bilateral relations with other Middle Eastern counterparts is that the UAE is the only country in the world that South Korea established a bilateral security partnership. The latter has been critical for the UAE to become the first country for South Korea to export its homegrown nuclear technology.

Chapter 5: This chapter maps South Korea's contributions to the post-war reconstruction efforts in Iraq following the Iran–Iraq War, the 1991 Gulf War, and the 2003 Iraq War. It delves into the economic and security implications of these conflicts on South Korea's commercial diplomacy with Iraq. The chapter also disentangles South Korean government's political dilemma in recent years as it has been increasingly been caught in the tug of war between the Iraqi federal government and the Kurdistan regional government. As the third-largest country with a foreign military contingent in Iraq, this chapter argues that the 2003 Iraq War has been a watershed event in reinforcing its image as a U.S. ally that has had profound security implications.

Chapter 6: This is the concluding chapter that provides a theoretical analysis on middle powers and South Korea's middle-power diplomacy. Based on the literature review, this chapter suggests that there are three types of middle powers: functional, behavioral, and ideational. It is argued that ideational facet is the prevailing feature of South Korea's middle-power diplomacy. In positioning Korea's middle power and Middle East policy, structural realism, the rise of China, and the declining U.S. hegemony are taken into account. The chapter also covers the factors underlying South Korea's resource diplomacy strategies and typologies and concludes by identifying areas of improvement and policy recommendations.

Notes

1 Jongsoo James Lee, *The Partition of Korea After World War II: A Global History* (New York, NY: Palgrave MacMillan, 2006), 13–15.
2 R.D. McLaurin & Chung-in Moon, "A precarious balance: Korea and the Middle East." *Korea and World Affairs* 8, no. 2 (1984), 235–264.
3 Patrick McEachern & Jaclyn O'Brien McEachern, *North Korea, Iran, and the Challenge to International Order: A Comparative Perspective* (New York, NY: Routledge, 2018), 89.
4 The Jordan Times, "Jordan cuts ties with North Korea," February 2, 2018.
5 Radio Free Asia, "North Korean workers in Kuwait face tight information controls as bulk of their pay goes to Kim regime," n.d., www.rfa.org/english/news/special/nkinvestigation/kuwait1.html; Agence France-Presse, "UAE stops issuing visas to North Koreans," October 12, 2017.
6 Richard J. Kilroy, *Threats to Homeland Security: An All-Hazards Perspective* (Hoboken, NJ: Wiley, 2008), 155.
7 Mushahid Hussain, "U.S. retrenchment and China's rise: Pointers to a new emerging order," *Wall Street International Magazine*, September 5, 2020.
8 Jason W. Davidson, "The costs of war to United States allies since 9/11," *Brown University Watson Institute of International and Public Affairs*, May 12, 2021, 8.
9 Jong-Sup Lee & Uk Heo, "The U.S.-South Korea alliance: Free-riding or bargaining?," *Asian Survey* 41 (5) (2001), 823.
10 John Ford, "The pivot to Asia was Obama's biggest mistake," *The Diplomat*, January 21, 2017.
11 U.S. Department of State, "Countering Iran's global terrorism," November 13, 2018.
12 See Alon Levkowitz, "The Republic of Korea and the Middle East: Economics, diplomacy, and security," *Korea Economic Institute*, August 2010.
13 Chalmers Johnson, *MITI and the Japanese Miracle: The Growth of Industrial Policy, 1925–1975* (Stanford, CA: Stanford University Press, 1982), 4.
14 Johnson, *MITI and the Japanese Miracle*, 305–307.
15 Linda Weiss, "Developmental states in transition: Adapting, dismantling, innovating, not 'normalizing'," *The Pacific Review* 13 (1) (2010), 23.
16 Frederick Cooper, *Africa Since 1940: The Past of the Present* (Cambridge: Cambridge University Press, 2002), 5–6.
17 Herbert Werlin, "Ghana and South Korea: Lessons from World Bank case studies," *Public Administration and Development*, 11 (3) (1991), 245.
18 Alice Amsden, "Diffusion of development: The late-industrializing model and Greater East Asia," *The American Economic Review* 81 (2) (1991), 282.
19 Robert Wade paints a more nuanced picture when it comes to describing the relationship between trade liberalization and economic growth. According to Wade, an outward-oriented trade regime does not uniformly apply cross-sectorally and at a country-wide level. Instead, he contends that trade liberalization is not what makes the East Asian NICs rich, but that these countries only liberalize more as they become richer. See Robert Wade, "East Asia's Development Strategy: Lessons for Eastern Europe," in Michael Dauderstädt (ed.), *Towards a Prosperous Wider Europe: Macroeconomic Policies for a Growing Neighborhood* (Bonn: Friedrich Ebert Foundation, 2005), 15–24.

20 Ha-Joon Chang, "Kicking away the ladder: The "real" history of free trade," *Foreign Policy in Focus*, December 2003, https://fpif.org/kicking_away_the_ladder_the_real_history_of_free_trade/.
21 Ha-Joon Chang, "Kicking away the ladder: An unofficial history of capitalism, especially in Britain and the United States," *Challenge* 45 (5) (2002), 64–71.
22 Robert Wade, "Managing trade: Taiwan and South Korea as challenges to economics and political science," *Comparative Politics* 25 (2) (1993), 149.
23 Late industrializers refer to countries that developed on the basis of an agrarian economy that underwent learning process (i.e. borrowed technology) and include countries such as Japan, South Korea, Taiwan, Brazil, India, Mexico, and Turkey.
24 U.S. aid accounted for 70–75% of South Korean capital inflows between 1953 and 1966.
25 Amsden, "Diffusion of Development," 284.
26 Amsden, "Diffusion of Development," 283.
27 Alice Amsden, *Asia's Next Giant: South Korea and Late Industrialization* (New York, NY: Oxford University Press, 1992), 3.
28 Amsden, *Asia's Next Giant*, 8–10.
29 Ibid.
30 David C. Kang, *Crony Capitalism: Corruption and Development in South Korea and the Philippines* (Cambridge: Cambridge University Press, 2004), 9.
31 Chung-in Moon & Byung-joon Kim, "Modernization strategy: Ideas and influences," in Byung-Kook Kim & Ezra F. Vogel (eds.), *The Park Chung Hee Era: The Transformation of South Korea* (Cambridge, UK: Harvard University Press, 2011), 115.
32 Kang, *Crony Capitalism*, 99–102.
33 Kang, *Crony Capitalism*, 153.
34 Amsden, *Asia's Next Giant*, 10.
35 These include, in descending order, Samsung Group, LG Group, POSCO Company, Hyundai Group, and Doosan Group.
36 See Peter Evans, *Embedded Autonomy: States and Industrial Transformation* (Princeton, NJ: Princeton University Press, 1995).
37 Kang, *Crony Capitalism*, 3–7.
38 Park Chung-hee's second daughter was briefly married to Ryu Chung, the first son of Poongsan Corporation's founder in 1982.
39 Kyu-Sung Lee, *The Korean Financial Crisis of 1997: Onset, Turnaround, and Thereafter* (Washington DC: World Bank Publications, 2011), 85.
40 Lee, *The Korean Financial Crisis of 1997*, 58–61.
41 For more on this, see Chyong-Fang Ko, Kyeung Mi Oh & Tetsuo Ogawa, "Aging population in East Asia: Impacts on social protection and social policy reforms in Japan, Korea, and Taiwan," in James Lee & Kam-Wah Chan (eds.), *The Crisis of Welfare in East Asia* (Lanham, MD: Lexington Books, 2007), 43–70.
42 Global Innovation Index, "Global Innovation Index 2019: The Republic of Korea," 1–10, n.d., www.wipo.int/edocs/pubdocs/en/wipo_pub_gii_2019/kr.pdf.
43 Roger Owen, *State, Power and Politics in the Making of the Modern Middle East* (New York, NY: Routledge, 2006), 16.
44 Andrew J. Tabler, "Introduction," in Andrew J. Tabler (ed.) *The Lines that Binds 100 Years of Sykes Picot* (Washington DC: The Washington Institute for Near East Policy, 2016), 1.

22 State-building processes

45 Owen, *State, Power and Politics*, 17.
46 James Onley, Britain and the Gulf Shaikhdoms, 1820-1971: The Politics of Protection, *Center for International and Regional Studies Georgetown University School of Foreign Service in Qatar*, 2009, 3–5.
47 Mehran Kamrava, *The Modern Middle East: A Political History Since the First World War* (Berkeley, CA: University of California Press, 2005), 145–156.
48 Henry & Springborg, *Globalization and the Politics of Development*, 11.
49 Mustapha K. Nabli, Jennifer Keller, Claudia Nassif & Carlos Silva-Jáuregui, "The political economy of industrial policy in the Middle East and North Africa," *The World Bank*, March 2006, 2–15.
50 John Waterbury, "The Long Gestation and Brief Triumph of Import-Substituting Industrialization," *World Development* 27 (2), 334.
51 Owen, *State, Power and Politics*, 26.
52 Waterbury, "Brief triumph of import-substituting industrialization," 337; Bassam Yousif, *Human Development in Iraq: 1950–1990* (New York, NY: Routledge), 16–41.
53 Chad H. Parker, *Making the Desert Modern: Americans, Arabs, and Oil on the Saudi Frontier: 1933–1973* (Amherst, MA: University of Massachusetts Press, 2015), 4; Daniel Silverfarb, "The Revision of Iraq's Oil Concession, 1949–52," *Middle Eastern Studies* 32 (1) (1996), 69.
54 Foreign Relations of the United States, 1977–1980, Volume I, Foundations of foreign policy, Document 138.
55 Giacomo Luciani, "The resource curse and the Gulf development challenge," in *Resources Blessed: Diversification and the Gulf Development Model*, ed., Giacomo Luciani (Berlin: Gerlach Press, 2012), 6–7.
56 See Michael L. Ross, "Does oil hinder democracy?" *World Politics* 53 (3) (2001), 325–361.
57 Saudi Arabia Ministry of Planning, "Achievements of the five-year plans," 2005.
58 Toby Craig Jones, *Desert Kingdom: How Oil and Water Forged Modern Saudi Arabia* (Cambridge, MA: Harvard University Press, 2010), 4–6.
59 Kiren Aziz Chaudry, *The Price of Wealth: Economies and Institutions in the Middle East* (Ithaca, NY: Cornell University Press, 2015), 156–157.
60 Saudi Arabia General Authority for Statistics, "Gross domestic product by institutional sectors at current prices," 2019.
61 Gwenn Okruhlik, "Rentier wealth, unruly law, and the rise of opposition: The political economy of oil states," *Comparative Politics* 31 (3) (1999), 295–315.
62 Martin Hvidt, "The Dubai Model: An outline of key development-process elements in Dubai," *International Journal of Middle East Studies* 41 (3) (2009), 401.
63 Hisham Sharabi, *Neopatriarchy: A Theory of Distorted Change in Arab Society* (New York, NY: Oxford University Press, 1988), 3–5.
64 The lowest rate in the index is –2.0 and the highest rate is 2.0. On a scale of 2.0, it is better performing in the index the closer it gets to 2.0.
65 The World Bank, "Worldwide governance indicators 2018: Control of corruption," 2018.
66 UNDP, Human Development Report 2020, 343.
67 Sook Jong Lee, "South Korea aiming to be an innovative middle power," in Sook Jong Lee ed., *Transforming Global Governance with Middle Power Diplomacy* (New York, NY: Palgrave Macmillan, 2016), 5.
68 Lee, "South Korea aiming to be an innovative middle power," 3.

References

Agence France-Presse. "UAE stops issuing visas to North Koreans," *The Daily Star*, October 12, 2017, www.dailystar.com.lb/ArticlePrint.aspx?id=422479&mode=print.

Amsden, Alice. "Diffusion of development: The late-industrializing model and Greater East Asia," *The American Economic Review* 81 (2) (1991), 282–286.

Amsden, Alice. *Asia's Next Giant: South Korea and Late Industrialization* (New York, NY: Oxford University Press, 1992).

Beblawi, Hazem and Giacomo Luciani. *The Rentier State* (London: Croom Helm, 1987).

Brown, William. "Still one size fits all? Uneven and combined development and African gatekeeper states," *Third World Thematics* 3 (3) (2018), 325–346.

Chang, Ha-Joon. "Kicking away the ladder: An unofficial history of capitalism, especially in Britain and the United States," *Challenge* 45 (5) (2002), 64–71.

Chang, Ha-Joon. "Kicking away the ladder: The "real" history of free trade," *Foreign Policy in Focus*, December 2003, https://fpif.org/kicking_away_the_ladder_the_real_history_of_free_trade/.

Chaudry, Kiren Aziz. *The Price of Wealth: Economies and Institutions in the Middle East* (Ithaca, NY: Cornell University Press, 2015).

Cooper, Frederick. *Africa since 1940: The Past of the Present* (Cambridge: Cambridge University Press, 2002).

Davidson, Jason W. "The costs of war to United States allies since 9/11," *Brown University Watson Institute of International and Public Affairs*, May 12, 2021.

European Patent Office. "Republic of Korea: European patent application." n.d., www.epo.org/about-us/annual-reports-statistics/statistics.html#applicants.

Evans, Peter. *Embedded Autonomy: States and Industrial Transformation* (Princeton, NJ: Princeton University Press, 1995).

Ford, John. "The pivot to Asia was Obama's biggest mistake," *The Diplomat*, January 21, 2017, https://thediplomat.com/2017/01/the-pivot-to-asia-was-obamas-biggest-mistake/.

U.S. Department of State, Foreign Relations of the United States, 1977–1980, Volume I, Foundations of Foreign Policy, Document 138, 2014, Kristin L. Ahlberg (Ed.), 692–699.

Global Innovation Index. "Global Innovation Index 2019: The Republic of Korea," 1–10, n.d., www.wipo.int/edocs/pubdocs/en/wipo_pub_gii_2019/kr.pdf.

Henry, Clement M. and Robert Springborg. *Globalization and the Politics of Development in the Middle East* (Cambridge: Cambridge University Press, 2004).

Hillbom, Ellen. "Botswana: A development-oriented gate-keeping State," *African Affairs* 111 (442) (2012), 67–89.

Hussain, Mushahid. "U.S. retrenchment and China's rise: Pointers to a new emerging order," *Wall Street International Magazine*, September 5, 2020.

Hvidt, Martin. "The Dubai model: An outline of key development-process elements in Dubai, *International Journal of Middle East Studies* 41 (3) (2009), 397–418.

Johnson, Chalmers. *MITI and the Japanese Miracle: The Growth of Industrial Policy, 1925-1975* (Stanford, CA: Stanford University Press, 1982).

Jones, Toby Craig. *Desert Kingdom: How Oil and Water Forged Modern Saudi Arabia* (Cambridge, MA: Harvard University Press, 2010).

24 State-building processes

Kamrava, Mehran. *The Modern Middle East: A Political History Since the First World War* (Berkeley, CA: University of California Press, 2005).

Kang, David C. *Crony Capitalism: Corruption and Development in South Korea and the Philippines* (Cambridge: Cambridge University Press, 2004).

Kilroy, Richard J. *Threats to Homeland Security: An All-Hazards Perspective* (Hoboken, NJ: Wiley, 2008).

Ko, Chyong-Fang, Kyeung Mi Oh and Tetsuo Ogawa. "Aging population in East Asia: Impacts on social protection and social policy reforms in Japan, Korea, and Taiwan," in James Lee and Kam-Wah Chan (Eds.), *The Crisis of Welfare in East Asia* (Lanham, MD: Lexington Books, 2007), 43–70.

Lee, Jongsoo James. *The Partition of Korea After World War II: A Global History* (New York, NY: Palgrave MacMillan, 2006).

Lee, Jong-Sup and Uk Heo. "The U.S.-South Korea alliance: Free-riding or bargaining?," *Asian Survey* 41 (5) (2001), 822–845.

Lee, Sook Jong. "South Korea aiming to be an innovative middle power," in Sook Jong Lee (Ed.), *Transforming Global Governance with Middle Power Diplomacy* (New York, NY: Palgrave Macmillan, 2016), 1–13.

Lee, Kyu-Sung. *The Korean Financial Crisis of 1997: Onset, Turnaround, and Thereafter* (Washington DC: World Bank Publications, 2011).

Levkowitz, Alon. "The Republic of Korea and the Middle East: Economics, diplomacy, and security," *Korea Economic Institute*, August 2010.

Luciani, Giacomo. "The resource curse and the Gulf development challenge," in Giacomo Luciani (Ed.), *Resources Blessed: Diversification and the Gulf Development Model* (Berlin: Gerlach Press, 2012), 1–28.

McLaurin, R.D. and Chung-in Moon. "A precarious balance: Korea and the Middle East," *Korea and World Affairs* 8 (2) (1984), 235–264.

Moon, Chung-in and Byung-joon Kim. "Modernization strategy: Ideas and influences," in Byung-Kook Kim and Ezra F. Vogel (Eds.), *The Park Chung Hee Era: The Transformation of South Korea* (Cambridge, UK: Harvard University Press, 2011), 115–139.

Nabli, Mustapha K., Jennifer Keller, Claudia Nassif and Carlos Silva-Jáuregui. "The political economy of industrial policy in the Middle East and North Africa," *The World Bank*, March 2006.

Okruhlik, Gwenn. "Rentier wealth, unruly law, and the rise of opposition: The political economy of oil states, *Comparative Politics* 31 (3) (1999), 295–315.

Onley, James. Britain and the Gulf Shaikhdoms, 1820–1971: The politics of protection, *Center for International and Regional Studies Georgetown University School of Foreign Service in Qatar*, 2009.

Owen, Roger. *State, Power and Politics in the Making of the Modern Middle East* (New York, NY: Routledge, 2006).

Parker, Chad H. *Making the Desert Modern: Americans, Arabs, and Oil on the Saudi Frontier: 1933–1973* (Amherst, MA: University of Massachusetts Press, 2015).

Patrick McEachern and Jaclyn O'Brien McEachern. *North Korea, Iran, and the Challenge to International Order: A Comparative Perspective* (New York, NY: Routledge, 2018).

Radio Free Asia. "North Korean workers in Kuwait face tight information controls as bulk of their pay goes to Kim regime," n.d., www.rfa.org/english/news/special/nkinvestigation/kuwait1.html.

Ross, Michael L. "Does oil hinder democracy?" *World Politics* 53 (3) (2001), 325–361.

Sadowski, Yahya. "Scuds versus butter: The political economy of arms control in the Arab world," *Middle East Report* (1992), 2–13.

Sales, Nathan A. "Countering Iran's global terrorism," U.S. Department of State, November 13, 2018, www.state.gov/countering-irans-global-terrorism.

Saudi Arabia General Authority for Statistics. "Gross Domestic Product by Institutional Sectors at Current Prices," 2019.

Saudi Arabia Ministry of Planning. "Achievements of the Five-Year Plans," 2005.

Sharabi, Hisham. *Neopatriarchy: A Theory of Distorted Change in Arab Society* (New York, NY: Oxford University Press, 1988).

Sparks, Grace. "Majority say US should not withdraw from Iran nuclear agreement," *CNN Politics*, May 9, 2018, https://edition.cnn.com/2018/05/08/politics/poll-iran-agreement/index.html.

Sorenson, David S. *An Introduction to the Modern Middle East: History, Religion, Political Economy, Politics* (Boulder, CO: Westview Press, 2014).

Tabler, Andrew J. "Introduction," in Andrew J. Tabler (Ed.), *The Lines that Binds 100 Years of Sykes Picot* (Washington DC: The Washington Institute for Near East Policy, 2016), 1–2.

The Jordan Times. "Jordan cuts ties with North Korea," February 2, 2018, 489.

The Heritage Foundation. "2019 index of economic freedom: Iraq," 2019, www.heritage.org/index/country/Iraq.

The World Bank. "Worldwide governance indicators 2018: Control of corruption," 2018.

UNDP. "Human Development Report 2020."

US Central Intelligence Agency. "Iraq economic data (1989–2003): Regime finance and procurement annex D," April 2007.

US Department of Agriculture Economic Research Service. *Developing Economies: Agriculture and Trade – Situation and Outlook Series* (Rockville, MD: US Department of Agriculture, 1990).

Wade, Robert. "Managing trade: Taiwan and South Korea as challenges to economics and political science," *Comparative Politics* 25 (2) (1993), 147–167.

Wade, Robert. "East Asia's development strategy: Lessons for Eastern Europe," in Michael Dauderstädt (Ed.), *Towards a Prosperous Wider Europe: Macroeconomic Policies for a Growing Neighborhood* (Bonn: Friedrich Ebert Foundation, 2005), 15–24.

Waterbury, John. "The long gestation and brief triumph of import-substituting industrialization," *World Development* 27 (2) (1999), 323–341.

Weiss, Linda. "Developmental states in transition: Adapting, dismantling, innovating, not 'normalizing'," *The Pacific Review* 13 (1) (2010), 21–55.

Werlin, Herbert. "Ghana and South Korea: Lessons from World Bank case studies," *Public Administration and Development* 11 (3) (1991), 245–255.

2 From Tehran boulevard to post-JCPOA Iran

Introduction

Since Iran and South Korea established diplomatic relations back in 1962, bilateral relations between the two countries have been predominantly shaped by their respective alliances with the U.S. and North Korea. The trajectory of diplomatic relations between Seoul and Tehran has been contingent upon geopolitics, nuclear programs, economic sanctions, and America's Middle East policy. Despite the tumultuous regional events since the Iranian Revolution and Tehran's relations with Pyongyang since the Iran–Iraq War and the challenges stemming from therein, South Korea has largely been able to maintain pragmatic relations with Iran leading up to the assassination of Qasem Soleimani in January 2020. In light of the broader interregional and geopolitical relations, this chapter is aimed at shedding light on Korea's role as a middle power in the Iranian context and the political, diplomatic, and economic implications against American foreign policy and Iran's nuclear program.

South Korea's amicable ties with Iran are symbolically embodied through the naming of the Tehran street (*Teheran-ro*) and Seoul street in northern Tehran during the late mayor of Tehran Gholamreza Nikpey's visit to Seoul in June 1977. The Tehran boulevard in Seoul is an affluent district in Gangnam that is likened to California's Silicon Valley as a hub of information technology (IT) industry with glitzy skyscrapers.[1] On the occasion of Tehran mayor's visit, a sisterhood relations pact was signed between Nikpey and the former mayor of Seoul Koo Ja-choon where the two mayors agreed to exchange street names between the two countries.[2] Mayor Nikpey, who attended the completion ceremony of Hoehyeon overpass, and upon realizing that construction costs in Korea were only half of that of Tehran, floated the possibility of attracting Korean civil engineers to Tehran. As an economy characterized by human capital abundance and natural resource deficit, Tehran has assumed strategic importance as a key source of energy supply and a market for the South Korean construction industry. South Korea's participation in Iran's construction industry dates back to the 1973 oil embargo.

DOI: 10.4324/9781003092100-2

ROK–Iran relations were fraught with political and economic predicaments since the Iranian Revolution and the U.S. withdrawal from Iran nuclear deal during the Trump administration. At the same time, bilateral relations were intermittently buoyed by the inception of *Hallyu* (K-Wave). Marking the 40th anniversary since the advent of diplomatic relations between the two countries, the Seoul Park was opened in Tehran in 2003. As South Korea's film industry gained reputation since the early 2000s in parallel with Hallyu boom, in December 2018, a delegation of South Korean filmmakers and performers met with Director-General of Iran's Farabi Cinema Foundation to discuss the opportunities for co-production.[3] At a diplomatic level, the ROK–Iran relations took to new heights in 2016 during the Park Geun-hye administration as Park became the first South Korean president to visit Tehran. Park's visit in May 2016 followed the signing of the Joint Comprehensive Plan of Action (JCPOA) in October 2015, which raised hopes for better investment prospects with the lifting of sanctions on Iran.

Cold War diplomacy: The UN, Islamic Revolution, and Iran–Iraq War

On the eve of formalizing diplomatic relations with Iran in 1962, South Korea's Middle East friendship delegation headed by Ambassador Yun Chi-chang held a meeting with former Iranian Prime Minister Ali Amini and the Acting Minister of Iranian Foreign Ministry Hossein Ghods-Nakhai in Tehran in August 1961. In the following year, Seoul's Cold War diplomacy took off as Kim Yong-woo, the Director of Asian Peoples' Anti-Communist League (APACL, which was renamed to World League for Freedom and Democracy in 1966), headed 22 delegates from APACL member states on a two-week tour to promote anti-communist sentiment in the MENA and the organization.[4] Ministerial meetings held in 1966 also helped in strengthening bilateral ties as Foreign Minister Lee Dong-won awarded Iranian Foreign Minister Abbas Aram the highest order of medal in Korea, and in return, Minister Lee was also awarded an Iranian royal medal of honor by Reza Shah at the Sa'dabad Palace. Throughout the Cold War era, the UN served as a key avenue for advancing South Korea's Cold War diplomacy. During his five-day official visit to Korea in 1969, Iranian Foreign Minister Ardeshir Zahedi issued a joint declaration with Seoul in asserting Iran's commitment to support South Korea's accession to the UN and agreed to strengthen bilateral relations to promote lasting peace. Historical claims of glory and ceremonial grandeur were prevalent in Iran's nation-building practices; the latter provided a channel for international partners to engage Tehran. In 1971, the Park Chung-hee regime sent a special envoy to Tehran at the 2500th National Day celebration. In a ceremony attended by 65 Heads of State, royal families, and special envoys from 28 countries, Mohammad Reza Shah provided eulogy at the tomb of King Cyrus the Great in Pasargadae on the occasion of the national day celebration.

In tandem with nation-building, Tehran and Seoul's cultural and public diplomacy flourished during the nascent days of diplomatic relations between the two countries in the 1960s and 1970s. Impressed by classical Korean music which he heard at a concert, Iranian-American composer and ethnomusicologist Hormoz Farhat visited Korea in 1969 to invite traditional Korean *Gugak* artists to perform at the third Shiraz International Music Festival. In the same year, two Korean members of Taekwondo boys club were invited to demonstrate Taekwondo performance before Reza Shah in the Marmar Palace, Tehran, on the occasion of his 56th birthday. Sports diplomacy offered an avenue for South Korean athletes to engage with their Iranian counterparts and Iranian military officials. Korean martial art Taekwondo became a popular sport that helped promote South Korea's sports diplomacy well into the turn of the century. Korean Taekwondo players, alongside Korean athletes in four other winter sports, participated in a sports competition in 1989 that commemorated the Iranian Revolution. Furthermore, the Iranian Armed Forces Brigadier General and the Commander of the Iran's Imperial Guard Ezzatollah Zarghami attended the 21st International Military Sports Festival hosted by the International Military Sports Council (CISM) earlier in Seoul in 1966. There he attended the air show at the Han River and pledged to support South Korea's participation in the International Olympic Committee meeting that was scheduled to be held in Tehran the following year.

South Korea's diplomacy with Tehran in 1975 was driven by its need to counter the expansion of North Korean influence internationally and expand export markets as Iran was the second largest oil-producing country in the mid-1970s. Cold War politics was most commonly manifested at the UN. There was a great sense of trepidation for South Korea at the 29th session of the UN General Assembly, as Pyongyang received double the support by the pro-communist countries (30 in favor and 12 against) than the votes Seoul received from pro-Western countries (17 in favor and 26 against) for the UN resolution on the question of Korea.[5] By then, Pyongyang was ahead of the Cold War diplomatic competition since it was recognized by three more countries than Seoul, by establishing diplomatic relations with 19 countries.

Since the second visit that followed after special envoy Choi Kyu-hah's diplomatic tour to the Middle East in the aftermath of the 1973 oil embargo, the 1975 summit held with Iran provided a window of opportunity for deepening bilateral economic collaboration. In 1975, Korea Overseas Development Corporation signed a contract with Pars International Container Company and agreed to hire 500 Koreans as tractor trailer drivers at a construction site in Tehran and the southern port city of Khomeyn. More importantly, Seoul also won the contract to build 100,000 housing units in Iran and agreed to send 5,200 technical experts to Tehran.[6] Deputy Prime Minister Nam Duck-woo and Minister of Commerce and Trade Jang Ye-jun's visits to Iran in the preceding years paved the way for the Korea–Iran economic summit. Since the 1973 oil shock, the South Korean government preferred to seek oil and gas exploration opportunities rather than relying on oil imports from the

Middle East. For South Korea, Iran became the second most sought after country to secure energy resources after Saudi Arabia. After the Vietnam War, South Korea's receding economic interests in Vietnam led to the pivot to the oil producers in the Middle East. This was demonstrated through the promotion of the level of joint economic committee to a ministerial level. South Korean private companies and civil engineers were also highly regarded by the Iranian society for their work ethics, which facilitated ministerial meetings and economic collaborations between the two countries. As was the case with South Korea's ties with the rest of the Middle East, complementary structural characteristics between the two countries greatly abetted bilateral economic cooperation. The Iranian counterpart also took great interest in South Korea's shipping industry and expressed their intent to purchase six cargo ships from Hyundai Heavy Industries. The Korean delegation, however, lacked diplomatic tact and savviness at the time and directly delved into the issue of oil prices, which puzzled the Iranian counterpart over the fixation with the exploitation of energy resources.

Between 1975 and 1977, South Korea and Iran expanded bilateral relations to include trade, capital, and technical cooperation. Both parties signed the social security agreement and fisheries cooperation agreement. The Iranian side agreed to buy 300,000 tons of cement, 100,000 tons of fertilizers and ships from Korea, import human resources from Korea, and establish a joint refinery facility in Seoul. Korea agreed to repair the 1,000 km Tehran–Mashhad Railway and support Iran's agricultural and fisheries development by establishing a joint fisheries company.[7] Technological cooperation was also enabled through the Ministerial Committee of Korea–Iran Economic and Technological Cooperation established in 1976. On the political front, interparliamentary exchanges between the two countries since the mid-1970s facilitated political discussions. Across several occasions, both parties expressed support and sympathy for peaceful reunification on the Korean Peninsula and declaration of non-nuclear zone in the Middle East and on recognizing legitimate rights of the Palestinians. As a way of reflecting these trends in robust diplomatic, commercial, and political cooperation, Iran's local daily *Ayandegan*, which was a popular daily newspaper during Reza Shah's rule, featured the South Korean Embassy as having the most active embassy and best public relations among Asian embassies in Tehran. In the West, British and German embassies were identified as among the most active, while the Soviet Consulate was ranked as the most active in the East.[8] On the occasion of the Korean delegation's visit to Tehran in 1977, the Minister of Commerce and Industry Jang Ye-jun praised the Shah's White Revolution and rural development in Iran. The South Korean delegation drew a resemblance between the White Revolution and South Korea's legacy of *Saemaul Undong* Movement.

While commercial ties had only just started to take off, economic cooperation had abruptly been grounded to a halt with the inception of the Islamic Revolution. In 1976, Ssangyong Yanghoe Industry (which was renamed to Ssangyong C&E in 2021) and National Iranian Oil Company (NIOC) embarked on a joint venture of Korea–Iran Oil Company. However, with the onslaught of the Iranian Revolution, Iran's NIOC withdrew capital from the joint venture in 1980. In the same year, the company changed the name to Ssangyong Oil Refining Co., Ltd. (which was renamed to S-Oil in 2000). Ssangyong Oil Company became nationalized when it became the sole shareholder of the company. By 1991, however, Saudi Arabia's state-run oil company Saudi Aramco purchased 35% of Ssangyong Oil Company's equity and became the largest shareholder.

There was a great degree of confusion and uncertainty over Iran's foreign policy vision under the Islamic Republic. A reversal of the pro-American policy under the deposed Pahlavi regime was inevitable. Amid tumultuous geopolitics and political unrest, the safety of Korean companies and employees was at risk. There were also some lingering questions as to whether Iran under Velayat e-Faqih would steer toward modernization or whether it would stick to its religious dogma and regress ten years.[9] As South Korea was perceived as neutral, no Korean lives were lost during the revolution. Some anti-Shah demonstrators were also told to have held signs demanding the French, which hosted Ayatollah Khomeini during his exile under the Shah, and Koreans to remain in Iran. Shortly after the Iranian Revolution, Kim Dong-hui, a former Korean Ambassador to Tehran, met with Ayatollah Khomeini, the de facto ruler of Iran from July 1979, and handed over President Park Chung-hee's letter describing that Kim Il-sung's uncompromising attitude had been an impediment to pursuing a peaceful resolution to the situation on the Korean Peninsula. Since Iran's exports of crude oil resumed on March 5, 1979, a month after the conclusion of the revolution, South Korea resumed construction projects that were stalled for ten months. To support the operation of 12 South Korean construction companies involved in 24 suspended construction projects worth $580 mn, the Iranian government guaranteed payments for accounts receivable to the South Korean counterpart.[10]

Throughout the 1970s, Kuwait and Saudi Arabia comprised 90% of crude oil imports and Iran and Iraq combined constituted the remaining 10% of South Korea's crude oil imports. The fact that both Gulf and (Texas) crude oil were part of the U.S. petroleum conglomerate and direct targets of the OPEC embargo put added pressure on the South Korean economy which prompted the urgency for diversifying the crude oil markets and increasing crude oil inventories.[11] During the same period, there was a construction boom in the Iranian construction market but was oversaturated. While South Korean construction companies were dealing with logistical barriers in executing construction projects and the bidding process, South Korea's Shinwon Construction Company, which became the first South Korean construction company to set foot in the Iranian soil, successfully completed the construction of Khorramshahr Port in southwest of Iran in 1976. As a result, Korean construction companies were able to enhance their credibility and boost their overseas construction orders. In the area of bilateral trade,

South Korea's commercial ties with Iran were burgeoning as exports to Iran (mostly consisting of building materials, textiles, and food products) increased by 293% between 1973 and 1974.[12]

When the Iranian Revolution took place, Park Chung-hee, the incumbent president at the time, directed the crisis management team to put human lives first before commercial interests and encouraged Koreans in Iran to voluntarily flee the country and advised those staying behind to stock up on six months' worth of food supply and not to leave their homes. The Iranian Revolution also had political ramifications during the Cold War era. Apart from logistical and safety concerns, South Korea was also cognizant of the ramifications that an abrupt withdrawal would have on diplomatic relations with the post-Shah regime in Tehran. As longstanding American ally, Seoul had enough reasons to be concerned about an imminent rise in anti-U.S. sentiments in the Iranian streets. Given the drastic shift in political orientations, Iran became a member of the NAM immediately following the Islamic Revolution of 1979 and later chaired the NAM from 2012 to 2015.[13]

Throughout the 1980s, NAM quickly emerged as a key avenue for political competition during the Cold War between Pyongyang and Seoul as the former sought to enhance its diplomatic leverage by rallying the hardline members of NAM around a pro-North Korea-centered political vision on the Korean Peninsula, an agenda that was to flounder by the seventh non-aligned summit hosted in New Delhi in 1983.[14] However, the NAM member states were also sharply divided over political ideologies and views and had lack of political will in resolving differences. In practice, NAM member states were divided between being a neutral member state both in theory and practice, and a nominally non-aligned country. As Seoul worked to gradually close the economic gap with Pyongyang, it was also straddling the divide between political and economic interests. The security of the Korean Peninsula was high on the agenda, but economic interests were equally at stake. Therefore, despite diverging political views with NAM, South Korea was also keen on strengthening ties with oil-exporting NAM member states, which was dubbed "non-aligned diplomacy."

Following the U.S. hostage crisis, the U.S. and its allies downgraded economic and diplomatic relations with Iran and implemented sanctions against Iran. And with the outbreak of the Iran–Iraq War, as an oil-dependent economy, South Korea became apprehensive about the possible closure of the Strait of Hormuz, a major oil chokepoint.[15] It was equally concerned about the repercussions of Iraqi attack on Iran's Abadan Oil Refining Company as the latter was estimated to comprise 5% of South Korea's crude oil supply at the time.[16] As the Iran–Iraq War progressed, there were additional concerns about the repercussions of geopolitics in the region and the safety of Korean expatriates in the war-torn Iran and Iraq. In 1985, the South Korean Embassy in Tehran coordinated with Korean Air to evacuate 450 South Korean residents and 1,700 Korean workers.[17] However, two Korean sailors were found dead in a Maltese tanker attack by an Iraqi rocket while it was transiting the Strait of Hormuz on May 13, 1985, and on July 1, 1988, 45 Korean workers were wounded and 12 were killed by an Iraqi air raid on South Korea's Daelim Industrial Company's construction site in Iran.[18]

Despite the sluggish economic recovery in the initial few years after the Iran–Iraq War, the post-war reconstruction efforts after the Iran–Iraq War also created a fertile market for FDIs and engineering, procurement, and construction (EPC) concessions as the Middle East comprised 78.1% of all overseas construction contracts.[19] In the aftermath of the Iran–Iraq War, Iran ($1 bn) had the highest value of EPC contracts in the Middle East followed by Saudi Arabia and Iraq (both $5.5 mn).[20] The energy sector, as well as free trade zones, offered viable investment opportunities. In the post-war Iran and Iraq, it was projected that South Korea would receive between $45 bn and $50 bn from the construction sector in Iran and export $5.3 bn of goods to Iran and Iraq combined.[21]

With the outbreak of the Iran–Iraq War, South Korea was apprehensive about the potential blockage of the Strait of Hormuz. Although the U.S. initially adopted a position of non-interference and neutrality in the Iran–Iraq War, it shifted course in 1982 when it was apparent that the war was progressing in favor of Iran. Conflict escalated in 1983 when Iraq threatened to target Iranian oil facilities and shipping for military assault, while Iran threatened to close the Strait of Hormuz should Iraqi attacks ensue.[22] While the Iranian Ambassador to South Korea Hassan Taherian singled out Iraq's unilateral reneging from the 1974 Algiers Agreement as the main cause for the conflict, he reassured South Korea that there would be a steady stream of crude oil shipments. In 1982 and 1984, two South Korean cargo ships, including Sambo Banner, which was loaded with oil and returning from Bandar Khomeini port, and the other vessel which was loaded with 9,000 tons of steel bound to Bandar Khomeini port in northern Iran, were destroyed by missile attacks and artillery shelling by the Iraqi Air Force.[23] In November 1985, it was also reported that Iran captured a vessel flying a Panamanian flag near a port of Iran that detained 24 Korean crew members on-board. At the time of the war, 450 Korean expatriates and 1,700 Korean laborers in Iran had fled the country, while there were also other Koreans hired by local Iranian companies who chose to remain in Iran.[24]

By the end of the Iran–Iraq War, Korean companies swarmed into the market in anticipation of rising demands for post-war reconstruction projects. As was the case with Iraq, political instability in Iran which lasted a decade created opportunities for Korean companies to participate in post-conflict reconstruction projects. Following the Iran–Iraq War in 1988, South Korean representatives from major construction companies had visited the Middle East 18 times to explore the possibility of contributing to post-war reconstruction projects. The post-Iran–Iraq War was thus informally referred to as the era of the second Middle East boom after the 1973 oil crisis. There were PPPs between Korean government officials and Korean businesses to spur economic activities in Iran. The South Korean government provided institutional frameworks conducive for trade and participated in large-scale EPC projects. Seoul continued to import Iranian oil throughout the Iran–Iraq War and was regarded as a neutral and economically reliable partner with high levels of technological competence. In 1990, the third Korea–Iran joint committee meeting was held in which the Iranian government invited the South Korean government and companies to contribute to Iran's five-year plan. The Iranian government guaranteed payment to Korean construction companies participating in suspended projects, including the post-war reconstruction project for the port city of Bandar-e Emam Khomeyni. The total amount for reconstruction projects and other deals in oil tanker, crude oil storage tank, and the basic design of a hydroelectric power plant was worth $7 bn.[25] Apart from business opportunities, there were additional risks that followed in the aftermath of the war. Iran and Iraq were both facing shortages of foreign currency and commercial interests were also intertwined with political considerations. For instance, Hyundai Engineering & Construction (Hyundai E&C), which had completed ten construction projects in Iraq, was cautious not to irk Iraq and make a hasty decision of entering into a business partnership with Iran. On the other hand, post-war reconstruction projects also encouraged the chairmen of South Korea's conglomerates and senior government officials to frequent the Middle East more often since then.

The Pyongyang–Tehran nuclear factor

Pyongyang and Tehran's nuclear programs that continued to dominate political discussions domestically as well as internationally had profound political and economic implications. While economic relations thrived between the two states, Iran was unable to pay its exports receivables by 1993, similar to what had happened with Saudi Arabia during oil bust. There was a shortage of foreign exchange since the previous year when the U.S. signed the Iran–Iraq Arms Nonproliferation Act into effect in October 1992. The act imposes sanctions on foreign entities that supply Iran with weapons of mass destruction (WMD) technology or destabilizing numbers and types of advanced nuclear weapons.[26] Tehran's Central Bank requested an extension of the repayment period for imports amounting to $220 mn by one year. If the extension were to be granted, Tehran was required to pay South Korea 10% of the total amount it owed within the ten days of signing the deferment agreement of exports receivables, with the remainder to be paid by the date of maturity.[27]

There were high hopes for expanding commercial ties with Iran when Iran emerged out of economic sanctions in the 2000s, during which a reformist Mohammad Khatami was in power from 1997 to 2005. As the South Korean government conceived of its relations with Iran in pragmatic terms, Iran served as a springboard for ushering in the second Middle East boom. When former South Korean Minister of Commerce, Industry and Energy Shin Kook-hwan visited Iran in February 2001 as part of a wider Middle East tour to discuss economic cooperation, he took great interest in Iran's South Pars gas field development project. In the following year, Hyundai E&C won the contract for constructing phases 2 and 3 as well as phases 4 and 5 of Iran's South Par gas field construction, among a total of 12 phases. During Shin's visit to Tehran, EPC projects worth $5.5 bn were under negotiations, and both parties agreed to establish a Korea–Iran enterprise cooperation committee to strengthen investment and technical cooperation. Iranian Deputy Minister of Industry, Mine and Trade Gholamreza Shafei expressed Iran's interests in entering a joint venture with Samsung Electronics and Hyundai Motors in the semiconductor and automotive industries. Iran was keen on cooperating with Seoul in the field of semiconductors, automobiles, shipbuilding, machinery, and electronics, whereas Seoul's policy preference was in facilitating the Korean companies' entrance into Iran's petrochemical and steel industries. In the previous year, the head of the trade bureau at the Ministry of Foreign Affairs Han Duck-soo also led a public–private economic delegation to expand economic cooperation in the aforementioned areas. In order to support commercial activities of South Korean companies in Iran, Korea Eximbank signed an agreement with Central Bank of Iran to provide a credit limit of $50 mn and agreed to collaborate on Iran's third five-year economic development plan.

While South Korea and Iran managed to maintain pragmatic relations in economic field, there were considerable debates on how to engage countries with nuclear weapons programs. The U.S. President George W. Bush's Axis of Evil speech during his State of the Union address on January 29, 2002 insinuated diverging views on North Korea with the Kim Dae-Jung administration's Sunshine policy. Bush reiterated that there would be no concessions lest Pyongyang meets the prerequisites of decreasing conventional military power, resolve the missile issue, and consent to nuclear inspections. Bush's speech dashed the hopes for an improvement in inter-Korean relations. At the same time, Seoul was apprehensive about the possibility of the U.S. attacking Iraq, Iran, and Libya as it did with Afghanistan. The U.S. War in Afghanistan disrupted trade flows to neighboring countries in South Asia and the Middle East, and business trips to Iran, Saudi Arabia, Jordan, and the UAE were banned as Korean companies set up a contingency plan for possible emergencies. As a country bordering Afghanistan, Iran was closely following the developments on the ground, as the state-owned Islamic Republic News Agency reported that the U.S. bombed the Shindand Air Base near the border shared with Iran. Shortly after the 9/11 attack, travel restrictions were also put in place in Iraq, Iran, Libya, and Sudan, the countries where anti-U.S. sentiment was on the rise. While South Korea also contributed a contingent of troops and police officers to Afghanistan in October 2009, the South Korean government had its misgivings about the North Korean issue being relegated to the backburner in the Obama administration's grand strategy. Despite South Korea's top policy priority in North Korea's nuclear issue, Pyongyang's renege on its denuclearization commitments and the collapse of six party talks had cast shadows over the prospects for a peaceful resolution of the North Korean nuclear issue.

Despite being featured in George W. Bush's Axis of Evil speech, bilateral economic cooperation which strengthened between the two countries in the early 2000s indirectly served as a soft power tool. In Tehran, South Korean automotive, home appliances, and football were popular among the Iranian people, and Mahan Air's direct flights from Tehran and Seoul in 2002 brought the two countries closer together. Iran's automotive industry was fully opened to foreign competition by September 2003. Although South Korea was Iran's second largest trading partner by 2001, the U.S. State Department's designation of Iran as state sponsor of terrorism was an impediment to ROK–Iran bilateral relations. As such, there were increasing calls among business communities and average citizens calling for a need to separate politics from business by adopting a pragmatic approach to business diplomacy.

People's diplomacy and cultural exchange had momentarily been promoted between the two countries under the Lee Myung-bak administration, as Ayatollah Mahmoud Hashemi Shahroudi, a senior Iranian cleric and former head of the judiciary, visited Korea at the invitation of former South Korea's Chief Justice Lee Yong-hun in March 2009. This was the first meeting held between the chief judiciaries of the two countries. Ayatollah Shahroudi also accompanied 11 other senior Iranian judiciary and legal officials in a high-level meeting, including Gholam-Hossein Elham, former Minister of Justice and former Vice President of Iran. During his visit, Ayatollah Shahroudi delivered a lecture on Islamic Sharia Law to Korean law students and met with President Lee Myung-bak. Since then, South Korea also took increasing interest in the social and cultural development of Iran. In August 2009, Iranian lawyer and human rights activist Shirin Ebadi, who became the first Muslim woman to receive the 2003 Nobel peace prize, visited Korea at the invitation of Asian Journalist Association. Ebadi gave a lecture on interfaith dialogue at Kyungdong Church in Seoul and became the first Muslim woman to deliver a public lecture at a Korean church.

Despite these efforts, on the international front, people's diplomacy became overshadowed by the considerable misgivings that non-NWS continued to express about the nuclear weapons programs in Iran and North Korea. By the mid-1990s, *Jane's Defence Weekly* revealed a classified information held by the U.S. Department of Defense which contained eight simulation scenarios for launching a simultaneous war on the Korean Peninsula and in the Gulf. In these scenarios, plans were drawn to deploy military transport aircraft and maritime transport to transport goods in both wars, as well as for the national command authority to divert maritime and air transport resources to Kuwait after the U.S. carried out a counterattack on the Korean Peninsula.[28] As South Korea looked to deter nuclear proliferation on the Korean Peninsula, it expressed support for an indefinite extension of nuclear nonproliferation treaty (NPT) at the 1995 NPT Review and Extension Conference for which Russia also voted in favor. In return for an indefinite extension of NPT, Libya and Syria, which are known for possessing WMDs claimed that Israel, which is suspected of possessing nuclear weapons, should also accede to NPT. Iran and Egypt also urged nuclear weapon states (NWS) to ratify the Comprehensive Nuclear-Test-Ban Treaty (CTBT) and conform to the provisions of the NPT treaty to which they have agreed to. North Korea was staunchly opposed to the U.S. proposition for an indefinite exten nuclear weapon states on of NPT treaty, while China abstained from voting on the issue.[29] In addition to this, diplomatic efforts were also aimed at engaging in political discussions regarding the prospects for peaceful reunification and security on the Korean Peninsula. As soon as former South Korean President Kim Young-sam took office, and briefly after the former Iranian President Akbar Hashemi Rafsanjani was elected as new president, the two countries discussed politics and security on the Korean Peninsula. Given Tehran's close diplomatic relations with the two Koreas, during a bilateral foreign ministerial summit between Seoul and Tehran in 1993, South Korea urged Iran to support the deterrence of North Korea's nuclear weapons program through political dialogue.

As Iran's relations with the two Koreas came increasingly under scrutiny, allegations and refutations were abound on possible nuclear cooperation between the two countries. In the mid-1990s, Iranian foreign ministry's APAC Department Director Hassan Taherian commented that Iran's relations with Pyongyang had improved and its relations with Seoul was satisfactory. While Taherian had hoped for South Korean Foreign Minister to visit Iran as a way of improving economic ties with Asia, around the same time, former Iranian National Assembly speaker Ali Akbar Nateq-Nouri also made plans to visit Pyongyang. In 1997, the incoming Iranian Ambassador to South Korea acknowledged major South Korean companies that stayed after for their contribution to Iran's economy during the Iran–Iraq War while emphasizing that Tehran's arms trade with North Korea was solely for the purpose of national defense.[30]

In 2002, there were allegations that North Korea used Pakistan and Iran as surrogates in testing intermediate-range missiles using North Korean technology, which were denied by Iranian and Pakistani authorities.[31] While Pakistan served as North Korea's procurement network for centrifuge, which is essential for manufacturing nuclear weapons, there were accusations that North Korea secretly developed uranium enrichment technology using centrifugal separators in Iran. In less than a decade later, Congressional Research Service's Larry Niksch suggested that it is necessary to suspend flights between Tehran and Pyongyang by pointing to the evidence that bilateral trade between Iran and North Korea amounted to $2 bn annually.[32] Though China had been reluctant to use leverage with North Korea, Iran, Syria, and Myanmar were among North Korea's main customers. Scientists and technicians and missile components were also transferred through Iran–North Korea flights. Additional reports insinuated arms cooperation between Pyongyang and Tehran. In January 2010, the Thai government reported to the UN Security Council (UNSC) that a plane that transported North Korean weapons was detained in Thailand on December 12, 2009. The plane which was loaded with rocket detonators, launchers, and rocket-propelled grenade launchers that departed from Pyongyang was bound to Mehrabad International Airport. This was the second violation of UN sanctions since Pyongyang conducted a second nuclear test in May 2009. Following the ROKS Cheonan sinking incident on March 26, 2010, it was also revealed that North Korea has been exporting CHT-02D torpedo, which was used during the attack on the ROKS Cheonan corvette, to Iran and Latin American countries.[33]

By virtue of pursuing nuclear weapons programs as rogue regimes, Tehran and Pyongyang have presented a unified front in antagonizing Washington. In 2010, during a meeting in Tehran between former Iranian President Mahmoud Ahmadinejad and a North Korean ambassador, Ahmadinejad urged the officials of two Koreas to "end their differences and not to allow enemies to sow discord between them." Further to this, Ahmadinejad also echoed North Korea's position which had been reiterated in the past that "the U.S. officials [should] avoid provocative measures and to pull out their forces from the region and let the people in both Koreas resolve their own problems."[34] Seen as encroaching on inter-Korean affairs, both countries had pressed the U.S. to stay out of the Korean Peninsula.

The passage of the Comprehensive Iran Sanctions, Accountability, and Divestment Act (CISADA) of 2010 coupled with sanctions mandated by the UNSC resolutions put a great pressure on South Korea. South Korea took great pains to impose additional sanctions against Iran. However, in his interview with BBC Persian, President Obama and international media outlets were quick to frame the action as "voluntary" and in Obama's words, perceiving Iran as a "threat."[35] In spite of Iran and North Korea's missile cooperation, as evidenced by Iran's acquisition of 19 BM-25 missiles from North Korea in 2010, South Korea perceived Iran first and foremost as a business partner rather than as a threat.[36] The CISADA was enacted while Iran was South Korea's fourth largest supplier of crude oil and when bilateral trade with Iran reached $10 bn in the preceding year. As a revitalizing measure, South Korea arranged two banks, Woori Bank and the state-run Industrial Bank of Korea (IBK), to resume financial transactions with Iran by activating won-denominated accounts held by Central Bank of Iran. This, in turn, paved the way for furthering commercial ties between South Korea and Iran. Both countries pursued joint investments and technology transfers on the industrial towns in Qom, in late 2010 and GS E&C re-entered the South Pars gas field project with Qatar six months after withdrawing from the project in June. Tehran was also keen on strengthening bilateral cooperation in science and technology. Leading up to the JCPOA agreement, South Korea continued to alternate between trade and sanctions, including in December 2012 while the import of Iranian oil fluctuated on a year-over-year basis. In the long-term, Iran sanctions have only served to create political dilemmas and failed to make a significant dent in inducing intended behavioral change in the Iranian regime.[37]

Legally binding UNSC resolutions and ramped-up sanctions on Iran also served as an implicit warning to North Korea in the aftermath of the ROKS Cheonan incident. A draft UNSC resolution on imposing additional sanctions against Iranian banks and arms embargo by the U.S. were approved by the permanent members of the UNSC, including Russia and China. The draft resolution of additional sanctions also included a provision on freezing Iranian Revolutionary Guard Corps (IRGC)'s assets overseas. By December 2011, the ROK Ministry of Economic and Finance designated an addition of 99 entities and six individuals as allegedly linked to Iran's nuclear program.[38] After the Cheonan incident, it was expected that the U.S. would submit a draft resolution condemning North Korea's attack and impose additional sanctions on North Korea. Though no evidence has been officially presented by Iranian and North Korean authorities to suggest a direct linkage between North Korea and Iran's nuclear program, nuclear programs of both countries have suggested a symbiotic relationship. Accusations were frequently raised against possible exchange between North Korea's missile technology and Iran's uranium enrichment technology. South Korea's participation in Iran sanctions also created political and diplomatic repercussions. North Korea's state news agency, the Committee for the Peaceful Reunification of the Fatherland, slammed South Korean government's participation in Iran sanctions. Likewise, the Iranian government denounced South Korean government's decision to comply with sanctions against Iran and vowed to raise tariffs on foreign goods by countries participating in sanctions, including South Korea, by 200%. Such measures were adopted to dissuade Iranian customers from buying goods produced by so-called Iran's enemies. Political rhetoric on the latter had sharpened as former Iranian Vice President Mohammad Reza Rahimi refused to trade with countries trading in dollars and euros, calling them "dirty currencies.[39]"

Several items of importance were also discussed on the agenda of the 2010 NPT Review Conference, including CTBT, Fissile Material Cut-off Treaty, ways of strengthening the nuclear nonproliferation regime, and the Middle East Non-Nuclear Zone. In particular, there were controversies surrounding the principles of nuclear disarmament, nuclear nonproliferation, and the right to peaceful use of nuclear weapons among non-NWS. Although the Middle East denuclearization zone was on the agenda, this too generated frictions between Iran and Israel as well as between Iran and the Gulf Arab states.

South Korea's foreign and security policy nevertheless was at odds with Iran's nuclear program. In 2003, Korea Eximbank reported that Iran downgraded economic relations with South Korea after the then Secretary of the Supreme National Security Council (NSC) and Iran's Chief Nuclear Negotiator Hassan Rouhani classified the latter as an unfriendly country alongside Japan, Australia, New Zealand, and Canada. This was due to

Rouhani's accusation that American allies had acted in solidarity with the U.S., which according to his view presumably led to the fallout of Iranian nuclear talks at the International Atomic Energy Agency (IAEA). Iranian Ministry of Foreign Affairs further warned that countries that adopt a hostile policy against Iran will have to bear the consequences. As a result, Iranian Petroleum Minister explicitly warned American allies that contracts would be thwarted for construction orders from the Iranian Petroleum Ministry. Commercial stakes were high considering that LG Construction was participating in phases 9 and 10 of the South Pars gas field development project. Iran was the 27th largest export market for South Korea by 2002, and South Korea's exports to Iran had witnessed an exponential growth by doubling between early and mid-2000s and increased to $30 bn by 2003.[40] South Korea also signed a double taxation prevention agreement and trade agreement with Iran in 2006 on the occasion of the 10th Korea–Iran economic joint committee meeting hosted by Seoul.

By the mid-2000s, ROK–Iran bilateral relations continued to be centered on economic cooperation. During a ministerial meeting held in January 2006, Tehran asked for South Korea's support in future IAEA board meetings, including an upcoming session that was scheduled for later during that year. Seoul, on the other hand, was chiefly concerned with resolving the delay in eight cases of import customs clearance for Korean goods in October 2005. The latter was assumed to be a form of commercial retribution for approving the resolution on Iranian nuclear issue at the IAEA board meeting in September 2005. Shortly after the Iranian government restricted the import of Korean goods, however, Iranian buyers that participated in Korean Machinery Exhibition Export Conference anticipated that import restrictions would be lifted in three to four months. Disagreements over nuclear programs persisted as former Iranian Deputy Foreign Minister for Economic Diplomacy Mahdi Safari emphasized the peaceful nature of Iran's nuclear program while former South Korean Minister of Foreign Affairs Yoo Myung-hwan conveyed South Korean government's concerns over Iran's resumption of nuclear program and reaffirmed South Korea's position in supporting the international community's efforts in upholding nuclear nonproliferation.

Concerns over nuclear proliferation were frequently raised in high-profile international conferences. North Korea nuclear program was high on the agenda in the World Economic Forum held in 2004. Former IAEA Director-General Mohamed ElBaradei pointed out that North Korea's nuclear program is the most dangerous nonproliferation problem facing the world today. In the meantime, Iranian President Mohammad Khatami denied all nuclear-related allegations with North Korea at a press conference on the first day of the annual meeting. Former Iranian Foreign Minister Kamal Kharazi echoed Khatami's claim of denying Tehran's nuclear cooperation with Pyongyang during his subsequent visit to Korea a few months later. In the following year, the then Foreign Minister Ban Ki-moon met with Muammar Qaddafi, who implored North Korea and Iran to follow in Libya's footsteps and renounce WMDs. However, in return, Qaddafi claimed that the international community would have to offer incentives to persuade other countries to follow suit. Qaddafi also stressed the importance of South Korea's role in promoting the nuclear nonproliferation initiative. Minister Ban offered to provide economic and energy support and multilateral security guarantee in return for Pyongyang ending the country's nuclear weapons program. Given the national security interests at stake, all eyes were on the foreign policy blueprint in the second term of George W. Bush administration. The first term of the Bush administration's unilateral, neoconservative, and hawkish approaches to foreign policy was sharply attacked by critics and the international community. Though the Bush administration had considered continuing diplomatic engagements based on the six party talks as a policy option, fundamentally it was suspected that Washington would continue in the same line of policy.

On November 20, 2004, Iran withdrew its previous claim that it would freeze 20 centrifuges for the country's uranium enrichment program. Amid reports that Iran was building a secret tunnel for its uranium enrichment activities, former Chairman of the Iranian Parliament Gholam-Ali Haddad-Adel protested IAEA's approach to the nuclear issues as a double standard and discriminatory. In fact, President George W. Bush had refused to engage with Iran in direct talks while issuing a stern warning that Iran would be internationally isolated if it continues to pursue its nuclear program. America's alliance with Israel was one of the main reasons that Bush objected to seeking a diplomatic solution to the nuclear issue. More importantly, the Bush administration expressed fewer misgivings over India's nuclear weapons capabilities and potential nuclear proliferation threat for the latter as a democracy with better accountability and transparency. However, at the same time, Bush admitted that Iran's nuclear program had been subjected to NPT's mandate and IAEA's nuclear verification and monitoring activities to a greater extent than North Korea, which expelled the IAEA inspectors in December 2002 and withdrew from the NPT in January 2003.

While there is a general consensus that there should not be a differential approach to countries that are committed to the nuclear NPT for peaceful uses of nuclear energy, Pyongyang violated this premise by withdrawing from the NPT in 2003. Six party talks and inter-Korean and U.S.–North Korea summits bore little fruit as Pyongyang declared itself as a "responsible nuclear weapons state." Though South Korea's nuclear dilemma has drawn relatively little attention, South Korea violated nuclear NPT safeguards agreement by failing to report Korea Atomic Energy Research Institute (KAERI)'s nuclear activities. In the past, Seoul had conducted chemical uranium enrichment experiments and manufactured depleted uranium munitions between 1979 and 1987 and experimented with laser uranium enrichment in 2000.[41] In November 2004, the IAEA board decided not to refer South Korea and Iran's nuclear tests to the UNSC. In a private IAEA board meeting held in Vienna, 21 out of 35 country representatives had spoken out against Seoul's clandestine nuclear material tests conducted in the past. Though the U.S., UK, and France took a tougher stance toward the violation than others, none of the member states treated South Korea's nuclear activities on par with the Iranian or North Korean counterparts or insisted on referring South Korea's case to the UNSC. While the South Korean government asked the IAEA to downgrade the warning by releasing Chairman's summary in lieu of a Chairman's statement, the U.S. vowed to push for a resolution on referring Iran to the UNSC if it were to resume nuclear enrichment activities in the future.

South Korea's strategic interests in Iran mainly lie in securing a continued supply of crude oil and expanding South Korea's participation in large-scale construction projects in Iran. As such, it joined Turkey, Iran, France, and India in participating in post-war reconstruction projects in Iraq. While Iran emerged as a major construction market in the Middle East, the election of hardliner Mahmoud Ahmadinejad as the new Iranian president in June 2005 was worrisome for the business community. Korean companies involved in major construction projects in Iran were concerned about subjecting Korea's commercial activities to erratic politics. Seoul was cognizant that the Supreme Leader enjoys overriding influence over Iran's foreign and economic policy under the Velayat e-Faqih regime. In particular, Mahmood Ahmadinejad's intent of resuming nuclear activities since uranium enrichment was last suspended in November 2004 stoked public debates about the instability in global oil production and supply and the future U.S.–Iran relations. Moreover, Ahmadinejad made a public declaration denying foreign capital and technology for developing Iran's oil field. Iran's pivot to the East was greatly facilitated by Iran's oil reserves and Iran's deteriorating relations with the West since the Iranian Revolution and the Kurdish Democratic Party of Iran (KDPI)-led insurrection in Iranian Kurdistan from late 1989 to 1996. While Iran had hoped that enticing customers for energy-hungry China and India would bolster its political cause, these energy-deficit economies, including South Korea, for the most part had been able to maintain pragmatic relations with Iran by separating politics from economics.

While Tehran remained South Korea's strategic partner for energy trade and construction industry and has been a key re-export hub, it also assumed strategic importance as a diplomatic gateway for negotiating on the Taliban issue in Afghanistan, the Iraqi Kurdistan, and the Strait of Hormuz. Politically, given its geographic proximity and social and cultural affinities with the Kurdish population, South Korea also sought Iran's endorsement on Seoul's dispatch of additional troops to the Kurdistan autonomous region in northern Iraq. In 2007, 23 Kandahar-bound Korean nationals in Afghanistan were abducted by Taliban. Two Koreans were killed in the process and the remaining 21 abductees were released after 42 days since abduction. The prisoner swap option was already ruled out in the negotiations held between the U.S. and Afghanistan. The South Korean government continued to make a humanitarian appeal at a tribal elders meeting held in Kabul and launched a public diplomacy campaign to help release hostages. In addition to these avenues, President Roh Moo-hyun met with the President of African Union (AU) while Minister of Foreign Affairs Ban Ki-moon met with Iranian Foreign Minister Manouchehr Mottaki, who condemned Taliban for kidnapping and killing Korean abductees and vowed to cooperate with the Afghan government and the UN to help release South Korean hostages.

During his visit to South Korea in January 2009, former Iranian Foreign Ministry spokesman Hasan Gashgavi denied Iran's intention of possessing nuclear weapons that could potentially lead to a nuclear arms race in the region. And while the U.S. demanded Iran's cessation of nuclear enrichment as a prerequisite for a dialogue, Iran denied such accusations and claimed that it was pursuing a peaceful nuclear program, and that uranium enrichment is a sovereign right that signatories of the nuclear NPT are entitled to.[42] While Iran's nuclear program was at the centerpiece of press coverage, Gashgavi stated that promoting media and cultural cooperation was the chief purpose for his visit to Seoul. The popularity of South Korea's *Hallyu* (Korean Wave) and Korean TV shows Dae Jang Geum and Jumong, which recorded above 85% ratings in Iran, promoted cultural and media cooperation between the two countries.[43] As such, Gashgavi brushed off any concerns about unilateral U.S. sanctions or UN-imposed sanctions to be a hindrance to ROK–Iran bilateral relations. This was particularly true on the commercial front, as bilateral trade exceeded $12 bn by 2008.[44]

While Iran remained cautiously optimistic to Obama's Middle East policy, based on his presidential campaign slogans of "Change" and "Change We can Believe in," it did not make haste in giving a downright optimistic prognosis for the incoming administration's Middle East policy. Obama had entered his presidency by declaring that he would use direct diplomacy with Iran with the possibility of seeking improved relations and a resolution to resolve differences over the nuclear issue. But in declaring the resolve to pursue direct engagements with all countries regardless of political differences, the Obama administration also signaled greater interests in introducing tougher measures on international sanctions that violate the NPT, including Iran and North Korea. During his State of the Union address delivered at a joint session of the U.S. Congress, Obama also reverberated George W. Bush's declaration that Iran would be internationally isolated if the Iranian leaders ignore their international obligations.

Occasional discussions on South Korea's political cooperation with Iran have never gone beyond political rhetoric. While Iranian and South Korean governments were in unison in condemning terrorism and extremism, international efforts to combat violence and counterterrorism were often linked to political motives. Iranian officials went into great lengths at denouncing not only the terrorist attacks in Kuwait, Tunisia, and France but also Saudi Arabia's operation in Yemen.[45] Iran had hosted the inaugural World Against Violence and Extremism (WAVE) conference in December 2014 after the proposal for this conference initiated by Hassan Rouhani received an approval from an overwhelming majority of participants in the UN General Assembly in December. Though South Korea rhetorically joined the international community in supporting counterterrorism initiatives, in practice both sides were unable to prioritize on a converging set of geostrategic interests. Moreover, Seoul had very little interest in getting involved in geopolitics of the Middle East. When it eventually did so by sending troops to the Strait of Hormuz in January 2020 and obliged sanctions on Iran, it did so mostly at the pressure of the U.S. and at the expense of prioritizing political and economic ties with Iran. As a result, collateral damage has been inflicted on South Korea including a South Korean tourist who was sentenced to seven years in prison on espionage charges in October 2013 as well as the seizure of the South Korean oil tanker MT Hankuk Chemi in 2021. Reiterating its position on the peaceful use of nuclear energy and slamming Israel as the only nuclear weapons-possessing country in the Middle East, Iranian President Hassan Rouhani emphatically stressed in the joint press conference with President Park Geun-hye in May 2016, "Iran seeks peace and stability in the Korean Peninsula and is against the production of any types of WMDs. We want a world free from WMDs, especially in the Korean Peninsula and the Middle East.[46]"

Interparliamentary exchanges between Iran and South Korea also flourished since the Lee Myung-bak administration. Interparliamentary meeting has served as a secondary point of contact between the two countries in the event of political and economic tensions, as demonstrated through the discussions held between former Prime Minister and Speaker of National Assembly Chung Sye-kyun and Iranian authorities over the diplomatic spat and seizure of an oil tanker linked to frozen Iranian assets in South Korea in 2021. Former South Korea's National Assembly speaker Kang Chang-hee became the first South Korean parliamentary speaker to visit Tehran in January 2014. In his historic visit, Kang met with President Hassan Rouhani and the Iranian parliamentary speaker Ali Larijani following the Geneva Agreement. A memoranda of understanding (MOU) was signed between the Head of Iranian parliament's research center and the South Korean counterpart in June for legislative cooperation.[47]

The provision "peaceful uses of nuclear energy" sparked a great deal of controversy even after the interim agreement, Joint Plan of Action (JPOA), was signed into effect on November 24, 2013. Fear was widespread among Israel and the neighboring Gulf states that the nuclear deal would set a precedence for condoning uranium enrichment, which would allow for Iran to produce nuclear fuel and potentially for military use. There was a general sense of trepidation that doing so would set forth a reverse effect – fueling mistrust among the neighboring countries and encouraging more countries to demand rights to enrich uranium and purchase nuclear weapons as a countermeasure.

As the Geneva agreement facilitated commercial ties with Iran, by June 2014, South Korea's oil imports from Iran more than doubled to 604,402 tons per barrel from the previous month.[48] Seoul rushed to expand business opportunities by sending business delegations through the Korea International Trade Association and strengthening cooperation in the shipping and maritime sector. With the nuclear deal underway, discussions were held on launching South Korean automotive and home appliance assembly lines in Iran, promoting economic cooperation through Iran's free trade zones, including investing in Pars Special Economic Energy Zone (PSEEZ) in Siraf. There were also renewed interests in investing in Iran's Qazvin province as well as an ease in the transfer of humanitarian goods and government-to-business and business-to-business (B2B) transactions.[49] Interparliamentary relations between the two countries continued to serve as a core avenue for facilitating high-level exchanges in political, trade, and cultural cooperation.

Sanctions and lawsuits: Bank Mellat and the Dayyani family

Iran's Bank Mellat, which opened a foreign branch in Seoul in June 2001, was at the center of controversy of the ROK–Iran spat over frozen oil assets. South Korea was one of the six branches it established apart from the UK, Germany, Turkey, and Armenia. Bank Mellat has been responsible for processing remittances for Iranian workers and looked to strengthen activities in trade finance with a capital of $100 mn. To boost South Korea's exports in automobile parts, machinery, and electronic products, Korea Eximbank increased the short-term deferred financing costs by 100% from $50 mn to $100 mn through the Seoul branch of Bank Mellat in 2004.[50]

In August 2010, the American government pressed Seoul to impose sanctions on the Seoul branch of Bank Mellat, which was suspected of operating as a base for international financial transactions related to nuclear and missile development. Therefore, in consultation with Iranian and American governments, South Korean government sought to pursue diplomatic efforts to support commercial activities such as in crude oil imports and South Korean construction companies doing business with Iran. It proposed creating a clearing account as a countermeasure against Iran sanctions. Deputy Governor of Iranian Central Bank also met with officials at Korea Central Bank to discuss such measures. In order to proceed with the plan, South Korean government stressed that it intended to exclude trading items prohibited by the U.S. including WMDs using the clearing account. South Korean government was also faced with a dilemma over the closure of Bank Mellat's Seoul branch, which was accused of providing financial support to Iran's nuclear activities, including to Iranian entities that had been designated by Executive Order 13382.

The CISDA of 2010, which came into effect on July 1, 2010, mandated that sanctions be imposed on financial institutions supporting the Iranian government's WMD and terrorist activities, violating Iranian sanctions imposed by the UNSC, supporting money laundering by Iranian financial institutions, and offering financial support to the IRGC. As a result, Bank

Mellat's Seoul branch, Iran Petro Capital Korea branch, and Cisco Shipping Company were among the Iranian entities in Korea that faced sanctions by the U.S. Department of Treasury. With the passage of the UN Security Council Resolution 1929 (2010), the State Department's Special Advisor for Nonproliferation and Arms Control Robert Einhorn demanded its East Asian allies, Japan and South Korea, to cooperate in sanctions against Iran to help deter Iran's nuclear ambitions.[51] Alternative measures to Iran sanctions were to be introduced in tandem with EU and Japan's policies. Iran sanctions inhibited Seoul's commercial activities and in winning contracts in Iran's oil and gas industry and prohibited transactions with Iranian companies and financial institutions. South Korea, however, was left with little option but to comply as violating sanctions would equally restrict South Korea's transactions with U.S. banks.

Sanctions against Iran not only disrupted South Korea's procurement of energy resources and restricted trade but also led to tangible financial losses. According to the government audit data submitted by the Korea Trade-Investment Promotion Agency (KOTRA), South Korea's participation in Iran sanctions led to increased trade receivables amounting to KRW 250 bn. Moreover, South Korea's trade with Iran by October 2010 had declined by 43% with trade deficits totaling KRW 730 bn.[52] Even while Iran was the fourth largest crude oil supplier in the world in 2010, South Korea was mulling options such as stockpiling energy reserves and diversifying sources of crude oil imports in order to better prepare for economic sanctions against Iran.[53] Iranian sanctions, however, had a much larger impact on private South Korean businesses. In 2009 alone, there were roughly over 2,150 local small and medium enterprises (SMEs) that traded with Iran.[54] Therefore, South Korean government also had to improvise additional measures to help liquidate South Korean SMEs impacted by Iranian sanctions. In response, the ROK Ministry of Knowledge Economy (renamed to Ministry of Trade, Industry and Energy in 2013) offered South Korean SMEs with rollover loans for maturing debts and soft loans amounting to $418,300.[55]

Iran sanctions hurt South Korea's economy with the suspension of Hyundai and KIA motors exports and the termination of GS Construction's contract on phases 6–8 of South Pars gas project. As a result of sanctions, South Korea's imports of Iranian crude oil declined in May 2012 by 47.3% from the previous month.[56] Iranian crude oil, which was a cheaper source of crude oil by two to four dollars per barrel, accounted for 9.6% of South Korea's total oil imports.[57] Though South Korea's sanction on Iran had greatly restrained crude oil imports, some relief and exemptions were provided for trade and commercial activities in non-oil sectors. By December 2013, the Obama administration extended sanctions waiver by six months. Sanctions waiver was granted to countries that had significantly reduced Iranian oil imports for the past 180 days. In the following year, Iran's Deputy Foreign Minister Abbas Araghchi designated South Korean, Japanese, and Swiss banks for international trade, specifically for purchasing food, drugs, and medical equipment. Despite sanctions imposed on Bank Mellat's Seoul branch, Seoul and Tehran were able to establish financial cooperation through a MOU that was signed between Korea Securities Depository and Iran's Central Securities Depository in 2014.

With frozen Iranian assets held in South Korea, a South Korean trader was arrested on charges for violating the Foreign Exchange Transactions Act and the Customs Act in 2012. The culprit was caught transferring over KRW 1 tn to nine overseas bank accounts from an Iranian Central Bank account in Korea. The South Korean trader established a ghost company and deceived Korean financial authorities and set up a fraudulent transaction invoice worth KRW 1.9 tn between Iran and a Dubai-based company. The trader abused the Iran Central Bank's KRW account set up with a Korean bank when the account was originally opened for the purpose of bypassing USD and resuming bilateral trade with Iran by trading in Korean Won since 2010. It was speculated that the Korean trader had colluded with the Iranian authorities in exchange for a commission considering that the payment instructions sent by Iranian commercial banks were not forged and the money remitted to nine countries were also designated by Iranian authorities. Following restrictions placed on financial transactions with Iran, Iran's Central Bank asked two South Korean banks, Woori Bank and IBK, to open a time deposit account with an interest rate of 3% per annum in lieu of opening a trade settlement account with an interest rate of 0.1% per annum. If the request were to be rejected, the Iranian authorities threatened to suspend deposit transactions, which would cut off the settlement of export payments to Iran and inflict damage on 2,700 Korean companies exporting to Iran. The amount of Iran's assets held by two South Korean banks reached KRW 5 tn.[58]

Since its operation was suspended due to UN sanctions in September 2010, Bank Mellat's Seoul Branch resumed its operation in March 2016 following relief in sanctions in January 2016. It finalized the establishment of a SWIFT system and opening transactions with Korean banks such as KEB Hana Bank and Woori Bank. The South Korean government also consulted the U.S. government in establishing an alternative payment system that would use the euro for trade with Iran. With the resumption of Bank Mellat's operation in Seoul, Persia International Bank, which is a trading bank headquartered in London through the joint investment between Iranian Banks, Bank Mellat and Tejarat Bank, sought to open a second overseas branch in Seoul, after Dubai.

In addition to Iranian assets frozen in South Korea, the South Korean government faced a third I dispute (ISD) case against an Iranian entity. In 2015, Entekhab Industrial Group, a consumer electronics group run by Mohammad Reza Dayyani, filed an ISD suit against the South Korean government as a request for the creditors to return down payment. In 2010, Entekhab Industrial Group agreed to purchase the equity of Daewoo Electronics for 540 bn Won and paid 10% of the agreed price to creditors in November, but creditors terminated the deal with Entekhab Industrial Group after it missed the deadline for full payment and over concerns about the impact of economic sanctions against Iran.[59] When Daewoo Electronics was later sold to a South Korean conglomerate DB Group the creditors refused to return the down payment for the purchase of Daewoo Electronics. The Dayyani family won the ISD case against the Korean government in 2015 and seized assets of Korean government bonds held by Korean companies, including Samsung, LG, and KEB Hana Bank, in the Netherlands. As of June 2018, the International Trade Law Commission arbitral tribunal ordered the Korean government to compensate interests on late refunds and contract deposit.

The South Korean government filed a cancellation lawsuit with the British High Court related to the merger and acquisition of Daewoo Electronics in July 2018. Due to sanctions against Iran, the sticking points to the ISD suit were over the plaintiffs and defendants of the dispute. The South Korean government maintained that the legal dispute with the Dayyanis was not subject to the ISD case since Entekhab Industrial Group had invested in a Singapore company called D&A Holding, which the Dayyanis acquired to change the identity of the purchaser to a non-Iranian entity with the sole purpose of buying Daewoo's assets and liabilities.[60] South Korea lost the ISD suit against the Dayyanis in 2019 and announced that it will present its objections to a British court ruling. There are far-reaching implications of the ISD case. International regulatory regimes are important for South Korea, which is an export-oriented economy and a conglomerate-led economy. South Korea has significantly higher bilateral investment treaties and treaties with investment provisions than Japan and is short of one-fifth of those of China.[61]

The JCPOA agreement and Park Geun-hye's high-profile Tehran visit

Shortly after the JCPOA was enacted on January 16, 2016, Park Geun-hye became the first South Korean president to visit Iran in May. Fifty-four years ago, her father and President Park Chung-hee invited Reza Shah to attend a Korea–Iran bilateral summit in August 1978. However, Park failed to convene the summit that year due to Islamic Revolution and the assassination of Park Chung-hee in the same year. Prior to the official state visit in May 2016, Park had hosted former Iranian Prime Minister Manouchehr Eghbal during his visit to Seoul in the 1970s while she served as a first lady to her father, Park Chung-hee.

Based on mutual economic and diplomatic interests, Park and Rouhani welcomed the JCPOA agreement reached between Iran and the P5+1 on June 14, 2015. The two leaders issued a joint statement on comprehensive partnership in the political, economic, cultural, inter-regional cooperation, and judiciary and security domains.[62] For the aim of advancing the stability and prosperity of the Korean Peninsula, the Middle East, and the international community, both leaders recognized the need to enhance bilateral cooperation by institutionalizing high-level meetings at a ministerial level and promote economic cooperation and mutual investments and expand bilateral trade in energy by convening Iran–Korea joint economic commission. Further agreements were made to strengthen collaborations in science and technology and in health sciences. Both countries also agreed to boost cultural cooperation and people-to-people connectivity, which have been a strength in bilateral relations. In recognizing the importance of promoting and strengthening international peace and security, both parties supported the fundamental values and principles contained in the UN Charter and NPT treaty. Both countries also reaffirmed their commitment to combating terrorism and violent extremism in the strategic framework recognized by the draft UN resolution, "A World against Violence and Violent Extremism (WAVE)" proposed by Rouhani.[63]

During Park's visit to Tehran in May 2016, Rouhani agreed in principle that both countries are opposed to North Korea's nuclear program. In reference to North Korea's nuclear program, Rouhani declared that nuclear weapons must be eliminated from the Korean Peninsula. As Park explained South Korean government's position on North Korea's nuclear program to the Iranian counterpart, the latter expressed support for Korea's aspiration for denuclearization and the peaceful reunification of the Korean Peninsula. Park's high-profile visit to Tehran was the first high-level meeting held between the two countries following the Iran nuclear deal. Following the meeting with Iran's Supreme Leader Ayatollah Khamenei and President Hassan Rouhani, Park expressed hopes to work closely with Iran to realize the vision of cooperating with the international community as the only way for achieving stability and prosperity that Pyongyang desires.[64]

On the commercial front, Park's visit to Tehran raised fresh hopes for buttressing economic cooperation between the two countries. Park led the largest economic delegation in the history of South Korea's commercial diplomacy. Representatives from 146 conglomerates and SMEs, including the chairmen of Korean conglomerates, including SK Corporation, GS Group, POSCO, and LS Group, were among those who accompanied the president during the visit. Following the bilateral summit held in the Sa'dabad Palace in Tehran, both countries agreed to collaborate on 30 projects worth $37.1 bn. Economic cooperation was discussed in the fields of transportation and infrastructure, water management, oil and gas, health care, and information and communication technology. Dubbed as the "second oil-boom," former top economic aide for Blue House Ahn Jong-beom acclaimed Park's state visit to Tehran as "the greatest economic and diplomatic milestone in history."[65] South Korea looked to restore the volume of bilateral trade to the pre-sanctions level, which stood at $17.4 bn in 2011 and plummeted to $6.1 bn in 2015.[66] Following the JCPOA agreement, Yoo il-ho, former Deputy Prime Minister of Economy and Minister of Strategy and Finance, aimed to double South Korea's exports to Iran in the following two years after the sanctions were lifted on Iran. Around the same time as President Park's visit to Tehran, the Central Bank of Iran and the Korea Development Bank renewed their ties as they signed an MOU to strengthen their cooperation in trade, banking, and investments. Capital market cooperation opportunities were also discussed between Korea Exchange and Securities and Exchange Organization of Iran to avail of sanctions lifted on Iran.

As the first female president to visit Iran, Park Geun-hye's veiled appearance caught the attention of the media. In parallel with Tehran Street and Seoul Park, both countries also agreed to build K-tower and I-tower in Tehran and Seoul to symbolize bilateral relations. During Park's visit, Korean culture week was held in Tehran's landmark Milad Tower. In commemoration of Park's visit, cultural performances were held as well as Iranian and Korean traditional martial arts performances in Zurkhaneh and Taekwondo. An MOU on exchange and cooperation in cultural technology and creative industries was signed at a ministerial level to promote cultural cooperation between the two countries. National Museum of Korea and National Museum of Iran also signed an MOU to hold a special exhibition highlighting the history of cultural exchanges between the Persian empire and the Silla Dynasty. In addition, both countries agreed to establish a Korean Cultural Center in Iran in 2017.

Tehran and Seoul also discussed ways to broaden energy cooperation in renewable energy, including a $10 bn project in Khuzestan province, and hydro-electric power plants following the P5+1 agreement. Little known at the time was that talks were also held between Iran's Atomic Energy Organization and South Korea's Ministry of Trade, Industry and Energy for nuclear energy cooperation in 2016. Among potential partners that were being discussed for the possible collaboration on Iran's nuclear power plant included China, France, Japan, Germany, and Italy. South Korea and Iran also explored joint ventures in refinery and petrochemical projects which received a major boost from the lifting of sanctions. Iran sought to reopen Bank Mellat's Seoul branch and resume direct flights between Seoul and Tehran. South Korea's imports of Iranian oil also surged since the JCPOA as Iran became the second largest supplier of crude oil to South Korea by April 2017.

Iran's population potential, with a population of 78 mn, and major reserves of natural resources are the prime factors that have made Iran an attractive market. By 2011, South Korea and Iran were included in two new acronyms, coined by the former chairman of Goldman Sachs Asset Management Jim O'Neill, denoting emerging markets aside from BRICS – the first which includes South Korea is MIKT (Mexico, Indonesia, South Korea, and Turkey) and the "Next 11," which includes the four MIKT countries and Bangladesh, Iran, Pakistan, the Philippines, Egypt, and Nigeria.[67] However, the controversies surrounding Iran's nuclear program have been a major impediment from realizing that potential. Referred to as "Iran effect," Park's Iran tour also gave a boost to her approval rating akin to rally-round-the-flag effect. According to Gallup Korea, Park's approval rating increased by

4.6 percentage points and spiked from 29% to 35.6%, which had initially plummeted due to the defeat in the April 13 legislative elections.[68]

Following Park's historic visit to Tehran in 2016 and a surge in high-level visits from South Korea to Iran during the Lee Myung-bak administration, delegations from Iranian and South Korean private enterprises signed 22 MOUs on technological transfers in innovation sectors in December 2017. According to the ROK MOFA, to date, there have been 41 high-level visits from Seoul to Tehran and conversely there have been 34 high-level visits from Tehran to Seoul between 1998 and 2019.[69] The Iranian Ambassador to South Korea Hassan Taherian commended the strengthening of bilateral ties and South Korea's traditional strengths in automotive and EPC sectors.[70] By the early 2010s, Iran was the largest export market for South Korea in the Middle East; by 2018, South Korea was Iran's fourth largest trading partner for exports ($3.64 bn) and fifth largest trading partner for imports ($2.29 bn).[71] The volume of trade for Iranian exports to South Korea had far exceeded South Korea's exports to Iran but the former was less diversified relative to the latter. Iran's crude oil exports in 2018 accounted for 95.9% of the total exports to South Korea.[72]

At the same time, there were also concerns regarding a possible drop in oil prices caused by an increase in Iran's oil production and a reverse oil shock. Furthermore, skeptics warned about over-optimism considering the heated competition in the Iranian market against the U.S., Japan, China, and India. Institutionally, Iran's financial sector is heavily indebted with a less advanced legal system. The challenges of settling on an alternative payment system for Iran are also an inhibiting factor. Although South Korea established a Korean won-denominated payment system for bilateral trade with Iran since 2010, the payment system, which had a lump sum of Iranian funds deposited in the account, became unavailable due to sanctions imposed against Iran. Investment plans were also scrapped due to the pharmaceutical company's deficit from economic sanctions. Chungbuk province had failed to attract $2 bn as a foreign investment from Tuba, an Iranian traditional medicine company, which had agreed to build a traditional Iranian medicine research institute in Osong Bio Valley in Chungcheong province and invest $2 bn over the course of a decade.

Trump's maximum pressure campaign and unilateral U.S. sanctions

As the Trump administration launched the maximum pressure campaign on Iran and announced withdrawal from the JCPOA in May 2017, fresh rounds of economic sanctions and punitive measures toward Iran loomed around the corner. Even when South Korea was initially exempted from sanctions, alongside China, India, and Japan, the U.S. sanctions stifled banking cooperation as well as in economic exchanges between the two countries. South Korea's relations with Iran suffered a setback following a series of geopolitical conflicts that flared up in the Gulf, including the attacks on oil tankers off the Fujairah coast, the attack on Saudi Aramco's oil facilities in Abqaiq and Khurais, and the downing of the U.S. drone in 2019, which culminated with the assassination of the former IRGC commander Qasem Soleimani. As South Korea was mulling over the options for dispatching troops to the Strait of Hormuz, Iran's Ambassador to South Korea Saeed Badamchi Shabestari was summoned due to the concern that the decision might negatively affect bilateral ties. Shabestari was quoted saying, "this moment is the biggest crisis in [1,000 years] of our [bilateral relations] history."[73]

By July 2019, the IAEA confirmed that Iran had exceeded 4.5% in uranium limits set by Iran nuclear deal. In August, Iranian Foreign Ministry spokesperson tried to dissuade South Korea from joining the U.S.-led maritime coalition in the Gulf by advising Seoul from exercising restraint and neutrality as a country in commercially friendly terms. In March 2020, Iranian Foreign Minister Mohammad Javad Zarif posted pictures of Iranian children dying from rare diseases and denounced U.S. sanctions as "economic terrorism." In accusing the U.S. of imposing "inhumane sanctions," Zarif also criticized South Korea for cutting off humanitarian aid and medicine supplies as part of U.S.-imposed sanctions. As a consequence, a joint public–private Korean delegation met with U.S. government officials in the same month to discuss Iran sanctions on humanitarian items, including medicines, medical devices, agricultural products, and food. To provide governmental support for Korean companies doing business with Iran under sanctions, the Ministry of Foreign Affairs hosted a company briefing session for 40 Korean companies at the Korea Chamber of Commerce and Industry on ways to expand trade with Iran using humanitarian goods. The South Korean government also launched a special task force, which consisted of relevant government ministries and KOTRA to support the expansion of humanitarian trade between the two countries. At one point, in July 2020, the Iranian government also threatened to take legal actions against Korean financial institutions for its frozen assets. In response to the Iranian government's request for humanitarian aid for the global pandemic, South Korea followed "Swiss mechanism" which refers to a transaction mechanism in which information is reported to the U.S. Treasury for validation to ensure that transactions with Iran are not in violation of sanctions. In April 2020, South Korea was able to send medical and quarantine equipment to Iran for Covid-19 relief. And by January 2021, South Korea received special approval from the U.S. Treasury Department to supply vaccines to Iran through COVAX facility, which is an international mechanism for the purchase and distribution of Covid-19 vaccines led by the World Health Organization (WHO), as an upfront payment.

Amid sanctions and geopolitical skirmishes, the ROK Ministry of Foreign Affairs arranged meetings with officials at the Office of Foreign Assets control at the U.S. Treasury Department and the U.S. State Department to discuss ways to resume humanitarian exports to Iran in February 2020. While humanitarian efforts were underway, the pressures stemming from U.S. sanctions undermined ROK–Iran relations. In August 2020, Tehran accused Seoul for blocking its funds in South Korea. Tehran has refused to accept South Korea's proposal to reimburse the frozen funds partially through medical supplies and food shipments. The Iranian Central Bank lodged an official complaint against two South Korean banks that have frozen approximately $8.5 bn Iranian funds following the ratcheting up of the U.S. sanctions on Iran. The U.S. sanctions fueled tensions between Seoul and Tehran as Iranian Foreign Minister Mohammad Javad Zarif retorted that Tehran would take necessary actions to reclaim frozen funds from Seoul. Slamming Seoul's compliance with the U.S. sanctions as "blind obedience,"[74] Zarif and Iranian Foreign Ministry spokesman Seyed Abbas Mousavi contrasted Seoul's decision with those of Beijing and Muscat. Blasting U.S. sanctions as "illegal," the governor of the Iranian Central Bank Abdolnaser Hemmati lambasted Seoul for blocking humanitarian exports and freezing Iranian funds. This is in spite of the $500,000 worth of hereditary disease treatment sent to Iran in May 2020 – the first humanitarian exports to Iran since the U.S. ramped up sanctions in 2019. Though South Korea is not the only country that has complied with U.S. sanctions, Iran's capture of South Korea's oil tanker MT Chemi highlighted the extent to which ROK–U.S. alliance has been a critical factor in shaping the shifting trajectory of ROK–Iran relations. The heightened tensions over frozen Iranian assets in South Korea also imply the extent to which the Iranian government was cash-strapped.

Payments for Iranian oil have equally been a source of friction in ROK–Iran relations. In 2012, South Korea had decided to introduce export quotas on steel, cars, and electronics to mitigate the risks associated with payment defaults in an economy crippled by sanctions. Moreover, after Seoul halted Iranian oil imports in August 2012, Tehran responded by threatening to retaliate against South Korea's ban on Iranian oil imports and trade quotas, only to revoke its decision within a matter of months. Initially, Iran cautioned that it would suspend imports of South Korean goods as a retaliation. Former Iranian Petroleum Minister Rostam Qasemi and former Iranian Ambassador to South Korea Ahmad Masumifar both warned that "relations with this country [South Korea] will be reconsidered" and that "oil importing countries will have to pay the price for these sanctions."[75] Transferring the $1 bn oil debt to Iran in two installments was not much of an issue when Iranian sanctions regime had eased following the interim Geneva Agreement back in November 2013.[76] However, stricter sanctions regime under the Trump administration have stirred political conflicts between South Korea and Iran even after Trump's departure from Washington.

The former commander of IRGC Qasem Soleimani was killed in a U.S. airstrike in Baghdad, Iraq on January 2, 2020. Three days later, the Iranian government announced that it would end nuclear commitments under the JCPOA. And in May 2019, the Iranian government issued a warning that it would block the Strait of Hormuz as a retaliation to restoring U.S. sanctions on Iran. Therefore, Seoul was concerned about the potential disruptions in the supply of crude oil. As a contingency measure, the South

Korean government also considered releasing 200 mn barrels of oil in case of emergency. As tensions escalated between the U.S. and Iran, South Korea was faced with a dilemma over the possibility of dispatching military troops to the Strait of Hormuz. As Seoul warily followed the situations on the ground, it was considering expanding the operational scope of Cheonghae unit from the Gulf of Aden to the Gulf of Oman and the Strait of Hormuz. The Cheonghae antipiracy unit were to be dispatched on a rotational basis for every six months and by deploying a navy destroyer ROKS Wang Geon. In addition, the South Korean government had plans to send a naval officer to Combined Maritime Forces in Bahrain. South Korea's worries had deepened over a potential involvement in an international conflict zone as the possibility of war in the Middle East was increasing.

The decision announced by the ROK Ministry of National Defense (MND) to dispatch Cheonghae naval unit to the Strait of Hormuz on January 21, 2020 raised Seoul's political, economic, and military stakes. The South Korean public was opposed to the decision citing thorny debates on potentially jeopardizing South Korea's national security and strained ROK–Iran bilateral relations. Apart from the UN peacekeeping operations, South Korea's alliance commitment to the U.S. has been the main cause behind sending its troops overseas. South Korea's history of military dispatch to the Middle East during the Roh Moo-hyun and the Moon Jae-in administrations were regarded as a bargaining chip for negotiating defense cost-sharing as well as the North Korean issue. Faced with a set of trade-offs, Seoul opted in for a subtle policy realignment as an alliance commitment to the U.S. in addition to claiming its geoeconomic stakes in the region to ensure continued access to Middle Eastern oil. The ROK MND took cautious steps to avoid vexing Tehran by opting out of joining the U.S.-led maritime coalition. As opposed to Japan's dispatch of their maritime self-defense force (SDF) which did not include the Strait of Hormuz, South Korea's dispatch of troops drew widespread criticism as the scope of its operation extended all the way to the Strait of Hormuz. To make matters worse, naming dispute resurfaced as Iran's foreign ministry slammed the ROK MND for citing Arabian Gulf in their official communications.

South Korea tried to straddle the divide between Tehran and Washington. Faced with the pressure to send troops, Seoul could not easily shake off America's demands as defense cost-sharing negotiations and North Korea issue were at stake. President Moon Jae-in presided over the NSC meeting and discussed the safety of local residents and directed the supply of crude oil to be closely monitored. Prior to finalizing the decision, former U.S. Ambassador to South Korea Harry Harris requested South Korea to send their troops to the Strait of Hormuz on the grounds of its energy dependency on the Middle East. Following the South Korean government's decision to dispatch the Cheonghae unit to the Strait of Hormuz, the South Korean antipiracy unit rescued a drifting Iranian vessel that was stranded in the Gulf of Oman on February 2. South Korea's decision to deploy troops to the Strait of Hormuz was justified on the grounds of individual deployment and defending national interests but it also elicited political debates over constitutionalism. The South Korean government sought to bypass National Assembly consent on the grounds of expanding the scope of Cheonghae unit's operation.

On January 4, 2021, Iran's IRGC seized South Korea's oil tanker MT Chemi off the Strait of Hormuz. Iran had accused the South Korean-flagged vessel of polluting the waters in the Strait, but the seizure was largely aimed at pressurizing Seoul into releasing $7 bn of Iranian assets frozen in South Korean banks amid U.S. sanctions on Iran. There was widespread resentment from the Iranian government about South Korea's compliance with U.S. sanctions and the oil tanker seizure was largely perceived as collateral damage. The pressure increased amid the shortage of medicines and difficulties in obtaining imported goods under Covid-19. In fact, the Governor of Iranian Central Bank Abdolnasser Hemmati called on South Korea to resolve frozen funds and accused the South Korean government for succumbing to U.S. pressure. Hemmati emphasized that the real issue is South Korean government's political will, which takes precedence over transferring remittances through INSTEX, a special purpose vehicle for bypassing U.S. sanctions. After several unsuccessful attempts of seeking a diplomatic solution, Iran released the South Korean oil tanker three months later. The Iranian government's resolve to restore the nuclear agreement presumably gave the impetus for the release of the Korean ship and captain. Throughout the negotiation process, ROK's 1st Vice Foreign Minister protested the Iranian authorities' detention of South Korean crew members and vessel and demanded the crew members to be released. Hemmati increased the pressure on South Korea and demanded that it pay interests on Iran's crude oil payment, its frozen assets. In January, the UN Secretary-General Antonio Guterres demanded ten countries, including Iran, to pay their dues or to have their voting rights restricted. Among these countries, Iran had the highest amount of unpaid dues totaling over $16 mn. As a result, Iran tried to pay overdue UN membership fees through its frozen assets in South Korea.

Conclusion

South Korea's relations with Iran have been characterized as pragmatic leading up to the Trump administration's maximum pressure campaign against Iran. Despite the strategic alliance between Iran and North Korea, both countries were able to work past political differences. Historically, cultural diplomacy and interparliamentary exchange between the two countries have been a buffer to divergences in political and security policies. While pragmatic cooperation has been largely possible since the Cold War era by pursuing mutual interests in economic cooperation, U.S. and UNSC-imposed sanctions and strained U.S.–Iran relations since the Iranian Revolution have been a major impediment in fostering bilateral relations. Park Geun-hye's historic visit to Tehran after the JCPOA led to a resurgence of commercial cooperation that was stalled under economic sanctions. However, the prospects for promising bilateral relations had been dashed with Park's impeachment and Trump's maximum pressure campaign. Frequent analogies have been drawn between Iran and North Korea vis-à-vis the regime types and efficacy of sanctions. While both countries have been subjected to sanctions as a primary measure for the deterrence of nuclear proliferation, fundamentally they differ in nuclear capabilities. North Korea already had nuclear weapons, whereas Iran did not. South Korea's approach to the two countries therefore has largely differed and predicated on a regionalist perspective. Due to geographical proximity, South Korea's chief concern is North Korea's nuclear program and security on the Korean Peninsula; nuclear proliferation of Iran and the Middle East is relegated to the backburner. Iran has therefore been treated primarily as a commercial partner rather than in strategic terms. The future of ROK–Iran relations is at a critical juncture with the recent turn of geopolitical events in the Gulf and is contingent upon the final outcome of Iran nuclear talks.

Notes

1 Seoul Metropolitan Government, *Seoul Tour Guidebook: Recommended Tour Courses in Seoul* (Seoul: Giljabi Media, 2015), 17.
2 The Korea Herald, "Tehran Street, Seoul Street stands as symbols of friendship," May 10, 2016.
3 Fars News Agency, "South Korean cineastes after joint film production with Iran," December 2, 2018.
4 Chosun-Ilbo, "Anti-communist Director Kim Yong-woo visits Iran," February 9, 1962, 1.
5 UN General Assembly, "Question of Korea," A/RES/3333(XXIX), December 17, 1974; Seong Han-pyo, "Third World politics from the Head of the Mission for Asia and the Middle East," *Chosun-Ilbo*, February 2, 1975, 2.
6 Chosun-Ilbo, "The ticket to Iran," November 23, 1975, 2.
7 Chosun-Ilbo, "Iran and Korea strengthen economic ties," December 11, 1976, 2.
8 Chosun-Ilbo, "The most active Korean diplomatic mission," July 1, 1976, 2.
9 Chosun-Ilbo, "The sentiment toward Korea is not bad," February 14, 1979, 2.
10 Chosun-Ilbo, "Resumption of construction work in Iran," September 28, 1979, 2.
11 Choi Chung-rim, "Impending oil price war: The impact of rising crude oil prices on the South Korean economy," November 23, 1976, *Chosun Ilbo*, 3.
12 Chosun News Library Centennial Archive, "Reduction in the inspection period for pending steel exports in the Middle East," September 26, 1974, 2.
13 Houman A. Sadri, "An Islamic perspective on non-alignment: Iranian foreign policy in theory and practice," in Stephen Chan, Peter Mandaville & Roland Bleiker (Eds.) *The Zen of International Relations: IR Theory from East to West* (New York, NY: Palgrave Macmillan, 2001), 157–174.
14 Shin Yong-suk, "Did North Korea give up on its agenda toward the Korean Peninsula?" *Chosun Ilbo*, February 10, 1981, 3.
15 Cf., Lee Chang-ryul, "Can Iran block the Strait of Hormuz? [in Korean]" *Dokdo Research Journal* (17) (2012), 76–77.

56 *Tehran boulevard to post-JCPOA Iran*

16 Chosun News Library Centennial Archive, "Concerns about disruption of crude oil import from Iran-Iraq War and the crisis after the blockade of Strait of Hormuz," September 25, 1980, 2.
17 Chosun News Library Centennial Archive, "South Korean residents in Iran and Iraq are safe," March 21, 1985, 4.
18 *The New York Times*, "The downing of Flight 655; South Korea Company halts work on an Iranian refinery," July 5, 1988, A10; Chosun News Library Centennial Archive, "Two South Korean sailors dead after a Maltese oil tanker attack," May 13, 1985, 11.
19 Chosun News Library Centennial Archive, "Low overseas construction orders last year," January 7, 1989, 7.
20 Chosun News Library Centennial Archive, "All overseas construction is $6.5bn," March 5, 1989, 7.
21 *The Wall Street Journal*, "South Korea estimates Iran-Iraq building orders – special to the Wall Street Journal," August 11, 1988.
22 Michael Sterner, "The Iran-Iraq War," *Foreign Affairs* 63 (1) (1984), 129.
23 Chosun-Ilbo, "Three wounded by Korean cargo ship in Persian Gulf," July 3, 1984, 1.
24 Chosun-Ilbo, "Koreans are safe in Iran and Iraq," March 21, 1985, 4.
25 Yonhap News Agency, "Economic cooperation between Korea and Iran likely to expand significantly," February 23, 1990.
26 International Business Publications, U.S.–Iran: *Political and Economic Relations Handbook* (Washington DC: International Business Publications, 2018), 134.
27 Yonhap News Agency, "Iran requests deferral of repayment of imports," October 2, 1993.
28 Yonhap News Agency, "Classified document for countermeasure strategy for the Korean Peninsula and Gulf warfare," February 3, 1995.
29 Munir Ahmad Khan, "Toward a universal framework of nuclear restraint," in Joseph F. Pilat & Robert E. Pendley (Eds.) *1995: A New Beginning for the NPT?* (New York, NY: Springer Science + Business Media, 1995), 44–64.
30 Choi Jun-seok, "The arms trade with North Korea is an old story," *Chosun-Ilbo*, February 18, 1997, 41.
31 Shirzad Azad, "Iran and the two Koreas: A peculiar pattern of foreign policy," *The Journal of East Asian Affairs* 26 (2) (2012), 182; Larry A. Niksch, "North Korea's nuclear weapons program," *CRS Issue Brief for Congress*, February 21, 2006, 11.
32 Yonhap News Agency, "North Korea earns more than $2bn a year from trade with Iran," News Clip, 00:46, July 15, 2009.
33 Hong Yong-sik, "In the aftermath of ROKS Cheonan incident," *Hanguk Kyungjae*, May 21, 2010.
34 Iranian Diplomacy, "Iran calls on North Korea, South Korea to bury hatchet," August 18, 2010, www.irdiplomacy.ir/en/news/8411/iran-calls-on-north-korea-south-korea-to-bury-hatchet.
35 Cambridge University Press, "U.S. commends nations for joining in the enforcement of sanctions: Statement by President Obama, July 1, 2010," *Foreign Policy Bulletin* 20 (4), 34–55, DOI: https://doi.org/10.1017/S1052703610000559.
36 William J. Broad, James Glanz & David E. Sanger, "Iran fortifies its arsenal with the aid of North Korea," *The New York Times*, November 28, 2010, A12; nuclear

threat initiative, "North Korea," July 2020, www.nti.org/learn/countries/north-korea/.
37 Yun Sun-bo, "US sanctions on Iran and South Korea's decision: Suggestions for a mature alliance [in Korean]," *State of Affairs and Policy* (9) (2010), 14.
38 KTV, "Government announces additional sanctions on Iran," December 16, 2011, *News Clip*, 0:27.
39 Kim Sunwoo, "South Korea should be punished too by raising tariffs by 200%," *Donga-Ilbo*, August 11, 2010, A8.
40 Park Sun-ho, "Bad news in Middle East Exports," *Munhwa Ilbo*, December 6, 2003; Park Yong-beom, "Catch the Iranian market," *Maeil Kyungjae*, November 8, 2004.
41 Eunjung Lim, "South Korea's nuclear dilemmas," *Journal for Peace and Nuclear Disarmament* 2 (1) (2019), 307.
42 Hwang Ji-hwan, "The Iran nuclear deal and the North Korean nuclear issue [in Korean]," *Diplomacy* (115) (2015), 57.
43 Kwon Hee-suk, "The implications and milestones of President Park Geun-hye's visit to Iran," *Diplomacy* (118) (2016), 78.
44 Yonhap News Agency, "Interview with Iranian Foreign Ministry Spokesperson Gashgavi," January 30, 2009.
45 Asia News Monitor, "Iran, South Korea call for reinvigoration of int'l campaign against terrorism," July 1, 2015.
46 Fars News Agency, "Rouhani underlines Iran's emphasis on dismantling WMDs in Middle East, Korean Peninsula," May 2, 2016.
47 Fars News Agency, "Iran, South Korea underline widening ties in parliamentary research," November 22, 2014.
48 Fars News Agency, "South Korea's oil imports from Iran double in September," July 16, 2014.
49 Asia News Monitor, "South Korea seeks to enhance trade ties with Iran," February 19, 2014.
50 Maeil Economy, "Iran expands deferred payments to $100mn," February 24, 2004.
51 See UN Security Council, "Resolution 1929 (2010)," S/RES/1929 (2010); Ha Tae-won, "Obama takes care of South Korea's participation in Iranian sanctions," *Donga-Ilbo*, August 13, 2010, A8.
52 SME Export Support Center, "KOTRA national inspections," October 25, 2010.
53 Asia News Monitor, "South Korea mulling plans for possible U.S. sanctions on Iran's oil exports," August 5, 2010.
54 Asia News Monitor, "South Korea set to help local exporters to Iran," August 25, 2010.
55 Ibid.
56 Park Sang-jin, "Iranian oil imports declined by half in May," *SBS News*, July 1, 2012.
57 Park Yang-su, "The government prepares 'three-step countermeasures' for Iran sanctions," *Munhwa Ilbo*, January 13, 2012, 13.
58 Kim Eun-byeol, "Iran asks Korean companies to raise interest rates," *Asia Economy*, August 16, 2012.
59 Royal Courts of Justice, "High Court of Justice Business and Property Courts of England and Wales Commercial Court (QBD): In the matter of an arbitration and in the matter of the Arbitration Act 1996," Case No: CL-2018-999454, December 12, 2019, 3–6.

60 Ibid, 4–19; In-Sook Kim, "A case study on the investor-state dispute-relevant public policy and the domestic implications [in Korean]," *Legal Research* Vol. 55 (2018), 201–202.
61 Soo-Hyun Lee, "In the habit of giants: Fair and equitable treatment and structural risk factors in conglomerate-led newly industrialized countries," in Junji Nakagawa (Ed.) *Asia Perspectives on International Investment Law* (London: Routledge, 2019), 160–166.
62 ROK Ministry of Foreign Affairs, "Joint statement on the comprehensive partnership between the Islamic Republic of Iran and the Republic of Korea," May 2, 2016.
63 See United Nations General Assembly, "A world against violence and violent extremism," December 14, 2017, A/72/L.32.
64 Yonhap News Agency, "President Park meets with Iran's Khamenei," May 1, 2016.
65 See Shirzad Azad, "In quest of a second boom: South Korea's Middle East policy under Park Geun-hye," *Contemporary Arab Affairs* II (1–2) (2018), 257–278.
66 ROK Ministry of Foreign Affairs, "Iran's trade status," July 21, 2016.
67 Henry W. Lane, Martha L. Maznevski & Joseph J. DiStefano, *International Management Behavior: Global and Sustainable Leadership* (Cambridge: Cambridge University Press, 2019), 342.
68 "Iran effect" approval rating rebounds," *Kyunghyang Shinmun*, May 6, 2016, A4.
69 ROK Ministry of Foreign Affairs, "Iran: Islamic Republic of Iran," n.d.
70 Lee Kyung-sik, "'Tehran Street' in Seoul, 'Seoul Street' in Tehran symbolize strong bilateral ties," February 1, 2017, *The Korea Post*.
71 The Observatory of Economic Complexity, "Iran," 2019.
72 The Observatory of Economic Complexity, "South Korea/Iran," 2019.
73 Jeff Sung, "South Korea summons Iran envoy over diplomatic threat," *Arab News*, January 12, 2020, www.arabnews.com/node/1611686/world.
74 Fars News Agency, "Spokesman blasts S. Korea for blind obedience to US in blocking Iran's assets," June 15, 2020, https://en.farsnews.ir/print.aspx?nn=139 90326000323.
75 BBC Monitoring Middle East, "Iran to reconsider ties with South Korea if oil import suspended – minister," June 29, 2012.
76 Fars News Agency, "NIOC Official: India Paying Oil Debt," March 5, 2014, https://english.farsnews.ir/newstext.aspx?nn=13921214000430.

References

Asia News Monitor. "South Korea mulling plans for possible U.S. sanctions on Iran's oil exports," August 5, 2010.
Asia News Monitor. "South Korea set to help local exporters to Iran," August 25, 2010.
Asia News Monitor. "South Korea seeks to enhance trade ties with Iran," February 19, 2014.
Asia News Monitor. "Iran, South Korea call for reinvigoration of Int'l campaign against terrorism," July 1, 2015.
Azad, Shirzad. "Iran and the two Koreas: A peculiar pattern of foreign policy," *The Journal of East Asian Affairs* 26 (2) (2012), 163–192.
Azad, Shirzad. "In quest of a second boom: South Korea's Middle East policy under Park Geun-hye," *Contemporary Arab Affairs* II (1–2) (2018), 257–278.

BBC Monitoring Middle East. "Iran to reconsider ties with South Korea if oil import suspended – minister," June 29, 2012.

Broad, William J., James Glanz and David E. Sanger. "Iran fortifies its arsenal with the aid of North Korea," *The New York Times*, November 28, 2010, A12.

Cambridge University Press. "U.S. commends nations for joining in the enforcement of sanctions: Statement by President Obama, July 1, 2010," *Foreign Policy Bulletin* 20 (4) (2010), 34–55, doi: https://doi.org/10.1017/S1052703610000559.

Choi, Jun-seok. "The arms trade with North Korea is an old story," *Chosun-Ilbo*, February 18, 1997, 41.

Chosun-Ilbo. "Anti-communist Director Kim Yong-woo visits Iran," February 9, 1962, 1.

Chosun-Ilbo. "The ticket to Iran," November 23, 1975, 2.

Chosun-Ilbo. "The most active Korean diplomatic mission," July 1, 1976, 2.

Chosun-Ilbo. "Iran and Korea strengthen economic ties," December 11, 1976, 2.

Chosun-Ilbo. "The sentiment toward Korea is not bad," February 14, 1979, 2.

Chosun-Ilbo. "Resumption of construction work in Iran," September 28, 1979, 2.

Chosun-Ilbo. "Three wounded by Korean cargo ship in Persian Gulf," July 3, 1984, 1.

Chosun-Ilbo. "Koreans are safe in Iran and Iraq," March 21, 1985, 4.

Choi, Chung-rim. "Impending oil price war: The impact of rising crude oil prices on the South Korean economy," November 23, 1976, *Chosun Ilbo*, 3.

Chosun News Library Centennial Archive. "Reduction in the inspection period for pending steel exports in the Middle East," September 26, 1974, 2.

Chosun News Library Centennial Archive. "Concerns about disruption of crude oil import from Iran-Iraq War and the crisis after the blockade of Strait of Hormuz," September 25, 1980, 2.

Chosun News Library Centennial Archive. "South Korean residents in Iran and Iraq are safe," March 21, 1985, 4.

Chosun News Library Centennial Archive. "Two South Korean sailors dead after a Maltese oil tanker attack," May 13, 1985, 11.

Chosun News Library Centennial Archive. "Low overseas construction orders last year, January 7, 1989, 7.

Chosun News Library Centennial Archive. "All overseas construction is $6.5bn," March 5, 1989, 7.

Fars News Agency. "NIOC official: India paying oil debt," March 5, 2014, https://english.farsnews.ir/newstext.aspx?nn=13921214000430.

Fars News Agency. "South Korea's oil imports from Iran double in September," July 16, 2014, https://theiranproject.com/blog/2013/10/15/south-koreas-oil-imports-from-iran-double-in-september/amp/.

Fars News Agency. "Iran, South Korea underline widening ties in parliamentary research," November 22, 2014, http://english.farsnews.com/newstext.aspx?nn=13930901001584.

Fars News Agency. "Rouhani underlines Iran's emphasis on dismantling WMDs in Middle East, Korean Peninsula," May 2, 2016, www.farsnews.ir/en/news/13950213001173/Rhani-Underlines-Iran39-s-Emphasis-n-Dismanling-WMDs-in-Middle-Eas-.

Fars News Agency. "South Korean cineastes after joint film production with Iran," December 2, 2018, www.farsnews.ir/en/news/13970911000602/Sh-Krean-Cineases-afer-Jin-Film-Prdcin-wih-Iran.

Fars News Agency. "Spokesman blasts S. Korea for blind obedience to US in blocking Iran's assets," June 15, 2020, https://en.farsnews.ir/print.aspx?nn=13990326000323.

Foreign Policy. "A.T. Kearney / Foreign Policy Magazine Globalization Index 2002," January 2002, https://foreignpolicy.com/issue_janfeb_2002/global_index.html.

Ha, Tae-won. "Obama takes care of South Korea's participation in Iranian sanctions," *Donga-Ilbo*, August 13, 2010, A8.

Hong, Yong-sik. "In the aftermath of ROKS Cheonan incident," *Hanguk Kyungjae*, May 21, 2010.

Hwang, Ji-hwan. "The Iran nuclear deal and the North Korean nuclear issue [in Korean]," *Diplomacy* (115) (2015), 54–62.

International Business Publications. *U.S.-Iran: Political and Economic Relations Handbook* (Washington DC: International Business Publications, 2018).

Iranian Diplomacy. "Iran calls on North Korea, South Korea to bury hatchet," August 18, 2010, www.irdiplomacy.ir/en/news/8411/iran-calls-on-north-korea-south-korea-to-bury-hatchet.

Khan, Munir Ahmad. "Toward a universal framework of nuclear restraint," in Joseph F. Pilat and Robert E. Pendley (Eds.), *A New Beginning for the NPT?* (New York, NY: Springer Science + Business Media, 1995), 44–64.

Kim, Eun-byeol. "Iran asks Korean companies to raise interest rates," *Asia Economy*, August 16, 2012, www.asiae.co.kr/news/view.htm?idxno=2012081614075696226.

Kim, In-Sook. "A case study on the investor-state dispute-relevant public policy and the domestic implications [in Korean]," *Journal of Legislation Research* 55 (2018): 193–237.

Kim, Jae-myung. "A world without nuclear weapons? Nuclear weapons states first!" *Pressian*, May 4, 2010, www.pressian.com/pages/articles/2935.

Kim, Sunwoo. "South Korea should be punished too by raising tariffs by 200%," *Donga-Ilbo*, August 11, 2010, A8.

KTV. "Government announces additional sanctions on Iran," December 16, 2011, *News Clip*, 0:27.

Kwon, Hee-suk. "The implications and milestones of President Park Geun-hye's visit to Iran," *Diplomacy* (118) (2016), 77–85.

Kyunghyang Shinmun. "Iran effect" approval rating rebounds," May 6, 2016, A4.

Lane, Henry W., Martha L. Maznevski and Joseph J. DiStefano. *International Management Behavior: Global and Sustainable Leadership* (Cambridge: Cambridge University Press, 2019).

Lee, Chang-ryul. "Can Iran block the Strait of Hormuz? [in Korean]" *Dokdo Research Journal* (17) (2012), 76–77.

Lee, Kyung-sik. "'Tehran street' in Seoul, 'Seoul street' in Tehran symbolize strong bilateral ties," February 1, 2017, *The Korea Post*, www.koreapost.com/news/articleView.html?idxno=2705.

Lee, Soo-Hyun. "In the habit of giants: Fair and equitable treatment and structural risk factors in conglomerate-led newly industrialized countries," in Junji Nakagawa (Ed.), *Asia Perspectives on International Investment Law* (London: Routledge, 2019), 160–166.

Lim, Eunjung. "South Korea's nuclear dilemmas," *Journal for Peace and Nuclear Disarmament* 2 (1) (2019), 297–318.

Maeil Economy. "Iran expands deferred payments to $100mn," February 24, 2004.

Niksch, Larry A. "North Korea's nuclear weapons program," *CRS Issue Brief for Congress*, February 21, 2006.

Nuclear Threat Initiative. "North Korea," July 2020, www.nti.org/learn/countries/north-korea/.

Park, Sang-jin. "Iranian oil imports declined by half in May," *SBS News*, July 1, 2012.
Park, Sun-ho. "Bad news in Middle East exports," *Munhwa Ilbo*, December 6, 2003.
Park, Yang-su. "The government prepares 'three-step countermeasures' for Iran sanctions," *Munhwa Ilbo*, January 13, 2012, 13.
Park, Yong-beom. "Catch the Iranian market," *Maeil Kyungjae*, November 8, 2004.
ROK Ministry of Foreign Affairs. "Iran: Islamic Republic of Iran." n.d.
ROK Ministry of Foreign Affairs. "Joint statement on the comprehensive partnership between the Islamic Republic of Iran and the Republic of Korea," May 2, 2016.
ROK Ministry of Foreign Affairs. "Iran's trade status," July 21, 2016.
Royal Courts of Justice. "High court of justice business and property courts of England and Wales commercial court (QBD): In the matter of an arbitration and in the matter of the arbitration act 1996," Case No: CL-2018-999454, December 12, 2019.
Sadri, Houman A. "An Islamic perspective on non-alignment: Iranian foreign policy in theory and practice," in Stephen Chan, Peter Mandaville and Roland Bleiker (Eds.), *The Zen of International Relations: IR Theory from East to West* (New York, NY: Palgrave Macmillan, 2001), 157–174.
Seong, Han-pyo. "Third World politics from the head of the mission for Asia and the Middle East," *Chosun-Ilbo*, February 2, 1975, 2.
Seoul Metropolitan Government. *Seoul Tour Guidebook: Recommended Tour Courses in Seoul* (Seoul: Giljabi Media, 2015).
Shin, Yong-suk. "Did North Korea give up on its agenda toward the Korean Peninsula?" *Chosun Ilbo*, February 10, 1981, 3.
SME Export Support Center. "KOTRA national inspections," October 25, 2010.
Sterner, Michael. "The Iran-Iraq war," *Foreign Affairs* 63 (1) (1984), 128–143.
Sung, Jeff. "South Korea summons Iran envoy over diplomatic threat," *Arab News*, January 12, 2020, www.arabnews.com/node/1611686/world.
The Korea Herald. "Tehran Street, Seoul Street stands as symbols of friendship," May 10, 2016, www.koreaherald.com/view.php?ud=20160510000912.
The New York Times. "The downing of Flight 655; South Korea company halts work on an Iranian refinery," July 5, 1988, A10.
The Observatory of Economic Complexity. "Iran," 2019, https://oec.world/en/profile/country/irn.
The Wall Street Journal. "South Korea estimates Iran-Iraq building orders – Special to the Wall Street Journal," August 11, 1988.
UN General Assembly. "Question of Korea," A/RES/3333(XXIX), December 17, 1974.
United Nations. "2010 Review conference of the parties to the treaty on the non-proliferation of nuclear weapons: Final document," Volume I, 2010.
United Nations General Assembly. "A world against violence and violent extremism," December 14, 2017, A/72/L.32.
UN Security Council. "Resolution 1929 (2010)," S/RES/1929 (2010).
Yonhap News Agency. "Economic cooperation between Korea and Iran likely to expand significantly," February 23, 1990.
Yonhap News Agency. "Iran requests deferral of repayment of imports," October 2, 1993.
Yonhap News Agency. "Classified document for countermeasure strategy for the Korean Peninsula and Gulf warfare," February 3, 1995.
Yonhap News Agency. "Iran rises in the Middle East market," June 26, 2003.

Yonhap News Agency. "Interview with Iranian Foreign Ministry Spokesperson Gashgavi," January 30, 2009.

Yonhap News Agency. "North Korea earns more than $2bn a year from trade with Iran," *News Clip,* 00:46, July 15, 2009.

Yonhap News Agency, "President Park meets with Iran's Khamenei," May 1, 2016.

Yun, Sun-bo. "US sanctions on Iran and South Korea's decision: Suggestions for a mature alliance [in Korean]," *State of Affairs and Policy* (9) (2010), 13–25.

3 Oil, business diplomacy and Saudi–Korea Vision 2030

Introduction

As the largest supplier of crude oil to Seoul, bilateral relations between Saudi Arabia and South Korea had almost exclusively been centered on energy trade and construction for the first two decades. In 1962, Saudi Arabia was one of the first few countries in the MENA to establish diplomatic relations with South Korea. Saudi Arabia's strategic importance to South Korea which gradually expanded to non-oil sectors from the 1990s onward was energized by Saudi Arabia's oil-led economic growth. In addition to the booming construction sector, Saudi Arabia's burgeoning economic growth during the 1970s and 1980s led to greater demands for human resources and fostered people-to-people connectivity and educational exchanges at the institutional level. While economic cooperation has been the cornerstone of ROK–Kingdom of Saudi Arabia (KSA) relations, little is known about the political cooperation between the two countries during the Cold War which was grounded on shared ideational interests in countering communism. South Korea's rapid economic growth, referred to as "Miracle on the Han River," coupled with creative economy and Saudi Arabia's five-year planning and Saudi-Korea Vision 2030 served as the basis for complementing economic development over the span of six decades. People's diplomacy was also a principal means of deepening commercial ties through the channel of state-business relations and business networks established between South Korean entrepreneurs and Saudi Arabian business moguls and the Saudi national oil company, Saudi Aramco.

Diplomatic and political relations during the Cold War

A myth has it that South Korea's ties with the Arab world date back to the 11th century, when the first and second generation of Arab merchants arrived in South Korea between 1024 and 1040. These merchants bartered metal products and silk and other fabrics with Koreans.[1] In modern history, South Korea had informal exchanges with Saudi Arabia until diplomatic relations were formalized in 1962. Despite the formalization of diplomatic relations, it

DOI: 10.4324/9781003092100-3

took another 12 years for Saudi Arabia to open an embassy in Seoul. Saudi Arabia Minister of State for Foreign Affairs Sayyed Omar Saqqaf arrived in South Korea on a four-day visit on December 12, 1974 to sign an economic and technical cooperation agreement. Although there were no signs of technical-level discussions during the visit, a joint communiqué was issued stating Saudi Arabia's intent to become the first Arab country to open an embassy in Seoul and to form a joint committee and hold annual meetings and foster high-level exchanges.[2] While the occasion had not led to any substantive progress in economic cooperation, it laid the groundwork for expanding formal ties between the two countries. In a special statement on foreign policy for peace and reunification released in 1973, President Park Chung-hee declared that ROK will open its doors to all nations in the world on the basis of the principles of reciprocity and equality, regardless of political or ideological differences. Park identified peace and good-neighborliness as core principles of South Korea's diplomacy during the Cold War era.[3] South Korea's resolve to expand diplomatic ties was borne out of a strategic decision to enhance its international profile through diplomatic recognition and to counter the expansion of the communist influence abroad.

Further accounts of high-level diplomatic communications were revealed two days after the passing of King Faisal bin Abdulaziz Al Saud on March 27, 1975. In a meeting with the Deputy Saudi Ambassador to South Korea Mohammed al-Iraqi, Prime Minister Kim Jong-pil expressed his condolences to the Saudi government and thanked them for the favors extended by King Faisal during the 1973 oil embargo. As Kim pledged that South Korea would lend moral support to the Saudi state, the Deputy Saudi Ambassador to South Korea lauded South Korea's cutting-edge technology, human capital resources, and industrial development and expressed keen interests in expanding the strategic relations between the two countries.[4] At the peak of the oil embargo, Seoul sought to negotiate with the Saudi government, led by the special envoy for diplomacy Choi Kyu-hah, who met with King Faisal of Saudi Arabia to help ease oil production cuts and managed to secure 65% of all crude oil imports to South Korea from Saudi Arabia by 1973.[5]

Saudi Arabia's decision to be the first country to open an embassy in Seoul had a symbolic significance in augmenting South Korea's status as an emerging regional economic powerhouse and a sovereign nation-state. Prior to the inauguration of the Saudi Embassy in Seoul, diplomatic operations with South Korea were conducted through the Japanese Embassy and Saudi Ambassadors to Japan were simultaneously appointed as Chargé d'Affaires to Seoul. In December 1973, South Korea also issued a public statement supporting the Arab states in the Arab–Israeli conflict. On the political front, Minister Kim Jong-pil exchanged political support during a meeting held with Sheikh Nawaf bin Abdulaziz, who served as a commander of the royal guard between 1952 and 1956. Kim publicly endorsed Saudi Arabia's role in promoting peace in the Middle East, while the Saudi counterpart also supported South Korea's position on North Korea and the Korean

Peninsula. As the opening of the Saudi Arabian Embassy in Seoul became imminent, South Korean Ambassador to Saudi Arabia Yoon Kyoung-do boasted of Seoul's amicable ties with Riyadh by stating that Saudi Arabia is a "spokesperson" for South Korea in the Arab world. Seoul regarded Riyadh as a diplomatic gateway to the wider Gulf and the Middle East and sought to strengthen multilateral cooperation with the GCC states by hosting the GCC Secretary-General Sheikh Fahim bin Sultan Al Qassimi in Seoul in 1995.

South Korea and Saudi Arabia were better able to foster diplomatic ties by establishing a common social, political, and ideational outlook throughout the Cold War era. Shortly after formalizing diplomatic ties with Saudi Arabia in 1962, economic diplomacy and proactive neutrality were identified as among the five key pillars of South Korea's diplomatic vision under the directive of the then Minister of Foreign Affairs Choi Kyu-hah. To this end, the ROK Ministry of Foreign Affairs engaged with United Arab Republic, Jordan, and Saudi Arabia and sought to boost social and cultural ties with these countries, including in religious affairs. For instance, Saudi Minister of Interior Sheikh bin Abdulaziz Al Saud pledged $30,000 each year for three years during his visit to Panmunjeom in 1979, to support the construction of an Islamic university in Korea as well as to establish a field office for the Organization of the Islamic Conference in Korea.

In spite of the geographical remoteness between South Korea and Saudi Arabia, Seoul courted Riyadh, a leading oil producer and regional power in the Middle East, as it underwent rapid growth under the export-led industrialization strategy led by Park Chung-hee. In conjunction with South Korea's commercial interests in the region, as hitherto discussed in the previous chapters, regional politics and security on the Korean Peninsula since the Cold War had equally been a major thrust behind South Korea's foreign policy with the MENA. In the Middle East, the Baghdad Pact precipitated regional instability through the Arab–Israeli conflict, dynastic rivalry between the Hashemites of Iraq and Jordan and the Al Saud family, and the contest for regional leadership between Egypt and Iraq.[6] The Arab world was divided between Iraq, Britain, Turkey, Iran, and Pakistan which acceded to the Baghdad Pact in 1955, and formed a military alliance against the Soviet aggression, whereas Saudi Arabia, Egypt, and Syria sought to undermine it.[7] During the Cold War, Saudi Arabia was the only country in the Gulf that had not established diplomatic relations with North Korea. As an Arab state opposed to communism, Saudi Islamic Affairs Minister Sheikh Mohammed Kutbi affirmed Saudi Arabia's resolve to combat communism and expressed deep respect and fraternity with South Korea during his visit to Seoul in September 1972, at the invitation of South Korean Minister of Culture and Information Yoon Joo-young. Kutbi was confident in future prospects for promoting stronger bilateral ties while stressing the mutual bonds between peace-loving citizens from both countries. As South Korea prepared for a showdown in the wider security and political theater against communist North Korea, it presided over the World Anti-Communist League

(WACL) in 1962, As both parties reaffirmed their mutual aim of countering the pro-Communist bloc, Kutbi threw his support around the initiative led by Seoul and declared, "the Arab state cannot be a pro-Communist force, firstly because of religious reasons. The doctrine of Islam, the state religion, does not tolerate the cruel nature and destructive behavior of communism. Arab countries, including Saudi Arabia, are more anti-communist in the region."[8] For both countries, opposing communism was a political decision as much as it was a social decision.

Anti-communist political views became a compelling unifying force, binding the social and political views of the two seemingly disparate countries. In the mid-1970s, Prime Minister Kim Jong-pil expressed his fondness and solidarity with members of the Saudi royal family, King Khalid bin Abdulaziz Al Saud and Sheikh Fahd bin Abdulaziz Al Saud, for their anti-communist orientations as reflected by their views toward communist Vietnam.[9] While citing religious reasons provided sufficient grounds for rejecting communism, Arab countries were also reluctant in offering a full-fledged support to Washington due to its pro-Israeli policy. The fierce competition between the two blocs led by the Soviet Union and the U.S. in a bipolar world spilled over to the politics of UN voting practices as controversies surrounding Zionism emerged as a main source of friction at the UN General Assembly. In opposition to the pro-Israeli countries in the West, MENA countries stood up for the Palestinian cause by declaring political Zionism as a racist movement at the NAM. Middle Eastern countries voted in favor of the passage of UN Resolution 3379 on the "elimination of all forms of racial discrimination." In response, the U.S., a top contributor to the UN, which accounted for a quarter of the UN budget, threatened to withdraw funds from the UN to prevent the passage of the resolution. The resolution was adopted on a vote of 34 to 0, with eight abstentions; the U.S. delegation abstained from voting in objection to the resolution.[10] There was a trepidation about the potential repercussions for the UN General Assembly votes on North Korea in the event that NAM member states succumb to U.S. pressure, and also considering the tensions mounting in the Western Sahara.[11]

Despite the concerns that Arab countries were generally reluctant to offer a full-fledged support to the anti-communist crusade led by the U.S. due to the latter's pro-Israeli policy, Seoul considered Riyadh as a reliable ally and a bulwark of stability in an increasingly turbulent region. According to South Korean Ambassador to Saudi Arabia Yoon Kyoung-do, Saudi Arabia was skeptical of Pyongyang's motives and the need for engaging the latter in a dialogue while being supportive of South Korea's position in the UN.[12] Given that the Palestinian Liberation Organization (PLO) was officially recognized by the Arab League and the UN as the sole and legitimate representative of the Palestinian people, Seoul regarded the PLO as a key avenue for expanding diplomatic and commercial ties with the Arab world.[13] Minister of Foreign Affairs Park Dong-jin was cautiously optimistic about the prospects for strengthening ties with PLO with the aim of establishing ties with members of NAM such as Iraq, Libya, and Algeria. During his visit to Kuwait in September 1979, Minister Park formally recognized PLO as the only legitimate representative of the Palestinian people through a joint declaration with Kuwait. The South Korean government endorsed the key claims highlighted by the PLO and the right of self-determination of the Palestinian people which recognizes: first, the right of the Arab Palestinian people to the return of its homeland and its right of self-determination; second, recognizing the PLO as "the sole legitimate representative of the Palestinian people"; and third, the demands for Israeli withdrawal from territories occupied in 1967.[14]

During his subsequent visit to Saudi Arabia, Minister Park reiterated Seoul's commitment to supporting the Palestinian cause. While seeking to advance economic statecraft, South Korea adopted a pragmatic approach toward the Israeli–Palestinian issue in conjunction with the Camp David Accords signed in 1978. However, supporting a political decision required a delicate balancing act as it was equally concerned about championing the Palestinian cause without irking Israel. Seoul was wary of the fact that Pyongyang had expanded its diplomatic outreach with regional powers in the MENA and stood by the Palestinian people. Yet at the same time, anti-American sentiment in the post-colonial Middle East was also on the rise incited by the pro-Zionist leanings of the West and the rise of pan-Arab nationalism. In practice, South Korea's foreign policy alignment with the U.S. based on the legacies of the Cold War also posed challenges in straddling the pro-Western and anti-Western divide in the Arab world.

The 1973 oil crisis and economic and health cooperation

Though South Korea's diplomatic relations with Saudi Arabia were established in 1962, economic cooperation between Seoul and Riyadh only gained momentum after the 1973 oil crisis. This followed when South Korean construction companies pulled out of Vietnam close to the end of the Vietnam War. Seoul's fiscal deficit and shortage of foreign currency at the time had prompted its pivot to the Middle East. South Korea's penetration in the Middle Eastern construction market was facilitated by the easing of competition in the market, especially from the world's major powers at the time, namely the U.S. and Japan. At the same time, South Korea's budding construction sector generated a steady stream of cash inflow for purchasing crude oil from the Middle East and spurred economic growth. Saudi Arabia's construction sector accounted for a large proportion of South Korea's export earnings as demonstrated in the first quarter of 1979, which amounted to $19 bn out of the total export earnings of $24 bn.[15]

In 1974, Minister of Foreign Affairs Kim Dong-jo and Saudi Minister of Foreign Affairs Sayyed Omar Saqqaf signed a five-year memorandum on economic cooperation including the development and exploitation of natural resources, process manufacturing, the agricultural and fishery industry, capital investment, and cooperation in science and information technology.[16] In the following year, Prime Minister Kim Jong-pil held a meeting with Sheikh Nawaf bin Abdulaziz Al Saud, former Minister of Finance and commander of the royal guard between 1952 and 1956, and discussed opportunities for South Korea to contribute to Saudi Arabia's five-year development plan worth $150 bn, which was introduced in July 1975. Economic cooperation between the two countries was set out around the same time as discussing plans for opening the Saudi Embassy in Seoul.

However, South Korea's dependency on Middle Eastern oil was also a cause of concern due to its vulnerability to geoeconomic and geopolitical volatilities in the region. Since the 1973 oil embargo, securing oil from the Middle East required a great deal of diplomatic dexterity. By the time Iran–Iraq War broke out in September 1980, South Korea's priority concern was in meeting energy demands and ensuring uninhibited access to crude oil in the Strait of Hormuz, the world's most important energy transit. According to the former Vice President of the Korea Institute for International Economic Policy Kim Jeok-gyo, an estimate of 98% of Seoul's energy demands were directly transited from the Strait of Hormuz, which far exceeded the energy demands from the U.S., France, and Japan, which accounted for 25%, 70%, and 80%, respectively.[17] As the war progressed well into the late 1980s, Korean oil tanker Royal Colombo which navigated between the straits of Saudi Arabia and Sri Lanka was struck by a missile attack from an Iranian fighter aircraft on February 20, 1985. It was not until July 1997 that South Korea was able to export refined oil for the very first time through Ssangyong refinery, which signed a contract to export 10,000 barrels of refined oil products to Saudi Arabia.[18]

South Korea's business diplomacy with Saudi Arabia reached new heights in the nascent days of South Korea's industrialization, when it received public support from King Faisal bin Abdulaziz Al Saud, who took great interest in South Korea's proposal to develop economic and technological ties during the first Saudi official's visit to Seoul in February 1974.[19] Economic cooperation that was burgeoning in the 1970s was typically reached in exchange for guaranteeing the supply of Saudi crude oil. What usually takes several years to materialize only took four and a half months to sign an agreement on bilateral economic–technical cooperation. What was distinct about the ROK–KSA economic and technical cooperation agreement was that it was a comprehensive agreement on a level-playing field rather than being a typical one-sided agreement that characterized technical transfers between the Global North and South. It also went above and beyond the initiative of sending technical experts and included suggestions for creating a joint venture and building a petroleum refinery in Saudi Arabia. By December 1974, South Korea was the only country in East Asia to have signed an agreement on economic, trade, and technical cooperation with Saudi Arabia, and by December 1979, joint public–private delegates visited Saudi Arabia for the very first time to discuss 26 major construction projects that South Korea were to participate in Saudi Arabia in return for a stable supply of Saudi crude oil.

South Korea's pivot to the Middle East was energized by Saudi Arabia's booming construction and petrochemical industries. In the 1970s, Seoul closed a deal as part of a multinational consortium consisting of six companies from three countries, South Korea, Japan, and Saudi Arabia, to jointly build a petrochemical plant in Jeddah, Saudi Arabia. By the mid-1970s, market forecasts predicted that Saudi Arabia and Iran would be the most promising markets for large-scale construction projects. As an emerging economy, South Korea's priority concerns were in improving the balance of trade and exporting manpower. South Korea's human capital was a major asset for a resource-deficit economy looking to strengthen economic ties with major oil-producing countries. South Korea's edge in manpower skills and technical skills gained a strong reputation in the construction and petrochemical sectors, including in the Saudi royal family. In 1975, King Khalid bin Abdulaziz Al Saud was impressed with the work ethics of South Korean workers that he witnessed while he was passing by a construction site when the workers from Samhwan Company were working their night shifts at a highway construction. As a result, King Khalid entrusted the South Korean company with a large-scale construction project based on a voluntary contract.[20]

As Saudi Arabia accounted for more than half of South Korea's energy supplies since the 1970s and emerged as a major hub for construction, the Saudi government made a request to Seoul to send economic planning experts and professionals in the construction industry. By 1976, Saudi Arabia announced that it would bring in 500,000 workers from Asia, including 100,000 workers from South Korea.[21] In addition, construction export targets to Saudi Arabia exceeded by 70% in 1975, which reflects how the Middle East accounted for 90% of South Korea's total construction exports that year.[22] In 2010, Human Resources Development Service of Korea, which is a South Korean government agency, offered vocational training in South Korea to technical vocational delegations from the GCC council member countries. Human resources training was expanded to legal and patent expertise. Following on from the vocational training offered to the GCC Patent Office in 2012, Korea Intellectual Property Office also provided a short-term vocational training to ten Saudi patent examiners at the request of the Saudi Arabian Patent Office on patent administration system and intellectual property system in 2014.

Bolstered by the prospects for stronger diplomatic relations after the South Korean Embassy was opened in Riyadh in 1974, Korean engineers entered the Saudi Arabian market in the following year. By 1979, there were 66 South Korean companies in Saudi Arabia and 75,000 South Korean workers working in Saudi Arabia.[23] Ghaith Pharaon, the president of Saudi Research and Development Company, also requested South Korea to dispatch 7,000 Korean engineers to participate in the construction of five gas plants on a four-year contract.[24] The construction sector was resilient to the Iran–Iraq War. And in the mid-1980s, the then President of Hyundai construction Lee Myung-bak signed a $350 mn housing construction contract with the Saudi

Arabia Ministry of Housing. However, competitions also intensified among foreign and Korean companies entering the Saudi construction market. To illustrate, the dumping scandal that erupted in the mid-1990s by Korea Heavy Industries (KHIND) and Halla Heavy Industries lurked behind the shadows of a booming construction sector and was presented with its own set of challenges. South Korean construction companies operating in Saudi Arabia were also faced with corruption allegations and a host of other issues including the use of poor construction materials, improper supervision on construction sites, and violation of employment and labor law.

Entering the Saudi Arabian construction market was fraught with logistical and social challenges. Given that Korean companies had entered the Saudi construction market immediately after it pulled out of the Vietnamese construction market, historical analogies were frequently drawn between South Korea's experience in the Vietnamese and Saudi construction markets. South Korea's participation in the Vietnamese construction industry was mostly facilitated by South Korea's alliance with the U.S. and its contribution of troops to the Vietnam War. By contrast, South Korea's participation in the Saudi construction industry was unprecedented. Working in an arid desert climate in the Middle Eastern construction sectors brought with it its own set of challenges – geological, bureaucratic, and cultural. For instance, drawing groundwater from 800 m deep was not cost-effective, and there were glaring differences in construction methods between Korea and Saudi Arabia; cultural and linguistic barriers were also present.

Labor exports from Korea to Saudi Arabia were also expanded to the healthcare industry since the late 1970s. After South Korea sent the first batch of nurses to West Germany in the mid-1960s, 900 Korean nurses had entered the Saudi labor market between 1977 and 1982. At the request of Saudi Health Ministry, the Korean government agreed to send an additional 5,000 nurses and medical staff to Saudi Arabia in 1999, which was the largest number of overseas jobs created for a single profession that year.[25] In addition to recruiting Korean nurses in Saudi hospitals, Saudi representatives from the Royal Medical Center visited Seoul National University Hospital and met with local medical authorities at the Korean Nursing Association and the Korean Medical Association in 1998. Although subordinate to the interests generated by the construction sector, medicine has been a field that has historically facilitated bilateral cooperation by creating job opportunities for Koreans while helping fulfill manpower demands for Saudi Arabia. During Prince Alwaleed bin Talal Al Saud's visit to South Korea in 1999, meetings were held with Lee Min-hwa, President of Korea Venture Business Association and the Chairman of a South Korean pharmaceutical company Medicine, to request a supply of medical devices for Kingdom Hospital in Riyadh.

By 2010, South Korea attracted 200,000 patients from Saudi Arabia with medical revenues amounting to $60 bn.[26] Signing a comprehensive medical cooperation agreement between the two countries in 2013 led to establishing bilateral cooperation in vocational medical education and training between

King Saud University Medical City and Hyundai Asan Hospital in the subsequent year. Under the Park Geun-hye administration, both countries broadened the scope of medical cooperation by signing an agreement to introduce a Korean-style hospital in Saudi Arabia that was to be modeled after the Sheikh Khalifa Specialty Hospital operated by the Seoul National University Hospital in Ras Al Khaimah. In 2015, Yonsei Severance Hospital also became the first Korean medical institution to operate a woman's cancer center in Saudi Arabia, while SK Telecom and Seoul National University Bundang Hospital agreed to export hospital information system to Saudi Arabia in the same year.

South Korea reported its first case of Middle East Respiratory Syndrome (MERS) case on May 20, 2015 and became the country with the largest outbreak of MERS outside of the Middle East that year, with 185 confirmed cases and 38 deaths according to the WHO. In response, WHO activated the regional emergency operations center and an event management team, and a joint mission was established between the Ministry of Health and Welfare and WHO to monitor the outbreak and recommend emergency measures.[27] Becoming the third-hardest country hit by the epidemic also offered South Korea to strengthen bilateral cooperation on public health with Saudi Arabia, which was the first and largest outbreak country for MERS. The head of the Saudi Center for Disease Prevention and Control Ali Albarak attended a seminar hosted by the Seoul National University Hospital on MERS in June 2015. Both countries shared information on possible transmission routes and on the importance of raising public awareness on the disease.

In addition to sending skilled and semi-skilled workers in construction and medicine, at Saudi Arabia's request, the two countries stepped up their efforts in strengthening educational and technical exchanges by launching the Korea–Saudi human resources development committee following the discussions held on the sidelines of the economic ministerial meeting between the two parties in 1978. The Korea–Saudi committee for human resources development was to participate in construction projects in the Jubail and Yanbu industrial cities and promote economic planning development in coordination with Saudi Arabia Ministry of Science Research and Technology and Korea Development Institute (KDI).

The rise in demand for skilled workforce in Saudi Arabia generated opportunities for joint ventures. Discussing construction projects for building ports and roads was also on the agenda at a ministerial-level summit held in Korea in 1975. Apart from participating in the building of large-scale construction projects, there were talks about establishing an overseas joint venture through a trading company established as a merger between the two countries. In addition, the joint construction of a fourth refinery in Korea and joint ventures in the petrochemical sector were also discussed. The second joint committee meeting held at the Economic Planning Board in Korea in 1976 agreed to form four subcommittees on capital and joint venture, construction, trade, and human resources. The joint committee also agreed on a slew of measures, including plans to establish the Korea–Saudi Bank and sign the double-taxation avoidance agreement; contribute Korean labor force to Jubail and Yanbu industrial complexes; boost bilateral trade; sign a memorandum on labor relations and insurance agreement.[28] Saudi Arabia also became the first country in the Middle East to sign an aviation agreement with Korea in the same year.

Over the following two decades, South Korea commissioned five economic planning experts to assist with Saudi Arabia's public policy and to expand economic and technical assistance. Moreover, joint ventures in the construction and petrochemical sectors also provided a firm footing for attracting FDIs. Saudi Arabia invested $50 mn in South Korea's port development plan in 1983. With an eye to diversify his overseas investments to Asia, Prince Alwaleed bin Talal bin Abdulaziz Al Saud, the nephew of King Fahd and a high-profile business mogul, invested in Asia for the first time by acquiring 5.9% of Daewoo Group's total stock in 1997 and invested $100 mn in Daewoo in 1998.[29] It was estimated at the time that the stock acquisition would effectively render Prince Alwaleed as the largest single stockholder in a decade. There was also a surge in overseas investments on Korean businesses during the 1997 Asian Financial Crisis. Daewoo, the second-largest South Korean corporation, was among the South Korean conglomerates that experienced over-expansion and issues tied to poor corporate governance, such as corruption and moral hazard, which led to restructuring and government bailouts.[30] Daewoo was declared bankrupt on November 1, 1999 in what was known as the largest financial default in Korea's history as it failed to comply with the government-led reform initiatives.

The Gulf War, energy security, and the Saudi construction industry

With the outbreak of the 1991 Gulf War, the U.S. mounted pressures on its allies that import crude oil from the region and indirectly benefit from U.S. military operations, namely South Korea, Japan, and Germany, to increase burden-sharing. Following the Iraqi invasion of Kuwait, South Korea signed an agreement with Saudi Arabia to dispatch 314 contingent of medical and transportation personnel to Saudi Arabia[31]; the agreement stipulated that military medical personnel were to be granted the privilege equivalent to diplomatic immunity as laid out in the Vienna Convention as well as granting duty-free access to goods and medical equipment during the mission in Saudi Arabia and bearing all expenses that go into the operation. South Korea's decision to supply non-military procurements and deploy military medical support team to the Gulf War was primarily a decision to commit to the U.S. alliance, rather than a decision borne out of strategic calculations for enhancing ties with the Middle East. During early 1990s, South Korea faced pressures to comply with the UN-imposed sanctions on Iraq and to contribute troops to the U.S.-led coalition in the Gulf War. These were more of a symbolic act for boosting moral support to the U.S. initiatives in Iraq. Given the vestiges of Korean War, South Korea's contributions on both counts reflected the transactional nature of ROK–U.S. alliance in the post-Cold War era. President Kim Dae-jung who was then the head of the center-left Peace Democratic Party (which is today's equivalent of Open Democratic Party) opposed to deploying troops to the U.S.-led coalition forces but was ready to comply with sanctions imposed on Iraq as a way of peacefully resolving the 1991 Gulf War.

South Korea was also commercially hard hit by the outbreak of the 1991 Gulf War. Export markets contracted as shipments to the Middle East were partially suspended by the Ministry of Commerce and Industry. Based on the two categories of export markets in the region, exports bound to Saudi Arabia, Israel, Jordan and Syria were put on hold, whereas the other category of Middle Eastern countries such as Egypt, Turkey, Iran, the UAE, Qatar, Bahrain, Oman, and Yemen were under scrutiny in the event of potential escalation of conflict. As tensions escalated, it was estimated that South Korea's loss from disrupted trade would amount to over $1 bn a year.[32] While South Korea set up a contingency planning and emergency preparedness unit, it remained cautiously optimistic that the 1991 Gulf War would not escalate into an all-out-war involving the rest of the Middle East given that Saudi Arabia, Egypt, and Syria also joined the U.S.-led coalition force. As Korean companies were gearing up for withdrawal with the possibility of a military attack on the eastern province of Saudi Arabia, its priority concern was in minimizing the loss in the construction sector considering that Saudi Arabia was the largest overseas market for Korean construction companies in the Middle East. Following the outbreak of the War, Korea Exchange Bank also suspended exchange market operations and trading activities on three currencies: Saudi Riyal, Bahraini Dinar, and the UAE Dirham.

As the Gulf War drew to a close, Aramco, a Saudi oil company, entered the domestic refinery market through equity participation with Ssangyong Oil in 1991. In return, Ssangyong Oil secured the right to access Saudi Arabian crude oil for 20 years. Though Saudi Aramco's plans to build a joint refinery with Ssangyong Oil in South Korea were thwarted, both parties agreed to collaborate on a joint construction of the oil refinery project in Qingdao, China. Saudi Arabia was highlighted as South Korea's largest export market in the Middle East by the first quarter of 1991, followed by Iran, Egypt, and Jordan.[33] According to the International Construction Association of Korea, South Korea's entry into the Saudi Arabian construction market via highway and infrastructure projects helped overcome economic recession caused by 1973 oil shock. As overseas construction orders became the main engine behind South Korea's industrialization, Ministry of Construction and Transportation (which was renamed to Ministry of Land, Infrastructure and Transport in 2008) took appropriate measures to improve working conditions for overseas construction workers and facilitated entry into joint bidding and tendering among Korean companies as well as with foreign companies in a multinational consortium, and coordinate joint negotiations for overseas construction orders.

As there was a growing demand for power plant construction, KHIND successfully bid for the tender to build world's largest Shuaiba power and desalination plant in Mecca, Saudi Arabia as part of a multinational consortium consisting of six companies. However, Shuaiba power and desalination plant, which was initially reputed as a large-scale construction project in Saudi Arabia, received a poor performance report by late 1996. In October, KHIND reported the payments received from the Shuaiba project was at 17.7% of the total accounts receivable. Upon reviewing the audit log submitted by Korea Heavy Industries & Commerce, MP Maeng Hyung-kyu pointed out that the total accounts receivable amounted to $311 mn.[34] Maeng thus urged to file a formal complaint to Saudi Arbitration Commission and request a compensation scheme.

While bilateral cooperation in the energy and construction industries was robust, the growing trade deficit was pointed out as an endemic problem in bilateral trade from the Korean side during the ministerial meeting held in 1994. This was attributed to an upsurge in South Korea's import of Saudi Arabian crude oil relative to the Saudi purchase of Korean goods and commodities during the same period.[35] According to the Korea International Trade Association, Korea is one of the most vulnerable economies to rising oil prices and that trade balance to the GDP ratio diminishes by 1.7% for an increase of 10 dollars in oil prices per barrel.[36] Moreover, Saudi Aramco's cuts on heavy crude oil production in the mid-1990s had a debilitating effect on South Korea's economy. As a result, Seoul had requested Saudi Arabia to improve the terms of trade for oil and gas and to help stabilize international oil prices and increase oil production levels. By August 2000, oil prices skyrocketed by reaching the highest level since the start of the 1991 Gulf War and sent shockwaves to the Korean economy and other major oil importing countries by causing trade deficits. Though Saudi Aramco signed a contract with the Korean oil refining industry on the provision of crude oil, Saudi Aramco was promoting the export of light crude oil over heavy crude oil to increase foreign currency inflows. At the same time, Minister of Petroleum and Mineral Resources Ali Al Naimi offered investment incentives to stimulate South Korea's participation in the Saudi construction sector.

In the aftermath of the Gulf War, South Korea capitalized on its dispatch of medical military personnel to Saudi Arabia, which gave them an edge in driving up the demand for construction orders from Saudi Arabia. At the conclusion of the war, South Korea received a letter of appreciation from King Fahd bin Abdulaziz Al Saud who thanked South Korea for contributing a contingent of military medical personnel and air transport command for the coalition forces in Saudi Arabia, branding it as a "true ally" and praised President Roh Tae-woo for his decisive leadership which contributed to the success of Operation Desert Storm.[37]

South Korea took additional steps to bolster resource diplomacy with Saudi Arabia by resuming meetings at the ministerial level shortly after the Gulf War, and the Minister of Power and Resources (which was renamed to the Ministry of Trade, Industry and Energy in 2013) Lee Hee-il delivered a keynote speech representing oil consumer countries at an international conference held in May 1991 in Isfahan, Iran. Highlighted as a priority sector for bilateral cooperation, in 1995, South Korea's resource diplomacy delegation, jointly consisting of government and private representatives, was commissioned to meet with the ministers of energy in Saudi Arabia, Oman, Qatar, Kuwait, and Yemen. The formation of a working-level committee was designed to facilitate business deals such as agreeing on energy cooperation with Saudi Arabia, signing an LNG gas contract with Qatar, and participating in development projects in Marib, Yemen, and in energy plant construction projects in Kuwait. In the same year, South Korea established a resource cooperation committee with Saudi Arabia, Iran, Malaysia, Indonesia, Australia, the UAE, Qatar, Kuwait, and Libya. By establishing a resource diplomacy network with energy producing countries, Seoul sought to promote periodical high-level meetings and host summits at a ministerial level in the country.

Business diplomacy with the Al Sauds in the aftermath of the debt crisis

Despite the rapid industrialization and the remarkable level of economic growth underpinned by the statist economic paradigm led by Park Chung-hee that was sustained for more than three decades since the early 1960s, South Korea experienced a severe economic downturn with the inception of the 1997 Asian Financial Crisis.[38] The Korean Financial Crisis has been regarded as a watershed event not only for the sheer scale and severity of economic crisis, but also for marking South Korea's formal entry into the neoliberal economic regime. The psychosocial impact of the Asian Debt Crisis was too great insofar as being dubbed as "the second national day of humiliation" after the Japanese colonization of Korea on August 22, 1910. The general public was largely demoralized due to unprecedented layoffs and socioeconomic chaos.[39] In January 1998, the Korean government and foreign banks agreed to restructure nearly 95% of Korea's short-term debt by March 18, 1998, while charging extraordinarily high interest rates which were set to 2.25–2.75 percentage points above the six-month LIBOR interest rates.[40] As a result, South Korean businesses had to attract foreign capital to salvage their companies from economic plight during the onslaught of the Asian Debt Crisis.

Saudi Prince and business tycoon Alwaleed bin Talal Al Saud, a major shareholder of Citibank and Four Seasons hotel, was among the high-profile foreign investors that visited South Korea to discuss investment opportunities. Alwaleed's visit in April 1998 came shortly after South Korea applied for an IMF bailout. At a joint press conference held with Hyundai Group, Prince Alwaleed revealed that Kingdom Holding Company (KHC), a team of investment specialists that he directs, received investment requests from South Korean companies. Prince Alwaleed signed the letter of intent on the purchase of Hyundai Motor Company's convertible bonds. During the signing ceremony, Alwaleed underscored that he regarded his investments on the automobile sector as an investment on Korea.[41] Alwaleed's visit reinvigorated commercial diplomacy between the two countries and boosted business morale of South Korean conglomerates. The deal which was an emblem of the trust and confidence that underlies economic cooperation between the two countries emphasized the role of business in the new public diplomacy.

Despite suffering the worst economic blow, Prince Alwaleed expressed his interest in investing $200 mn in South Korea's Hyundai Group, i.e. Hyundai E&C, Hyundai Electric, and Hyundai Motors, given that the Korean economy was recovering at a faster rate with a high growth potential. Alwaleed's confidence in Hyundai Group was rooted in Hyundai E&C's history of building a $930 mn worth of Jubail Industrial Port project in 1976. Moreover, given his stakes in Four Seasons hotel, Prince Alwaleed also sought to invest in the leisure and hospitality industry in South Korea by building a hotel or acquiring an existing hotel to operate it as a chain of Four Seasons hotel. Though no further development was noted, pop star Michael Jackson and Prince Alwaleed took interest in acquiring Shilla Hotel in Seogwipo, Jeju Island, at a time when Jeju Island, a major tourist destination in the southwest of the Korean Peninsula, was also looking to attract foreign investments for tourism development. Business deals also reinforced people-to-people connectivity as Prince Alwaleed also received an honorary doctorate at Kyungwon University during his visit to South Korea in recognition for his entrepreneurial spirit and contribution to the recovery of the post-IMF crisis Korean economy. In 1999, Prince Alwaleed was also awarded a diplomatic medal of honor by the ROK Ministry of Foreign Affairs in recognition of advancing ROK–KSA business diplomacy.

The reeling effect of the 1997 Asian Financial Crisis was equally felt in other sectors such as the oil refining industry. As was the case with major businesses, the oil refining industry also faced major challenges caused by shortages in foreign exchange and heavy reliance on short-term foreign debt. Among the top five oil refining companies in South Korea, SK Energy, Ssangyong Oil, and Hanwha Energy held shareholder meetings in the aftermath of the debt crisis. In addition to the $58.35 bn conditional bailout loans arranged by the IMF, Ssangyong Oil and Hanwha Energy were looking to restructure debts by selling their stakes to foreign investors or pursuing a joint venture with foreign companies to improve their financial conditions. Ssangyong Oil (now renamed S-Oil) expressed its intent to sell 14% of equity to Saudi Aramco, in addition to the 35% of equity it had sold to Saudi Aramco. This would effectively render Saudi Aramco as the single largest stakeholder by increasing the shares to 49%.[42] As such, the South

Korean government had been pushing for the amendment of the Petroleum Business Act, in accordance with the stipulations set out by the IMF. In line with the company's strategy to strengthen its presence in the Asian market, Saudi Aramco announced in 2014 that it would acquire the entire shares of Hanjin Group, which owns S-Oil.

Politics has largely remained a marginal interest in Korea–Saudi relations; at best it was discussed on the sidelines of ministerial-level meetings and was usually brushed aside as being nothing more than symbolic reciprocations and verbal endorsements that have no bearing on actual foreign policy outcomes. Nevertheless, the news about Kim Young-sam's economic mismanagement made the headlines in Saudi Arabia's English-language daily *Arab News* and Jordan's Arabic daily *Al-Aswaq* in 1997. In spite of introducing political reform, economic liberalization, and welfare enhancement under the banner of "New Korea" reform initiative, Kim was unsuccessful in eradicating rampant corruption as the country's first democratically elected president, and instead, Kim's exit from his presidency ushered in an era of severe economic crisis.[43] Kim Young-sam's successor Kim Dae-jung's political views also gained attention from newspaper outlets in Saudi Arabia and the wider Arab world which republished an op-ed penned by Kim Dae-jung titled "Universal globalism.[44]" Kim's piece attracted readership from the developing and emerging economies in South Asia, Latin America, the Middle East, and SSA for representing the views of the developing countries based on South Korea's rapid transition from a developing economy to an industrialized country. Economic recovery was Kim Dae-jung's priority agenda during his first week as president-elect in late February 1998. While holding a chain of meetings with cabinet members in economics and finance, the Kim Dae-jung administration secured a $10 bn loan from the IMF. As the President-elect geared up to capture investments and generate economic interests on South Korean businesses by arranging meetings and receiving high-level delegates, Kim also received endorsements for the flagship Sunshine policy from his Saudi counterparts, namely former Saudi Minister of Defense Sheikh Sultan bin Abdulaziz Al Saud.

While Kim Dae-jung is better known for Sunshine policy, Kim also held frequent meetings with policy and business communities and engaged with Middle Eastern delegates to implement the vision for "Universal Globalism." In 1998, President Kim also met with Saudi King Fahd bin Abdulaziz Al Saud and Crown Prince Abdullah bin Abdulaziz Al Saud to discuss measures to promote economic cooperation between the two parties. Kim underscored how the two countries structurally complement each other given Saudi Arabia's drive for economic diversification and South Korea's capacity for technology, machinery, and experts for industrialization. In a high-level meeting held with Saudi Crown Prince Abdullah bin Abdulaziz Al Saud and the Saudi Minister of Foreign Affairs, and attended by South Korean business communities, political figureheads, and cabinet members, Kim brought up the perennial issue of Seoul's trade deficit with Riyadh by asking the Saudi counterpart to import more Korean goods, expand opportunities for South Korean companies to participate in Saudi construction projects, and discussed investment opportunities in Korea.[45] Between 2017 and 2018, trade deficits in South Korea's exports to Saudi Arabia were particularly acute in the automotive and electrical supplies.

During the Saudi Crown Prince Abdullah's visit to Korea in the same period, he also met with Prime Minister Kim Jong-pil as both parties agreed to upgrade the chief representative of the Korea–Saudi joint committee formed in 2008 from a vice-ministerial to a ministerial level. As a way of demonstrating the symbolic resolve to enhance bilateral ties, Kim was awarded with the Order of King Abdulaziz, which is the second highest honor awarded to Saudi citizens and foreign officials for their service to the Kingdom. Later President Kim delivered a letter addressing King Abdullah bin Abdulaziz Al Saud through his special envoy Prime Minister Lee Han-dong who visited Saudi Arabia in May 2001. In the letter, Kim underscored the rapidly expanding commercial ties between the two countries based on the fact that bilateral trade between the two countries had exceeded $10 bn for the first time in history.

However, by the early 2000s, Seoul was mired in yet another political and economic crisis. After Daewoo was put under court receivership in May 2001, Prince Al Waleed retracted $150 mn of investments in Daewoo and Hyundai Motors, including the interests, and also disposed $50 mn shares of Hyundai Motors following disagreements over dividends. In the subsequent year, the feud between the Chairman of Hyundai Motors Chung Mong-koo and the Chairman of Hyundai Asan Chung Mong-hun led to a crisis of Hyundai Group, which was amplified by the 2003 corruption scandal involving businessman Choi Kyu-sun and President Kim's two sons, MP Kim Hong-il and Kim Hong-geol. Three tapes released in May 2002 reveal that Kim Dae-jung's eldest son Kim Hong-il tried to dissuade his brother Kim Hong-geol from starting a joint venture investment fund with Choi Kyu-sun in the early 2000s, using a seed funding of $1 bn dollar supported by Prince Alwaleed. The plan, which was approved by the President and was to be publicly announced during Alwaleed's visit to Korea in July, was annulled after it faced staunch resistance from the eldest son Kim Hong-il. While MP Kim claimed that he tried to stop his brother from starting a business with Choi to preserve his father's honor and dignity, power struggle had developed between the two brothers, which also involved politicians and their close aides in government.

While government agencies sought every opportunity to improve market conditions, the specter of South Korea's debt crisis continued to linger on, as foreign investors and Bahrain's Arab Banking Corporation and Saudi Arabia's Riyad Bank exerted pressure on Seoul to withdraw their shares from SK Global. As for the former, the share accounted for 17% of the company's equity, and both banks demanded that the Korean government guarantee payment for SK Global's debts. Although controlling capital flight in South Korea became increasingly difficult in the early 2000s, in 2004, Saudi

Prince Bandar bin Sultan bin Abdulaziz Al Saud and his company Group Tech Corporation, which is involved in trade, IT, and security, submitted a letter of intent on acquiring stakes in Ssangyong Motors, the fourth largest automobile company. Prince Sultan's request was submitted alongside the Chinese company Shanghai Automotive Industry Corporation (presently SAIC Motor Corporation) which also entered the bid to overtake the Korean automobile company. Prince Sultan also discussed the business opportunities with Korean IT, construction, and textile companies as part of his plans to build a tourist and leisure complex in Saudi Arabia. Prince Sultan's plans to take over Ssangyong Motors were devised as a means to industrialize the Saudi economy by developing a homegrown automotive industry in Saudi Arabia. Though Prince Sultan expressed his interest in retaining production facilities and employees in South Korea and building an automobile assembly line in Saudi Arabia, negotiations were already underway with Shanghai Automotive Industry Corporation as a preferred negotiating partner. Eventually, however, India's Mahindra acquired a 75% stake in Ssangyong Motors in 2010. Regardless of the outcome of the bid and the debilitating effect of the financial crisis, Al Saud's business engagements with Seoul since the late 1990s turned out to be a silver lining from the Asian Debt Crisis of 1997.

Roh Moo-hyun's collaborative governance and Middle East diplomacy

South Korea's deployment of 18,000 troops to Iraq – in addition to the 2,500 noncombatant troops (Seohee, Jema, and Daiman units) – was the third-largest foreign military deployment in Iraq. As Korea's largest military dispatch since the Vietnam War, it was a policy decision that increasingly exposed Seoul to geopolitical volatilities in the region. By virtue of U.S. hegemony, the Middle East unwittingly became incorporated into South Korea's strategic calculations. As the military dispatch to Iraq was regarded as a political decision, diplomatic engagements with the neighboring countries in the region were critical to draw public support. Therefore, in 2004, the then Foreign Minister Ban Ki-moon toured three Middle Eastern countries – Saudi Arabia, Jordan, and Egypt – to discuss plans for dispatching additional troops to Iraq. Saudi Arabia and Jordan shared borders with Iraq, and the occupation of Iraq jeopardized Egypt's regional roles and interest; though the Hosni Mubarak government vehemently called for Saddam Hussein's ouster, they shifted their response once it became clear that the U.S. troops were facing resistance on the ground and Egyptian public opinion was turning against the war.[46] These countries, that were all linked to the war in Iraq one way or the other, had disagreements over the 2003 U.S. invasion of Iraq. Although Jordan was officially opposed to the war in Iraq, it served as a base of operations for American and British forces. It was supportive of South Korea's decision to send additional troops to Iraq and offered to provide medical and logistical support for Korean troops.

Regardless of their official positions toward the 2003 U.S. invasion of Iraq, Ban's diplomatic tour was fruitful in that it elicited nominal support from the Middle Eastern countries as a sovereign decision, ahead of dispatching additional troops to Iraq. South Korea was also able to generate interests among Middle Eastern countries on strategic issues that are vital to its national interests, namely security on the Korean Peninsula and six-party talks. Though Saudi Arabia Minister of Defense Sultan bin Abdulaziz Al Saud made it clear that Saudi Arabia adheres to the principle of non-interference, it unequivocally expressed that it "actively welcomes and supports" South Korea's decision to send additional troops to Iraq. During an interview with Yonhap News Agency in 2004, former Saudi Ambassador to South Korea Salem Al Rajhi also added that in order to receive international support for South Korea's additional deployment of military troops, it is critical for Zaytun unit to assimilate to the norms and culture of the Iraqi people and to focus on reconstruction efforts as the military medical support that Seohee and Jema units had contributed in the past.[47]

Ban's diplomatic tour was South Korea's first visit to Jordan and a second visit to Saudi Arabia since the former foreign Minister Park Dong-jin's visit in 1979. Though diplomatic engagements with the Middle East came much later in the process, Minister Ban's tour to the Middle East was instructive for signaling Seoul's intentions to adopt a proactive approach to foreign policy and strategic issues affecting the MENA as a member of the international community. Ban's diplomatic tour was significant in that it ushered in a new era of diplomatic diversification as part of South Korea's agenda for pursuing "sovereign diplomacy," which entails charting an independent diplomatic course that transcends the traditional emphasis on the diplomatic relations with the four states – the U.S., Japan, China, and Russia – whose ties are based on geographic proximity or are linked to the historical vestiges of Korean War. Korea's Middle East diplomacy, which comprised 12% of the Roh administration's diplomatic visits, was groundbreaking as it sharply contrasted with the previous two administrations that paid little or no attention to the region.[48] Following Ban's visits to the Middle East, further visits were planned with the cabinet members from the Ministries of Construction & Transportation; Defense; Science and Information and Communication Technology (ICT) and special envoys across 15 countries in the MENA.

Under the Roh administration, IT cooperation emerged as a key area of bilateral relations in a non-oil sector. Following on from the visit by Prime Minister Lee Hae-chan in November 2005, Minister of Information and Communication Chin Dae-jae, who held the position as the CEO of Digital Media Network Business at the Samsung Electronics and worked for major IT companies as a an engineer and researcher prior to his stint in public service, held a meeting with the ambassadors of five GCC member states in 2006 to strengthen exchange diplomacy, establish a common IT framework, and promote high-level meetings. Accordingly, the ROK Ministry of Education, in coordination with the Ministry of Foreign Affairs and the Saudi government, introduced a study abroad program that targeted 300 state-sponsored Saudi students, which accounted for 10% of all eligible students who were on government scholarship, to receive education on IT development in Korea. During his visit to South Korea in 2007, Saudi Arabia Education Minister Khalid al-Angari also expressed hopes for fostering exchange diplomacy at a professorial level between the two countries by sending 84 Saudi college students to six South Korean universities in a study abroad program as a way of promoting nationalization of local workforce by equipping Saudi nationals in IT, engineering, management, and natural sciences. As South Korea held the first study abroad fair in Riyadh later in the same year, Korea–Saudi Higher education cooperation laid the groundwork for strengthening people's diplomacy.

By July 2008, negotiations on the first Korea–GCC free trade agreement (FTA) were underway during Roh's meeting with the UAE Minister of Energy. Concluding the Korea–GCC FTA was anticipated to boost South Korea's efforts for supporting the non-oil growth in the GCC economies. As part of South Korea's broader economic blueprint in the Middle East, it sought to boost construction orders through the financial support of Korea Eximbank; attract FDI in refining and petrochemical activities abetted by the surge in oil prices in the region; increase exports in the automobile and electronics industries and machineries. Though procuring natural resources has been imperative to South Korea's industrialization, it lacked a comprehensive and proactive foreign policy vision and institutional capacity for activating business diplomacy. Informally dubbed as "sales diplomacy" in the policy circle, high-level visits were minimal leading up to the Roh administration, which spearheaded efforts at a governmental level to advance Middle East diplomacy beyond the traditional oil and gas and construction sectors.

South Korea's business activities in the mid-to-late 2000s received a boost from Prime Minister Lee Hae-chan's diplomatic tour to the Middle East in December 2005. Lee was likened to a "sales manager" as he was accompanied by 40 business delegations from Korea to promote resource diplomacy. Lee's visit to the Middle East came at a time when oil prices were soaring above $60 per barrel in the first two quarters of 2005, fueled by concerns over terrorist threats in Saudi Arabia, Iran's resumption of nuclear activities, and the passing of King Fahd bin Abdulaziz Al Saud in August 2005. It was a significant milestone for expanding the network and providing brokerage for establishing an environment conducive for trade and commerce. Establishing relations with local authorities and government officials in the Middle East has led to tangible results including bagging nine deals in construction and EPC and negotiating 48 projects and signing MOUs in energy and mineral cooperation and ICT. Lee Hae-chan's visit to Saudi Arabia which was the second high-level visit since President Choi Kyu-hah's visit in 1980 was planned in the eve of the second Middle Eastern construction boom. Investment briefings and business symposiums were held to promote FDIs, business consultations, and South Korea's plant construction capabilities. During Prime Minister Lee's two-day visit, he met with Saudi King Abdullah bin Abdulaziz Al Saud and attended joint Korea–Saudi economic conference of private sector representatives and Korean expatriates in Saudi Arabia.

In March 2007, President Roh Moo-hyun made subsequent visits to Saudi Arabia, Kuwait, and Qatar to strengthen business diplomacy. Roh became the second president in South Korea's history to visit Saudi Arabia after Choi Kyu-hah in 1980. In a tour accompanying 200 businesspersons, Roh pushed for enhanced business, political, and diplomatic partnerships with the GCC member states. Saudi Arabia and Qatar had expressed their intentions to invest in Korea ahead of Roh's scheduled visits to the Middle East. During his visit to Saudi Arabia, Roh met with King Abdullah to discuss strategies in expanding bilateral cooperation in energy, construction, IT, education, and science and technology. In a second high-level summit since the President Choi Kyu-hah's visit, both leaders signed MOUs in double taxation prevention agreement, higher education cooperation agreement, and IT cooperation agreement.

Roh also visited the *Majlis al-Shura* (consultative council) and delivered a speech titled "The future of 21st century Korea-Middle East relations" and addressed the speaker and 150 members of the council and expressed his intent to push for Korea–GCC FTA in the same year. Given Korea's energy dependence on the Middle East and the heightened competition in the Middle Eastern construction and export markets, concluding the FTA with the GCC was expected to reinforce mutual interests in economic cooperation while boosting South Korea's business competitiveness in the Middle Eastern market against the competitors from the EU, China, Japan, and America. If ratified, the Korea–GCC FTA was projected to boost Korea's construction order in the MENA by 100% in the next three years, which would also exceed the value of $100 bn in construction projects in 2005.[49] Though Roh highlighted the mutual interests in contributing to the development of human resources and non-oil sectors in the Gulf economies, negotiations for the Korea–GCC FTA had stalled since 2009.[50] In addition to the Korea–Saudi Economic Cooperation Committee meeting that was jointly held by the Korean Chamber of Commerce and Saudi Chamber of Commerce, Roh envisioned a holistic vision for promoting people-to-people connectivity and cultural exchange programs with the input of business, media, religion, and academic communities and offered to share Korea's industrialization experience and support technical transfers to the GCC countries. Roh's visits to the GCC countries coincided with the U.S. Secretary of State Condoleezza Rice's meeting with foreign ministers from Egypt, Jordan, Saudi Arabia, and the UAE in Aswan, Egypt ahead of the Arab Summit scheduled for March 28. In commemorating the first presidential-level meeting held in nearly three decades, Roh Moo-hyun was awarded the King Abdulaziz medal.

Roh's visits to the Gulf were further supported by ministerial-level visits to Saudi Arabia. Deputy Prime Minister and Minister of Education Kim Shin-il's follow-up visits to Saudi Arabia, Kazakhstan, and Uzbekistan were part of a broader governmental initiative to engage in educational diplomacy and promote academic exchanges in higher education. Education was revitalized as a new tool and chief strategy for diversifying bilateral cooperation and transferring Korea's knowledge-based economy to the Middle East by benchmarking Korea's education system. In the long term, the South Korean government directed its efforts in promoting internationalization of the country's higher education sector. The three-pronged strategies in higher education management include the plans for recruiting a higher number of international faculty to improve the international ranking of Korean universities; promoting the internationalization of Korean universities and offering financial incentives for encouraging evaluation and monitoring of internationalization; and easing restrictions for establishing foreign branches of Korean universities.[51] To support the country's transition into a knowledge-based economy, Saudi Arabia also coordinated with the KDI to create the Saudi Development Institute in 2012. Minister of Information and Communication Roh Jun-hyung also accompanied Roh to attend the Korea–Saudi IT business forum and Korea–Saudi civil economic cooperation committee and introduce WiBro, the world's first commercialized IT services developed by South Korea for the Saudi government and businessmen. The visit culminated with signing a MoU on IT cooperation with the Saudi counterpart Mohammed Jamil bin Ahmed Mulla.

South Korea's priority interests in energy security and economic development implied that bilateral cooperation was bound to be multifaceted. In addition to the steady provision of heavy crude oil as a feedstock in refineries, South Korea was equally concerned with oil price stability given the repercussions of the 1973 oil crisis. Therefore, Roh's Middle East policy was buttressed by a comprehensive set of government-led initiatives that promoted "sovereign diplomacy." While engaging with private business representatives, Roh called for government agencies to offer guidance and supportive role to Korean businesses operating in the construction sector in the Middle East and urged Deputy Minister for Economic Affairs at the Ministry of Foreign Affairs to play an oversight function in devising a methodical strategy for facilitating business activities in the Middle East. In doing so, the Roh administration recognized the need for making a systematic effort in laying the groundwork for fostering high-level meetings and providing governmental support for ensuring steady supply of energy resources. In spite of Korea's status as a resource-deficit country, Roh placed a high value on South Korea's abundance of human capital and recognized the local workforce as the main engine of economic growth and prosperity. As a President with a populist appeal, these principles were encapsulated in Roh's doctrine of participatory governance, with an emphasis on democratization and welfare development. To establish a systematic framework for facilitating the entry of Korean SMEs in the Middle Eastern market, South Korea's Small and Medium Business Corporation entered into a business cooperation agreement with Saudi Arabian General Investment Authority (SAGIA).

Roh's visits to the Middle East led to tangible outcomes in business development including the SK Group signing a MoU to participate in the construction of Saudi U-City (ubiquitous city) in Riyadh. The aim was to establish a cooperative framework with the Saudi government for creating a cutting-edge, high-tech city that is modeled after the construction of Hwaseong Dongtan city in Korea. In the mid-to-late 2000s, Saudi Arabia was investing in modernizing and industrializing its infrastructure by building industrial complexes and high-rise buildings and skyscrapers. To exploit the opportunities created by oil-boom, Korea Eximbank signed an agreement with SABIC, a Saudi state-run petrochemical company to finance the participation of South Korean companies in the construction of large-scale construction projects and to collaborate on future projects, while KOTRA signed an agreement of MOU for promoting trade cooperation with the Saudi Chamber of Commerce and Industry.

Korea–Saudi Arabia bilateral talks were also held at the ministerial level on the sidelines of the Asia Cooperation Dialogue (ACD) in Seoul in June 2007. IT cooperation was at the crux of the summit and Seoul IT Declaration, which aimed to close the gap in informational and technological divide in Asia, was adopted by 30 countries. The ACD made for a timely segue for South Korea for which IT cooperation was a key area of bilateral and multilateral relations with the GCC countries, and for enhancing South Korea's soft power capabilities by promoting Yeosu Expo and PyeongChang 2018 Winter Olympics. As it turns out, 19 of 30 countries participating in ACD were members of the Bureau International des Expositions and 13 of 30 participants were members of the International Olympic Committee. IT cooperation between the two countries provided a basis for supporting Saudi Arabia's innovation and future-oriented economic activities, as part of a broader blueprint to diversify its economy away from oil as set out by Saudi Vision 2030.

S-Oil, Hyundai E&C, and Lee Myung-bak's resource diplomacy

The MENA figured prominently in South Korea's energy diplomacy, which became the hallmark of Lee Myung-bak's foreign policy doctrine. Given his background as a former chairman of Hyundai E&C, Lee accorded a high priority to economic growth, privatization, deregulation, and took business-friendly measures.[52] Concluding FTAs with Japan, China, Russia, and the GCC and holding summits and high-level meetings figured high on the agenda for promoting resource diplomacy. By 2008, there was a total of 32 field offices for energy and resource bases operated by South Korean companies, including in Saudi Arabia and Russia, and there were plans to increase them to 50.[53] The inauguration of the Korea–Arab Society during the Lee administration was a driving force for enhancing South Korea's bilateral relations with the Middle East and was welcomed by Saudi Arabia. Korea–Arab Society's founding member states consisted of 22 countries from the MENA, including the GCC states. As an organization established under the public–private not-for-profit partnership, members of the ruling family and academic and business communities were invited to participate in events.

Lee Myung-bak's resource diplomacy focused on elevating relations with the oil-producing countries of the Middle East and Central Asia. In order to take practical and holistic approaches to diplomacy, the Lee administration launched the Korea–Arab Caravan Trade to promote public diplomacy and sent economic representatives to key oil-producing countries, including Saudi Arabia, to support investment opportunities in plant and equipment in South Korea. However, South Korea's resource diplomacy was lagging behind that of China and Japan. According to *Petroleum Intelligence Weekly*, three Chinese oil companies, including the state-owned China National Petroleum Corporation, which was ranked seventh, were among the top 100 oil companies globally, while five of Japanese oil companies were also ranked in the top 100, but the majority of them lie outside the top 50.[54] But while China and Japan have made considerable strides in resource development and South-South cooperation by extending their ties to SSA, Central Asia, Russia, and Iran, South Korea's strength mainly lies in the oil refinery industry.

S-Oil, whose largest shareholder is Saudi Aramco as of August 1991, is an emblem of the Korea–Saudi economic partnership in the oil refining industry. Metaphorically, S-Oil has assumed an intermediary role between the South Korean government and the Saudi construction market. It has indirectly contributed to winning construction tenders in nuclear power plant construction, city construction, oil tanker projects, and oil and gas projects. In March 2012, Lee Myung-bak attended the completion ceremony for the Onsan petrochemical production facility expansion project in Ulsan alongside Korean government officials and Saudi Minister of Petroleum and Minerals Ali bin al-Naimi and former CEO of Saudi Aramco Khalid al-Falih. On this occasion, Lee lauded Minister al-Naimi as "the first person in the history of Saudi Arabia as a CEO of Saudi Aramco to make a large investment in Korea." Moreover, he hailed S-Oil as a successful model of economic cooperation between oil-producing and oil-consuming countries.[55] Building on the history of 20 years of bilateral commercial relations, Saudi Aramco signed a 20-year crude oil supply contract with S-Oil in 2012. In 2015, the road at Onsan Refinery was named after former Saudi Minister of Petroleum Ali bin al-Naimi. Corporate relations also strengthened cultural affinity as the chairman of S-Oil Hussein al-Qahtani celebrated his first Korean Chuseok holiday in 2019 by giving himself a Korean name Ha Se-in, which means "a blessed person with an overflowing energy in a big house," and volunteered distributing songpyeon rice cakes to 800 underprivileged local households with his staff.[56] During Saudi Crown Prince Mohammed bin Salman's visit to Korea on June 26, 2019, S-Oil held an inauguration ceremony for a new petrochemical complex, which is the largest scale investment project completed in South Korea's refining and petrochemical industry.

Lee's credential as the former chairman of Hyundai E&C generated confidence in foreign investors. Dar Al Salam Holding Group, an investment company in Saudi Arabia, and S&C International Group showed great interest in investing in Korean businesses and attended Lee Myung-bak's inauguration ceremony. Dar Al Salam Holding Group, which signed an agreement with Gunsan in North Jeolla province to participate as a developer and investor in December 2007, expressed its intent to invest $6–$8 bn in Saemangeum Development Plant.[57] As the company's first foreign investment outside the Middle East, investing in tourism development in South Korea enhanced the future prospects for attracting diversified foreign investments in domestic construction and IT companies that operate in Saudi Arabia. Given the Saudi government's interests in the e-government industry, Saudi Arabia's S&C International Group likewise expressed its interests in investing in urban development and companies involved in intelligent and smart building.

The outbreak of the global financial crisis of 2008–2009 cast a shadow over the rosy economic forecast of what was initially to be sustained by oil revenues for at least another five years. The G20 convened an emergency meeting with governors and finance ministers of 20 countries, which includes South Korea and Saudi Arabia, at the request of Brazil which assumed the G20 presidency in 2008. In the face of global economic recession induced by the U.S. subprime mortgage crisis, high oil prices, and youth unemployment, President Lee was resolved to revitalize the economy and enhance corporate management and investment activities by improving labor-management relations, increasing export competitiveness, and strengthening diplomatic relations. At the G20 Summit held in November 2008, Lee called for extending currency swaps with advanced economies to ensure sufficient liquidity supply in emerging economies by strengthening partnerships between advanced and emerging economies in G20.

While construction projects were scaled back during the global financial crisis, the total number of orders for eight large-scale EPC industries for Korean companies in Saudi Arabia amounted to approximately $5 bn in 2009 and by 2012 negotiations were underway for participation in the construction of the $4 bn Riyadh metro project.[58] Signs of robust economic cooperation were evident when the Korea–Saudi customs agreement was signed during the first Korea–Saudi customs commissioners meeting in 2012, and around the same period, Korean Air started operation of its direct flights to Saudi Arabia for the first time in 15 years. In the same year, Saudi Arabia also recorded a budget surplus for the first time since the 2008–2009 financial crisis. Saudi Arabia thus earmarked 28% of its total budget in the construction of new hospitals and invested in the construction of 500,000 housing units. Buttressed by stable market conditions, South Korea also recorded the highest number of orders received for Saudi construction projects in 2012 which amounted to $72 bn and accounted for nearly a quarter of the total market share in the Saudi EPC industry.[59] Following on from signs of a second oil boom in the Middle

East, Lee Myung-bak made Saudi Arabia his first stopover among the Gulf countries in February 2012. Marking 50 years of Korea–Saudi diplomatic relations, the year 2012 also witnessed major milestones in the bilateral cooperation across a broad range of fields. Dubbed as "proprietary patent diplomacy," Lee met with the Saudi Oil Minister Ali al-Naimi regarding the supply of crude oil in case of emergency and shortage of crude oil production caused by Iranian sanctions.

At the same time, increasing attention was dedicated to engaging in multifaceted diplomacy at economic, cultural, and diplomatic levels. As former Saudi Ambassador to South Korea Abdullah al-Aifan noted during a meeting with the ambassadors from Arab countries presided over by the Lee administration in 2008, there was an increasing call to strengthen South Korea's diplomatic ties with Saudi Arabia and wider MENA in parallel with the well-established bilateral economic relations.[60] In response, Lee pledged to deepen ties with the MENA countries by holding frequent high-level meetings than his predecessors. Since taking office as the Minister of Land, Transport and Maritime Affairs in February 2008, Jeong Jong-hwan's first overseas business trips were to Saudi Arabia and the UAE, the largest construction markets. The construction market in these countries was relatively immune to the effects of global economic downturn in 2008 but experienced a sharp decline in the first quarter of 2009. The chairman of SK Group Choi Tae-won's private economic diplomacy at the Davos Forum in 2009 also played a vital role in furthering the governmental blueprint for improving resource diplomacy with the Middle East. In particular, Choi met with key political and business figures, including the head of SAGIA Khaled al-Saleh on the sidelines of the Davos Forum to discuss the role of the South Korean government and businesses in helping reinvigorate the global economy after the financial crisis.

Building on the legacies of educational cooperation initiatives from the previous administration, defense exchange and cooperation was also promoted through the visits by Saudi Arabian Command and Staff College and the Saudi defense cooperation delegation in 2009 and 2012. A defense cooperation agreement, which also led to a $500 mn worth of South Korean arms sales of ammunitions and howitzers to Saudi Arabia, was signed between South Korea and Saudi Arabia in February 2012 during Lee's visit to Saudi Arabia. The Saudi defense attaché's office also reopened in the same year in Seoul after it was closed in 1992 since the initial establishment in 1962. South Korea also sought to strengthen bilateral cooperation in defense and security in 2019 by launching the inaugural Korea–Saudi Defense Cooperation Committee in Saudi Arabia which followed from an agreement to establish the Vice-Ministerial Defense Cooperation Committee in December 2018 and the Defense Technology Committee and Military Cooperation Committee held in the previous month. In conjunction with Korea–Saudi Vision 2030, both parties discussed ways to foster military exchange and defense cooperation at the 2019 Seoul Security Dialogue. Discussions were held about security on the

Korean Peninsula as Vice Minister of National Defense Park Jae-min asked for Saudi support on the complete denuclearization of the Korean Peninsula and the establishment of a permanent peace regime. In July, Hanwha signed an agreement to embark on a joint venture with Saudi state-owned defense company Saudi Arabian Military Industries (SAMI) in Saudi Arabia under the label SAMI – Hanwha Logistics System, which paved the way for South Korean defense firms to enter the Saudi defense industry.

Park Geun-hye's creative economy and Rafiq diplomacy

The Park Geun-hye administration, which took office on February 25, 2013, embarked on an "inauguration diplomacy" and introduced an official development assistance policy that built on her father Park Chung-hee's *Saemaul Undong* (New Village) Movement. During the height of second oil boom in the Middle East in 2015, Park engaged in proactive summit diplomacy by visiting 17 countries and holding 43 summit meetings.[61] The Gulf states of Kuwait, Saudi Arabia, the UAE, and Qatar were among the first few countries that she visited that year. Despite the risk factors of low-cost construction project orders, excessive competition, and oversaturation of markets in the Middle East, South Korea accounted for nearly a quarter of the market share in the EPC sector in 2013. Saudi Arabia remained a hub for large-scale construction, shipbuilding, and power plant projects.[62] During her diplomatic tour to Riyadh in March 2013, Park also met with Prince Alwaleed to discuss investment opportunities. Alwaleed established ties with South Korean companies since the 1970s and visited South Korea four times by then.[63] In what was dubbed as "sales diplomacy," Park suggested launching a joint investment fund in the Middle East and asked Prince Al Waleed to invest in the South Korean cultural industry. As Park aspired to boost investment cooperation with Riyadh by establishing a joint investment fund in the Middle East, in addition to the booming construction sector, an investment cooperation agreement was signed between Korea Investment Corporation (KIC) and KHC. The Investment Cooperation Agreement embedded clauses on investing in technology and the Saudi real estate market as well as investing KHC's capital in KIC. During the same visit, Seoul agreed on exporting Korean-style System-integrated Modular Advanced Reactor (SMART) nuclear reactors worth 2 tn Won to Saudi Arabia and fostering bilateral nuclear and renewable energy cooperation by collaborating with King Abdullah City for Atomic and Renewable Energy (KACARE). The Korea–U.S. Nuclear Power Agreement which was signed during the Park administration facilitated the export of Korea's nuclear exports, which was ranked as the world's top five nuclear power plants in the world.

At a summit held with Saudi economic minister at the Korea–Saudi business forum during the same visit, Park referred to the Arab saying, "One hand cannot clap," and by alluding to the prospects for a "second miracle of the Han River," stressed that both countries should seek mutual interests by putting their hands together to clap in order to materialize a common vision.[64] By promoting a future-oriented growth strategy that is aligned with Saudi Arabia's economic diversification initiatives and Korea's three-year economic innovation plan, Park reiterated how Saudi and South Korean economies complement each other by combining Saudi capital and Korean technology. In taking a futuristic approach, Park emphasized in an interview with Saudi's leading local daily *Al-Riyadh* that Saudi Arabia is a long-term, strategic partner ("*Rafiq*") to South Korea. Park was especially keen on diversifying the scope of bilateral cooperation by referring to a Middle Eastern proverb, "Rainfall in desert starts with a drop of rain."[65]

Creative economy was the core philosophy and doctrine behind Park Geun-hye's business diplomacy. The aim was to resolve three major economic issues of slow growth, high unemployment, and economic disparity by promoting sustainable development and enhancing global economic alliance and solidarity. President Park delivered an opening speech on creative economy for Davos Forum 2014 which was held under the theme of "Reorganizing the world: Impact on politics, business and society." Park's speech highlighted the importance of promoting entrepreneurship and sustainable and inclusive growth by creating practical guidelines and strategies to innovate and restructuring an alternative global economic regime to Washington Consensus through the so-called Davos Consensus.

Creative economy, which became the flagship policy of the Park administration, equally served as the basis for promoting joint strategies in future-oriented sectors through the launch of joint innovation centers and vocational training programs. Seoul hosted the 2015 ministerial-level meeting held for the OECD Committee for Scientific and Technological Policy at the Daejeon Convention Center, which was also attended by the Saudi Minister of Science Research and Technology. In her opening speech at the OECD ministerial meeting, Park called for the adoption of Daejeon Declaration to cultivate a sustainable and inclusive growth through creative economy. Inspire U, the first Saudi grassroots ICT and digital innovation startup company, was modeled after Korea's creative economy initiative and established by Saudi Telecom Company (STC) in 2015. The CEO of Inspire U Saud al-Hawawi visited SK Creative Economy Innovation Center in Korea in the following year and expressed hopes for fostering bilateral knowledge and information exchange. Indirectly buttressed by the creative economy initiative, further strides were noted in bilateral partnerships in technology, business, and cultural sectors. Between 2014 and 2017, POSCO signed a MOU with the Saudi Arabia's sovereign wealth fund, Public Investment Fund (PIF) to pursue joint venture in the automotive industry, while Doosan Heavy Industries & Construction signed an agreement with the Saudi Seawater Desalination Agency (SWCC) to conduct joint research on seawater desalination technology. South Korea's legendary archery player Kim Soo-nyung was also appointed as a personal archery coach to King Abdullah's granddaughters.

The role of the private sector assumed importance in advancing commercial interests in parallel with the government-led commercial diplomacy led by the Park administration. As the largest shareholder of S-Oil, the board of directors of Saudi Aramco visited Ulsan to pay respect to the late founder of Hyundai Group Chung Joo-young and did a stopover to the Asan Memorial Exhibition Hall at the Hyundai Heavy Industries Cultural Center. Chung was remembered for his contributions to South Korea's economic growth and for constructing the Jubail Industrial Port in 1976. Informal business ties were also established between Seoul and Riyadh through the chairman of UI Energy Choi Kyu-sun, who forged 20 years of business ties with Prince Alwaleed. Choi visited Korea in May 2016 and discussed investment opportunities in the IT industry, specifically in the areas of artificial intelligence and robotics and digital media city. Previously, Choi was part of a business delegation that met with Prince Alwaleed alongside Li Xiao-lin, the chairman of the Chinese People's Association for Friendship with Foreign Countries and surveyed the construction site for the Jeddah project, which was contracted to a consortium led by a Chinese state-owned and private companies. Despite his embezzlement charges during the Kim Dae-jung administration, Choi was a savvy businessman who brokered business meetings at a governmental level through his far-reaching network of business connections. Choi vowed to contribute to the growth of Korean economy and expand business deals with Saudi Arabia in line with Saudi Vision 2030 by signing a defense contract for DoDaam Systems' unmanned security system which was introduced to Saudi Defense Minister and Crown Prince Mohamed bin Salman in October 2016. Around the same time, Prince Alwaleed and his son Sheikh Khaled bin Alwaleed Al Saud became the largest shareholders of SunCore Incorporation, a machinery manufacturing company, and Suntech International, a technology company, both run by Choi.

In line with Saudi Arabia's initiative to prepare for the post-oil era, Saudi Arabia's sovereign wealth fund, PIF acquired 38% shares of POSCO E&C in October 2015, which led to the advancement of joint ventures in Saudi local industries and construction projects. On the occasion of signing the agreement, which followed nine months after receiving the letter of intent from Saudi Arabia, Chairman Kwon highlighted 1,000 years of historical exchange between the two countries since Korea was part of Goryeo Dynasty and when Arab merchants came to Bekryung Island, which is 50 km away from Songdo, where POSCO E&C headquarter is based.[66] Despite these efforts, business dealings were also stymied by corruption charges in South Korea. Although the plans for establishing a joint construction company were underway in 2015, the Saudi national car project, which was designed to boost Saudi Arabia's crude oil exports to Korea – during which it was facing competitions from the American shale gas industry and cheap sources of crude oil from Iran – was scrapped as POSCO E&C was embroiled in a slush fund probe. Instead, the contract was later awarded to Ssangyong

Motors. Furthermore, former Prime Minister Lee Wan-koo stepped down in April 2015 after it was revealed that Sung Wan-jong, a construction mogul, left a suicide note which named the prime minister amid allegations on corruption charges. The incident proved to be a blow to the Park Geun-hye administration, which was besieged in Sewol ferry incident from the previous year. Park's so-called Rafiq diplomacy was noted for mobilizing large business delegations as part of her diplomatic visits to the Middle East, Latin America, Vietnam, and Germany since the inauguration in 2013. Notably, Park led 116 businesspersons to the Gulf in 2015 and a record 236 businesspersons to visit Iran in April 2016, which was unprecedented in scale. The accomplishments of Park's sales diplomacy were noteworthy as the total number of contracts signed following her visits amounted to $109 bn. Yet at the same time, as was the case with Roh Moo-hyun and Lee Myung-bak administrations, there was a lack of clarity as to whether the record achievements had fully materialized considering the non-binding nature of MOUs.

Saudi-Korea Vision 2030

Saudi Vision 2030 is a political, economic, and social reform plan led by Saudi Crown Prince Mohammed bin Salman in April 2016. As a comprehensive blueprint for social, economic, and educational modernization scheme, Saudi Arabia has had plans to improve economic diversification, localization of national industries, social and cultural welfare, and human capital development. Discussions were held over ways to deepen bilateral relations centered on Saudi Vision 2030 during the Saudi–Korea summit which was held on the sidelines of the G20 Summit in Hangzhou, China in 2016. As a result, both countries agreed to establish the Saudi–Korea industrial cooperation committee to advance strategic partnership in the automotive, shipbuilding, and electronics industries. Saudi Minister of Energy, Industry and Minerals Khalid al-Falih discussed a joint venture on shipbuilding between Saudi Aramco and Hyundai Heavy Industries. This followed from Saudi Ministry of Energy, Industry and Mineral Resources whose function was expanded to oversee science and technology in addition to energy, industrial policy, and mineral resources prior to the agreement.

In addition to South Korea's developmental blueprint for a creative economy, Saudi Vision 2030 served as a basis for signing multiple visa agreements and transportation cooperation and investment cooperation agreements during the Prime Minister Hwang Kyo-ahn's visit to Saudi Arabia in May. Hwang's visit to Saudi Arabia was scheduled as part of his attendance of the World Humanitarian Summit in Istanbul, but it also came against the backdrop of international sanctions lifted on Iran. Hwang's visit to Riyadh was part of a foreign policy calculus to pursue "balance diplomacy" which was sought to appease Saudi Arabia, in light of Park's visit to Tehran which led to a record number of business delegations on a diplomatic visit and to reassure Saudi Arabia of maintaining a strategic partnership. As the launch of Saudi Vision 2030 improved the outlook for a second oil boom, this led to the formalization of a strategic partnership between the Saudi Ministry of Trade, Industry and ROK Ministry of Trade, Industry and Energy through the formation of Saudi-Korea Vision 2030.

Saudi-Korea Vision 2030 was founded on complementary economic structures. Some of the core strengths that Saudi Arabia has to offer are in the areas of energy supply, sovereign wealth funds, strategic gateway to the MENA, and large-scale market. Based on Saudi Arabia's needs, South Korea is able to offer expertise in technological and manufacturing experience, training of human capital, and EOI.[67] Though the extensive gamut of partnership opportunities in smart infrastructure and digitization; capacity-building; healthcare and life sciences; SMEs and investment showed potential to varying degrees, bilateral cooperation in the nuclear power plant construction was thwarted by conflict of interest stemming from the South Korean government's nuclear phase-out policy under the Moon Jae-in administration as well as corruption scandal that culminated with Park Geun-hye's impeachment in March 2017.

Prior to Park's impeachment, Foreign Minister Yun Byung-se held a meeting with the Saudi Minister of Economic Planning and discussed strategies to implement Saudi Vision 2030 by recognizing Korea–Saudi joint committee formed in 1975 as a foundation for strengthening bilateral cooperation. During the first Korea–Saudi Vision 2020 summit held in May 2018, particular attention was given to the development of automobiles and renewable energy by exploiting sovereign wealth funds. In addition to expressing South Korea's interest in bidding for the Saudi nuclear power plant construction project and expanding cooperation in the pharmaceutical industry, both parties agreed to set up a platform to facilitate communication between government officials and research institutions from both sides and automotive companies in Korea. In accordance with Saudi-Korea Vision 2030, KOTRA signed a MOU with Saudi Aramco in April 2018 to cooperate in a multitude of fields including trade, investment, education, petrochemical industry, renewable energy, construction, shipbuilding, and IT. Saudi and Korean governments reviewed over 40 projects pertaining to manufacturing and energy, digital and smart infrastructure, health and life sciences, small and medium businesses and investment, and agreed to open a Vision Realization Office in Seoul in 2019.

Given that Hyundai Heavy Industries was awarded a contract to construct the Jubail Port project in 2015 and SK Global Chemical, a subsidiary of Korea's largest refinery company SK Innovation, has been operating a joint polyethylene plant along with SABIC since 2015, Ulsan city invited ambassadors of the GCC countries to South Korea to attend an investment conference. Although Saudi Arabia has been South Korea's largest trading partner in the Middle East, further efforts to engage in business diplomacy with Saudi Arabia were marred by South Korea's domestic politics. As President Park faced an impeachment trial in December 2016, South

Korea was excluded from King Salman's visits to Asian countries, which was carried out to drive investments in the Saudi economy battered by low oil prices. In order to boost investments in the Kingdom in the face of an unprecedented fiscal crisis, the Saudi government issued the first-ever dollar-denominated bonds that were sold to VIP investors in South Korea through domestic securities and investment corporations. Considering that Asian countries are Saudi Aramco's largest customers, Saudi Aramco negotiated with investors from South Korea, China, and Japan to decide on where to list Saudi Aramco's overseas stock market before it went public in October and November 2018.

Robot diplomacy was also instituted as Sophia, the world's first humanoid robot to be declared a Saudi citizen in 2017, attended a conference on the Fourth Industrial Revolution that was hosted by Seoul in January 2018. In a panel moderated by lawmaker Park Young-sun, David Hanson the CEO of Hanson Robotics, a Hong Kong-based company that developed Sophia, suggested that AI robots should be recognized as humans. Park later called on Seoul mayor's office to award an honorary citizenship to humanoid Robot Sophia as a symbolic act of cementing the Seoul's status as a hub of the Fourth Industrial Revolution. In order to grant citizenship to AI humanoid robots, Park proposed to enact the Basic Robot Act. The Fourth Industrial Revolution was also the main theme for the 15th meeting of Korea–Arab Society co-sponsored by South Korea Ministry of Foreign Affairs and the Emirates Center for Strategic Studies and Research (ECSSR) in Abu Dhabi in 2018. The meeting which was attended by Saudi, Jordanian, and Korean delegates discussed the outlook for economic and communication cooperation strategies between South Korea and the Middle East under the Fourth Industrial Revolution and ways to diversify cooperation in future-oriented sectors.

Further to these initiatives, Saudi Crown Prince Mohammed bin Salman's visit to South Korea in 2019 bolstered a common development blueprint founded on Saudi-Korea Vision 2020. The Crown Prince led an economic delegation of 300 people, which was comparable in scale to his earlier visit to China, including Saudi Aramco CEO Amin al-Nasser and the Deputy Governor of Investment Attraction and Development at the SAGIA Sultan Mofti. The Crown Prince met with Samsung Electronics Vice Chairman Lee Jae-yong and the CEOs of three major corporations, Hyundai, SK, and LG. In particular, the Crown Prince met with Samsung Electronics Vice Chairman Lee to discuss future collaborations in 5G wireless communication technologies and AI. Hyundai Motor Company and Saudi Aramco also held talks on the hydrogen infrastructure construction project and various other EPC projects in Saudi Arabia were also discussed on the table. As the chief architect behind Saudi Vision 2030, there were high hopes and expectations that the Crown Prince's visit would facilitate the entry of South Korean companies in nuclear power plant construction and other industrial projects. Ten memoranda worth $8.3 bn were signed on initiatives that combine ICT and urban development such as smart cities, electric vehicles, and renewable energy in Saudi Arabia.[68]

Korea's SMART nuclear reactor and nuclear energy cooperation

As part of the five areas of business cooperation under energy and manufacturing, as set out by the Saudi-Korea Vision 2030 initiative, both parties signed a nuclear energy cooperation agreement in 2011 that entails conducting joint nuclear R&D program between KAERI and KACARE. The nuclear agreement served as the basis for exporting South Korea's nuclear technology and for the development and operation of nuclear power plants. These initiatives were further supported by a three-week vocational training provided by Korea Advanced Institute of Science and Technology (KAIST) to top three Saudi graduates in the field of nuclear science in 2014. In late 2017, as the Saudi government began issuing request for information (RFI) as a preliminary step for inviting international bidding for two 1400 MW nuclear power plants, Korea Electric Power Corporation (KEPCO) and KEPCO's subsidiary Korea Hydro & Nuclear Power (KHNP) decided to participate in the bidding process as a consortium. In a meeting between the Minister of Trade, Industry and Energy Paik Un-gyu and Saudi Economic Planning Minister Adel Fakeih, Minister Paik stressed that South Korea has over 40 years of experience in the construction and operation of nuclear power plants and the only country with nuclear power plant construction experience in the Middle East.

There was a great deal of commotion as the Moon Jae-in administration sent mixed signals about the government's agenda to promote South Korea's entry for international nuclear power plant construction biddings in the future. Delivering on his presidential campaign pledge, Moon introduced the nuclear phase-out and renewable energy expansion policy with an eye to reduce the number of nuclear power plants in South Korea from 24 to 14 by 2038. The operations of Wolsong Nuclear Power Plant unit 1 and 14 other nuclear power plants were shut down ahead of schedule and the six nuclear power plants projects were scrapped. There were increasing concerns that the possibility of shutting down the operation of Shin Kori Units 5 and 6 would be an impediment to participating in international biddings. As a result, South Korea's local nuclear industry officials called on the South Korean government to resume nuclear power plant activities and stressed the need for government to re-establish nuclear energy development as a national priority.

Flying in the face of Moon's controversial nuclear energy policy, the Ministry of Trade, Industry and Energy continued to promote South Korea's intent to support its nuclear power plant projects abroad by meeting with the Saudi Minister of Economic Planning at Korea–Saudi Vision 2030 meeting. Hamstrung by politics, Moon's nuclear phase-out policy undermined the credibility of the South Korean nuclear power plant industry. In the absence of government support, the future of the Korean nuclear power plant industry remained bleak. Moon's directives significantly undercut efforts for advancing South Korea's "sales diplomacy" from the previous administrations and it remained uncertain as to whether the state-owned Korea Eximbank would be able to fund nuclear power plant projects after declaring the nuclear energy policy moot. Though South Korea's nuclear power plant industry outmaneuvered America, Japan, and France after winning the Barakah Power Plant bid in the UAE, the Chinese and Russian counterparts emerged as strong competitors in the nuclear power plant construction market. By 2019, the working-level negotiations between the UAE and KHNP did not follow through, while the U.S. confirmed that nuclear energy talks were underway with Saudi Arabia. South Korea initially held high hopes for pushing forth with the nuclear deal by offering incentives such as localizing manpower training and technical transfers to meet Saudi Arabia's future energy needs as well as through the U.S. Nuclear Regulatory Commission's certification of South Korea's APR-1400 nuclear reactor. However, the prospect for exporting South Korea's SMART nuclear reactors was dampened when U.S. Energy Secretary Rick Perry outwit Korea by approving six authorizations for nuclear power work for Saudi Arabia. While the critics slammed Moon's nuclear phase-out policy, the Moon administration followed a contradictory path in supporting the anti-nuclear movement in South Korea while pushing for nuclear power plant projects elsewhere, including the Czech Republic and Poland.

Moon's nuclear phase-out policy also had repercussions on the EPC sector. Though efforts were made at the ministerial level in leading a public–private business delegation to facilitate South Korean companies win large-scale EPC project contracts in Saudi Arabia and Oman, the EPC sector lost momentum in the initial months after the Moon Jae-in administration took office. Bureaucratic hurdles hindered efforts for furthering commercial diplomacy as travel bans were imposed on cabinet members to confirm supreme court judge. MP Kim Moo-sung of the main opposition party decried that national interests should be a priority concern for any government and denounced Moon for taking advice from non-nuclear experts in basing his policy decision.

Global strategic cooperation and the formation of a consortium became necessary to enhance South Korea's competitiveness in the nuclear power plant construction sector. In July 2018, KEPCO and the Ministry of Trade, Industry and Energy established the Saudi Nuclear Power Plant Support Center in Seoul and held a nuclear power plant export strategy meeting in the same month to discuss plans to pursue a strategic alliance with the U.S. and the UAE and export SMART nuclear power reactors to Saudi Arabia. South Korea discussed plans to jointly target the entry of the Saudi nuclear power plant market with the UAE during Mubadala CEO Khaldoon al-Mubarak's visit to Seoul during the meeting presided over by Minister Paek in January 2018. A few months later, Saudi Minister of Energy Khalid al-Falih conveyed his interests in collaborating with South Korea for the development of hydrogen and electric vehicles and for cooperation in the development of small- and medium-sized nuclear reactors with KAERI. Signing the Korea–Saudi service agreement in August 2015 synergized nuclear energy cooperation efforts as it led to Seoul's provision of technical training to 40 Saudi nuclear technology experts in the design of SMART nuclear power plants. The South Korea Ministry of Science and ICT presided over the third Korea–Saudi Nuclear Joint Committee and the fourth SMART Steering Committee meeting with KACARE in Riyadh in May 2019 to discuss nuclear manpower and technological cooperation. It also took necessary steps to promote SMART construction and commercial licensing in Saudi Arabia by establishing the Korea–Saudi joint nuclear research center.

As Seoul was navigating opportunities to expand cooperation in renewable energy development, solar power superseded nuclear energy in Saudi Arabia's energy mix. Expanding cooperation into renewable energy was inevitable given that nuclear energy development is preconditioned on renewable energy development to operate nuclear power plants. This is due to the importance accorded to power generation efficiency of nuclear power plants, which can be obtained as twice as much through solar power generation. In light of the current challenges in fossil fuel depletion, climate crisis, and nuclear safety, domestic nuclear energy officials equally stressed on the importance of complementing renewable energy development with solar power, wind power, and energy storage. The absence of clear guidelines over licensing the Saudi nuclear power plant and the Saudi government's decision to extend the invitation to all four major nuclear energy competitors, namely the U.S., China, France, and Russia, to participate in the pre-qualification round for tendering to build Saudi nuclear power plants also cast doubt over the prospects for proceeding with South Korea's export of SMART nuclear reactors.

Conclusion

Saudi Arabia's strategic importance to Korea continues to derive from its status as the largest supplier of crude oil. Conversely, South Korea's importance to Saudi Arabia lies in its economic competitiveness including human capital and its rapid industrialization and knowledge-based economy. However, as set out by Saudi-Korea Vision 2030, bilateral cooperation between South Korea and Saudi Arabia has diversified into non-oil sectors especially in the last two decades, including in the energy sector. The evolving nature of Korea–Saudi relations over the six decades has shown that commercial diplomacy between the two countries has pointed to the importance of people's diplomacy and B2B and business-to-government (B2G) ties, which transcends traditional diplomacy or government-to-government (G2G) ties. As discussed in this chapter, key business personalities and their firms and state-owned and private companies from both countries, notably Saudi's business tycoon Prince Alwaleed and the KHC, Saudi Aramco, and South Korea's prominent conglomerates, Samsung, Hyundai, SK, and LG, and SMEs have played an instrumental role in advancing business diplomacy.

The Roh Moo-hyun administration laid the groundwork for initiating "sales diplomacy" and proactive Middle East policy and efforts to promote resource diplomacy have continued during the Lee Myung-bak and Park Geun-hye administrations by making the latter a flagship policy and leading a record size of business delegations to the region. Given the strategic importance of oil, B2G relations have proven to be equally important as an intermediary between government and businesses. S-Oil and Saudi–Korean Vision 2030 also served as channels for revitalizing Korea–Saudi bilateral relations during the second oil boom. Yet at the same time, stalled discussions on the GCC–Korea FTA and South Korea's domestic politics and corruption charges and nuclear phase-out policy were hindrances to budding business ties and bilateral relations. As the outgoing Saudi Ambassador to South Korea Abdullah al-Aifan has pointed out, in the long term, it is critical for Seoul to continue to develop bilateral partnerships in non-oil sectors and go beyond "sales diplomacy" by deepening and diversifying diplomatic relations with Riyadh.

Notes

1 Research Center for Peace and Unification, Korea & World Affairs: *A Quarterly Review* 8 (1–2), 236; Kumja Paik Kim, *Goryeo Dynasty: Korea's Age of Enlightenment, 918–1392* (San Francisco, CA: Asian Art Museum, Chong-moon Lee Center for Asian Art and Culture, 2003), 316.
2 U.S. Department of State, "Korea and Saudi Arabia sign economic cooperation agreement," June 30, 2005, Electronic Telegram.
3 Byung-Hwa Lyou, "Peace and unification in Korea and international law," *University of Maryland School of Law*, 1986, 76.
4 Chosun-Ilbo, "What we can give is our sincerity," April 27, 1975, 2.
5 Chosun-Ilbo, "Arab countries lift restrictions on oil exports," December 27, 1973, 1.
6 Nigel John Ashton, "The Hijacking of a Pact: The Formation of the Baghdad Pact and Anglo-American Tensions in the Middle East, 1955–1958," *Review of International Studies* 19 (2) (1993), 125.
7 Harvey H. Smith et al., *Area Handbook for Lebanon* (Washington DC: American University Press, 1969), 182–184.
8 Chosun-Ilbo, "Peace-loving Koreans and Arab countries cannot be pro-Communist," September 3, 1974, 3.
9 Heo Mun-do, "Impressed by Saudi Arabia's view of Korea," *Chosun-Ilbo*, May 9, 1975, 2.
10 U.S. Department of State, *United States Participation in the UN: Report by the President to the Congress for the Year 1982* (Washington DC: Bureau of International Organization Affairs, 1984), 210.
11 "The UN Resolution on Palestine," *Journal of Palestine Studies* 5 (1/2) (1976), 252–254.
12 Sung Han-pyo, "Saudi Arabia is South Korea's representative," *Chosun-Ilbo*, January 9, 1975, 3.

13. Ann Mosely Lesch & Mark A. Tessler, *Israel, Egypt, and the Palestinians: From Camp David to Intifada* (Bloomington, IN: Indiana University Press, 1989), 17.
14. United Nations, "Right of self-determination of the Palestinian people – CEIRPP, DPR study," 1979, www.un.org/unispal/document/auto-insert-196558/; Chosun-Ilbo, "South Korea's Palestinian Policy," September 23, 1979, 2.
15. Song Hyeong-mok, "High energy dependency on the geopolitically volatile Middle East: An interview with KIEP Vice President Kim Jeok-gyo," *Chosun-Ilbo*, September 28, 1980, 4.
16. Chosun-Ilbo, "Saudi Embassy will be established," July 5, 1974, 5.
17. Song, "High energy dependency on the geopolitically volatile Middle East," 4.
18. Na Jong-ho, "Export of premium gasoline to Saudi Arabia," *Chosun-Ilbo*, July 11, 1997, 13.
19. Chosun-Ilbo, "New Stronghold Established in the Arab World," July 5, 1974, 3.
20. Chosun-Ilbo, "The King of Saudi Arabia, admiring the hard work of a Korean construction company," September 26, 1975, 2.
21. Chosun-Ilbo, "Inviting Koreans for manpower resources," April 13, 1976, 2.
22. Chosun-Ilbo, "Last year's construction export target exceeded by 70%," January 14, 1976, 2.
23. Chosun-Ilbo, "South Korean construction companies in Saudi Arabia," July 17, 1979, 6.
24. Chung In Moon, "Korean contractors in Saudi Arabia: Their rise and fall," *Middle East Journal* 40 (4) (1986), 623–624; Chosun-Ilbo, "A demand for road construction professionals," June 24, 1975, 2.
25. Yonhap News Agency, "Nurses to enter Saudi Arabia soon," January 23, 1999.
26. MBN, "Korea Tourism Organization attracts medical tourists from the Middle East," March 22, 2010, www.mbn.co.kr/news/culture/493905.
27. World Health Organization, "MERS outbreak in the Republic of Korea, 2015," n.d., www.who.int/westernpacific/emergencies/2015-mers-outbreak.
28. For more on the history of Korea's Economic Planning Board (EPB), see Byung-Kook Kim, "Economic policy and the economic planning board (EPB) in Korea," *Asian Affairs: An American Review* 18 (4) (1992), 197–213.
29. Bae Sang-bae, "Saudi royal family acquired 45 billion worth of convertible bonds from Daewoo Group," *Chosun-Ilbo*, October 16, 1997, 11.
30. Dong Gull Lee, "The restructuring of Daewoo," in Stephan Haggard, Wonhyuk Lim & Euysung Kim (Eds.), *Economic Crisis and Corporate Restructuring in Korea: Reforming the Chaebol* (Cambridge: Cambridge University Press, 2003), 150–180.
31. Spencer C. Tucker, *Persian Gulf War Encyclopedia: A Political, Social, and Military History* (Santa Barbara, CA: ABC-CLIO, 2014), 237–238.
32. Yonhap News Agency, "$1 billion in exports disrupted by the crisis," January 10, 1991.
33. Yonhap News Agency, "Korea exported $2.33 bn to five countries in Middle East this year," March 14, 1991.
34. Yonhap News Agency, "Receivables from Saudi construction project amounts to KRW 22 bn," October 12, 1996.
35. Yonhap News Agency, "Vice minister of commerce and industry Lee met with Saudi oil minister," May 19, 1994.
36. Lee Shim-gi, "Korea is most vulnerable to rising oil prices…GDP declines by 1.7% for every 10 dollar increase," *Hankyung*, September 19, 2000.

37 Yonhap News Agency, "Letter to President Roh from Saudi King," March 13, 1991.
38 Uk Heo & Sunwoong Kim, "Financial crisis in South Korea: Failure of the government-led development paradigm," *Asian Survey* 40 (3) (2000), 492–493.
39 Jesook Song, *South Koreans in the Debt Crisis: The Creation of a Neoliberal Welfare Society* (Durham, NC: Duke University Press, 2009), ix.
40 Kim Kihwan, "The 1997–98 Korean Financial Crisis: Causes, policy response, and lessons," *The International Monetary Fund*, 2006, 12.
41 Yonhap News Agency, "Press conference with the Chairman of Hyundai and Prince Waleed," March 16, 1998.
42 Saudi Aramco, *Saudi Aramco World: Volume 59* (Dhahran: Saudi Aramco, 1992), 46; 57; *The Wall Street Journal*, "South Korea's Ssangyong to sell stake in oil refinery to Aramco," November 23, 1998, www.wsj.com/articles/SB911721859442123500.
43 Victor D. Cha, "Politics and democracy under the Kim Young Sam government: something old, something new," *Asian Survey* 33 (9) (1993), 850–853; Sanghyun Yoon, "South Korea's Kim Young Sam government," *Asian Survey* 36 (5) 9 (1996), 511–514.
44 Yonhap News Agency, "President Kim's English contribution attracted the attention of international media," December 10, 1998; Barry K. Gills & Dong-Sook S. Gills, "South Korea and globalization: The rise to globalism?," *Asian Perspective* 23 (4) (1999), 220
45 Yonhap News Agency, "Luncheon between Saudi Prince Abdullah and President Kim," October 24, 1998.
46 Abdennour Benantar, "Egypt and the war on Iraq: Implications for domestic politics," *Journal of Third World studies* 24 (1) (2007), 229.
47 Hong Deok-hwa, "Interview with Saudi Ambassador Saleh al-Rajhi," *Yonhap News Agency*, September 23, 2004.
48 ROK Ministry of Foreign Affairs, "Participatory government's five-year diplomatic milestones," 2007, 31–32.
49 Yonhap News Agency, "President Roh promotes Korea-GCC free trade agreement," March 25, 2007.
50 Inkyo Cheong & Jungran Cho, "Republic of Korea," in Masahiro Kawai & Ganeshan Wignaraja (Eds.), *Asia's Free Trade Agreements: How Is Business Responding?* (Cheltenham: Edward Elgar, 2011), 134.
51 Kim Mi-ran, Hong Young-ran, Kim Eun-young & Lee Byung-sik, "Assessments and policy recommendations for internationalization strategies for higher education in Korea," *Korean Educational Development Institute*, 2013, 251–255.
52 Sunhyuk Kim, "Collaborative governance in South Korea: Citizen participation in policy making and welfare service provision," *Asian Perspective* 34 (3) (2010), 186.
53 ROK Ministry of Foreign Affairs, "Press release," March 11, 2008, www.mofa.go.kr/www/brd/m_4080/view.do?seq=310578&srchFr=&amp%3BsrchTo=&amp%3BsrchWord=&amp%3BsrchTp=&amp%3Bmulti_itm_seq=0&amp%3Bitm_seq_1=0&amp%3Bitm_seq_2=0&amp%3Bcompany_cd=&amp%3Bcompany_nm=&page=1101.
54 Energy Intelligence, "The energy intelligence top 100: Ranking the world's largest oil companies," 2008, n.p.
55 Ajou News, "S-Oil, completion ceremony for petrochemical expansion project," March 7, 2012, www.ajunews.com/common/redirect.jsp?newsId=20111020000241.

100 Saudi–Korea Vision 2030

56 Yonhap News Agency, "Saudi S-Oil CEO's Korean Name is 'Ha Se-in,'" September 4, 2019.
57 Hankyung TV, "Saudi company invests 8 trillion won in Korea," February 28, 2008, News Footage, 3:17, www.wownet.co.kr/WOWNET_404.html.
58 Asian Economy, "Plant industry receives orders from Saudi Arabia," September 4, 2009, www.asiae.co.kr/news/view.htm?idxno=2009090411191635538.
59 Hankyung TV, "A record orders received in the Saudi construction industry," March 8, 2012, 18.
60 Yonhap News Agency, "President-elect Lee to expand high-level meetings between Korea and the Middle East," January 31, 2008.
61 KTV News, "Summit diplomacy…17 countries visited, and 43 summit meetings held," New footage, 1:57, www.ktv.go.kr/content/view?content_id=516797.
62 Kim Hyun-kyeong, "Korean companies dominate the Saudi construction market," Herald Economy, January 9, 2013, http://news.heraldcorp.com/view.php?ud=20130109000192&md=20130112004444_BL.
63 Lee Yong-wook, "Middle East's Warren Buffett Saudi Prince Al Waleed meets with President Park to expand investments," Kyunghyang, March 5, 2015, A5.
64 Channel A, "President Park, 'I can't clap with one hand…' emphasis on partnership," March 4, 2015, News Footage, 1:41, http://news.ichannela.com/politics/3/00/20150304/69951746/1.
65 Oh Se-joong, "President Park, Saudi Arabia is a long-term partner," Money Today, March 3, 2015.
66 Yonhap News Agency, "POSCO E&C and Saudi Arabia's joint venture attracted 1.2 trillion won," June 15, 2015.
67 Saudi Ministry of Economy & Planning, "Saudi-Korean Vision 2030," 2016, 5; 8–12, https://mep.gov.sa/Documents/Content/KSA_Korean.pdf.
68 YTN, "President Moon attends the meeting with Crown Prince Mohammed bin Salman," June 26, 2019, News clip, 02:50, www.ytn.co.kr/_ln/0101_201906261614484786.

References

Ajou News. "S-Oil, completion ceremony for petrochemical expansion project," March 7, 2012, www.ajunews.com/common/redirect.jsp?newsId=20111020000241.
Ashton, Nigel John. "The hijacking of a pact: The formation of the Baghdad pact and Anglo-American tensions in the Middle East, 1955–1958," *Review of International Studies* 19 (2) (1993), 123–137.
Asian Economy. "Plant industry receives orders from Saudi Arabia," September 4, 2009, www.asiae.co.kr/news/view.htm?idxno=2009090411191635538.
Bae, Sang-bae. "Saudi royal family acquired 45 billion worth of convertible bonds from Daewoo Group," *Chosun-Ilbo*, October 16, 1997, 11.
Benantar, Abdennour. "Egypt and the war on Iraq: Implications for domestic politics," *Journal of Third World Studies* 24 (1) (2007), 227–247.
Cha, Victor D. "Politics and democracy under the Kim Young Sam government: something old, something new," *Asian Survey* 33 (9) (1993), 849–863.
Channel A. "President Park, 'I can't clap with one hand…' Emphasis on partnership," March 4, 2015, News Footage, 1:41, http://news.ichannela.com/politics/3/00/20150304/69951746/1.

Cheong, Inkyo and Jungran Cho. "Republic of Korea," in Masahiro Kawai and Ganeshan Wignaraja (Eds.), *Asia's Free Trade Agreements: How is Business Responding?* (Cheltenham: Edward Elgar, 2011), 130–158.
Chosun-Ilbo. "Arab countries lift restrictions on oil exports," December 27, 1973, 1.
Chosun-Ilbo. "New stronghold established in the Arab world," July 5, 1974, 3.
Chosun-Ilbo. "Saudi Embassy will be established," July 5, 1974, 5.
Chosun-Ilbo. "Peace-loving Koreans and Arab countries cannot be pro-communist," September 3, 1974, 3.
Chosun-Ilbo. "What we can give is our sincerity," April 27, 1975, 2.
Chosun-Ilbo. "A demand for road construction professionals," June 24, 1975, 2.
Chosun-Ilbo. "The King of Saudi Arabia, admiring the hard work of a Korean construction company," September 26, 1975, 2.
Chosun-Ilbo. "Last year's construction export target exceeded by 70%," January 14, 1976, 2.
Chosun-Ilbo. "Inviting Koreans for manpower resources," April 13, 1976, 2.
Chosun-Ilbo. "South Korean construction companies in Saudi Arabia," July 17, 1979, 6.
Chosun-Ilbo. "South Korea's Palestinian policy," September 23, 1979, 2.
Energy Intelligence. "The energy intelligence top 100: Ranking the world's largest oil companies," 2008.
Gills, Barry K. and Dong-Sook S. Gills. "South Korea and globalization: The rise to globalism?, *Asian Perspective* 23 (4) (1999), 199–228.
Hankyung TV. "Saudi company invests 8 trillion won in Korea," February 28, 2008, News Footage, 3:17, www.wownet.co.kr/WOWNET_404.html.
Hankyung TV. "A record orders received in the Saudi construction industry," March 8, 2012, 18.
Heo, Mun-do. "Impressed by Saudi Arabia's view of Korea," *Chosun-Ilbo*, May 9, 1975, 2.
Heo, Uk and Sunwoong Kim. "Financial crisis in South Korea: Failure of the government-led development paradigm," *Asian Survey* 40 (3) (2000), 492–507.
Hong, Deok-hwa. "Interview with Saudi Ambassador Saleh al-Rajhi," *Yonhap News Agency*, September 23, 2004.
Kim, Byung-Kook. "Economic policy and the economic planning board (EPB) in Korea," *Asian Affairs: An American Review* 18 (4) (1992), 197–213.
Kim, Hyun-kyeong. "Korean companies dominate the Saudi construction market," *Herald Economy*, January 9, 2013, http://news.heraldcorp.com/view.php?ud=20130109000192&md=20130112004444_BL.
Kim, Kihwan. "The 1997-98 Korean Financial Crisis: Causes, policy response, and lessons," *The International Monetary Fund*, 2006, 1-25.
Kim, Kumja Paik. *Goryeo Dynasty: Korea's Age of Enlightenment, 918-1392* (San Francisco, CA: Asian Art Museum, Chong-moon Lee Center for Asian Art and Culture, 2003).
Kim, Mi-ran, Young-ran Hong, Eun-young Kim and Byung-sik Lee. "Assessments and policy recommendations for internationalization strategies for higher education in Korea," *Korean Educational Development Institute*, 2013, 251–255.
Kim, Sunhyuk. "Collaborative governance in South Korea: Citizen participation in policy making and welfare service provision," *Asian Perspective* 34 (3) (2010), 165–190.

KTV News. "Summit diplomacy…17 countries visited, and 43 summit meetings held," *New footage*, 1:57, www.ktv.go.kr/content/view?content_id=516797.

Lee, Dong Gull. "The restructuring of Daewoo," in Stephan Haggard, Wonhyuk Lim and Euysung Kim (Eds.), *Economic Crisis and Corporate Restructuring in Korea: Reforming the Chaebol* (Cambridge: Cambridge University Press, 2003), 150–180.

Lee, Min-woo. "President Park Geun-hye's sales diplomacy achievements amount to 123 trillion won," *Sisa Journal No. 1649*, May 31, 2016, www.sisajournal.com/news/articleView.html?idxno=153190.

Lee, Shim-gi. "Korea is most vulnerable to rising oil prices…GDP declines by 1.7% for every 10 dollar increase," *Hankyung*, September 19, 2000.

Lee, Yong-wook. "Middle East's Warren Buffett Saudi Prince Al Waleed meets with President Park to expand investments," *Kyunghyang*, March 5, 2015, A5.

Lesch, Ann Mosely and Mark A. Tessler. *Israel, Egypt, and the Palestinians: From Camp David to Intifada* (Bloomington, IN: Indiana University Press, 1989).

Lyou, Byung-Hwa. "Peace and unification in Korea and international law," *University of Maryland School of Law*, 1986, 76.

MBN. "Korea Tourism Organization attracts medical tourists from the Middle East," March 22, 2010, www.mbn.co.kr/news/culture/493905.

Moon, Chung In. "Korean contractors in Saudi Arabia: Their rise and fall," *Middle East Journal* 40 (4) (1986), 614–633.

Na, Jong-ho. "Export of premium gasoline to Saudi Arabia," *Chosun-Ilbo*, July 11, 1997, 13.

Research Center for Peace and Unification. *Korea & World Affairs: A Quarterly Review* 8 (1–2): 110–340.

ROK Ministry of Foreign Affairs. "Participatory government's five-year diplomatic milestones," 2007.

ROK Ministry of Foreign Affairs. "Press Release," March 11, 2008, www.mofa.go.kr/www/brd/m_4080/view.do?seq=310578&srchFr=&amp%3BsrchTo=&amp%3BsrchWord=&amp%3BsrchTp=&amp%3Bmulti_itm_seq=0&amp%3Bitm_seq_1=0&amp%3Bitm_seq_2=0&amp%3Bcompany_cd=&amp%3Bcompany_nm=&page=1101.

Saudi Aramco. *Saudi Aramco World: Volume 59* (Dhahran: Saudi Aramco, 1992).

Saudi Ministry of Economy & Planning. "Saudi-Korean Vision 2030," 2016, https://mep.gov.sa/Documents/Content/KSA_Korean.pdf.

Smith, Harvey H. *Area Handbook for Lebanon* (Washington DC.: American University Press, 1969).

Song, Hyeong-mok. "High energy dependency on the geopolitically volatile Middle East: An interview with KIEP Vice President Kim Jeok-gyo," *Chosun-Ilbo*, September 28, 1980, 4.

Song, Jesook. *South Koreans in the Debt Crisis: The Creation of a Neoliberal Welfare Society* (Durham, NC: Duke University Press, 2009).

Sung, Han-pyo. "Saudi Arabia is South Korea's representative," *Chosun-Ilbo*, January 9, 1975, 3.

"The UN resolution on Palestine," *Journal of Palestine Studies* 5 (1/2) (1976), 252–254.

The Wall Street Journal. "South Korea's Ssangyong to sell stake in oil refinery to Aramco," November 23, 1998, www.wsj.com/articles/SB911721859442123500.

Tucker, Spencer C. *Persian Gulf War Encyclopedia: A Political, Social, and Military History* (Santa Barbara, CA: ABC-CLIO, 2014).

United Nations. "Right of self-determination of the Palestinian people – CEIRPP, DPR study," 1979, www.un.org/unispal/document/auto-insert-196558/.
U.S. Department of State. *United States Participation in the UN: Report by the President to the Congress for the Year 1982* (Washington DC: Bureau of International Organization Affairs, 1984).
U.S. Department of State. "Korea and Saudi Arabia sign economic cooperation agreement," June 30, 2005, Electronic Telegram.
World Health Organization. "MERS outbreak in the Republic of Korea, 2015," n.d., www.who.int/westernpacific/emergencies/2015-mers-outbreak.
Yonhap News Agency. "Nurses to enter Saudi Arabia soon," January 23, 1999.
Yonhap News Agency. "$1 billion in exports disrupted by the crisis," January 10, 1991.
Yonhap News Agency. "Letter to President Roh from Saudi King," March 13, 1991.
Yonhap News Agency. "Korea exported $2.33bn to five countries in Middle East this year," March 14, 1991.
Yonhap News Agency. "Vice minister of commerce and industry Lee met with Saudi oil minister," May 19, 1994.
Yonhap News Agency. "Receivables from Saudi construction project amounts to KRW 22bn," October 12, 1996.
Yonhap News Agency. "Press conference with the Chairman of Hyundai and Prince Waleed," March 16, 1998.
Yonhap News Agency. "Interview with Al Waleed, Prince of Saudi Arabia," March 17, 1998.
Yonhap News Agency. "Luncheon between Saudi Prince Abdullah and President Kim," October 24, 1998.
Yonhap News Agency. "President Kim's English contribution attracted the attention of international media," December 10, 1998.
Yonhap News Agency. "President Roh promotes Korea-GCC free trade agreement," March 25, 2007.
Yonhap News Agency. "President-elect Lee to expand high-level meetings between Korea and the Middle East," January 31, 2008.
Yonhap News Agency. "POSCO E&C and Saudi Arabia's joint venture attracted 1.2 trillion won," June 15, 2015.
Yonhap News Agency. "Saudi S-Oil CEO's Korean Name is 'Ha Se-in,'" September 4, 2019.
Yoon, Sanghyun. "South Korea's Kim Young Sam government," *Asian Survey* 36 (5) (1996), 511–522.
YTN. "President Moon attends the meeting with Crown Prince Mohammed bin Salman," June 26, 2019, News clip, 02:50, www.ytn.co.kr/_ln/0101_201906261614484786.

4 Nuclear energy and security cooperation with the UAE

Introduction

The UAE and ROK celebrated 40 years of diplomatic relations in 2020. On the occasion of ROK's National Liberation Day on August 15, 2019, Burj Khalifa, the world's tallest tower built by a Samsung C&T-led consortium, lit up the South Korean flag and N Seoul Tower reciprocated by lighting up the UAE flag in celebration of the UAE National Day on December 2. Apart from the longstanding history of bilateral partnerships in energy and construction sectors, security and nuclear energy cooperation have become increasingly relevant to meet future strategic and economic challenges in light of the 40 years of diplomatic history which was punctuated by watershed regional and international events. At the same time, much less is known about the nexus of internal and external drivers and the historical underpinnings of the bilateral relations which were elevated to special strategic partnership on March 26, 2018. In mapping the history of ROK's emergence as a middle-power diplomacy, this chapter aims to contextualize the socioeconomic, strategic, and political trajectories. In this chapter, the UAE–ROK relations will be examined against three points: first, the extent to which turbulences in regional security theaters and transnational threats have strengthened strategic linkages; second, the ways in which state capacities and economic competitiveness have deepened commercial ties; third, how future challenges in economic diversification and energy demands have broadened the scope for bilateral partnership in nonconventional areas.

A history of ROK and UAE's economic cooperation and regional security

ROK's diplomatic relations with the UAE were established on June 18, 1980. While this dates back to four decades ago, bilateral ties between the two countries were at a standstill, mainly constricted to crude oil exports and the construction sector in the initial two decades. Leading up to the industrialization in the late 1980s, South Korea was transitioning from

DOI: 10.4324/9781003092100-4

an agrarian to a manufacturing economy based on Park Chung-hee's heavy and chemical industry (HCI) drive. From 1967, the South Korean government took loans from foreign banks, including the World Bank and its subsidiary, International Finance Corporation, to invest in educational and infrastructural development (i.e. railway, highway, port, agricultural credit, and various rural infrastructure projects).[1] Departing from the statist roots, South Korea instituted economic liberalization and market-oriented reforms in the 1980s.[2] During the same period, Gulf states were investing its petrodollars in public works projects and modernizing its port facilities. Oil was first discovered in commercial quantities in Abu Dhabi in 1958, and the first cargo of oil was exported in 1962. As a federation system, oil production has been mostly confined to the emirates of Abu Dhabi, Dubai, and Sharjah. Abu Dhabi is the political and administrative capital of the UAE, while Dubai is a regional commercial hub. The size of oil reserves is proportionate to the order oil was discovered in these emirates and was later discovered in Dubai in 1966 and in Sharjah in 1972. By 2004, Abu Dhabi held 92.2% of oil reserves, while Dubai and Sharjah had 4.0% and 1.0% of the total oil reserves in the UAE.[3] Considering that the UAE's state-building process in the incipient days coincided with the advent of the oil economy, the ROK–UAE bilateral relations also developed on the basis of an oil economy and South Korea was one of the five major importers of crude oil from the UAE in the 1980s. Furthermore, ROK's status as the fourth largest economy in Asia and the 11th largest economy in the world meant that its energy demands would remain on the rise as the world's ninth-largest oil consumer.[4] However, the conditions at the time were not ripe for deepening bilateral relations since the UAE–ROK diplomatic ties were formed only nine years after the UAE was established as a federation on December 2, 1971, while South Korea was only two decades in from emerging out of poverty. Despite the humble beginnings, it is important to contextualize the diplomatic history between the two countries as the history of bilateral relations was not established in insolation from surrounding geopolitical events.

Emerging from poverty and the tumult of Korean War, as a divided country, South Korea also kept a close watch at the recent developments in Yemen at the time, a country in Arabian Peninsula which was ravaged by Civil Wars: North Yemen Civil War (1962–1970) and the South Yemen Civil War (January 1986). As the only remaining Marxist–Leninist regime in the Arab world following the independence from Britain in 1967, South Yemen was ruled by a Maoist regime under Salim Rubai Ali from 1969 to 1978 and thereafter by a pro-Soviet regime under Ali Nasir Muhammad from 1980 to 1986. However, from a South Korean perspective, South Yemen was perceived more as a nationalist regime than a socialist regime as a protest to the British rule. Seen through an ideological lens of Cold War, South Korean media outlets painted a rosy picture on the prospect of a unified Yemen on May 22, 1990. As will be explained below, the history of South Yemen's political development is important for understanding the regional context that gave rise to a booming maritime economy in Dubai and the broader Gulf states.

Before South Yemen's declaration of independence from Britain in 1967, Aden was a bustling entrepot next to New York and Liverpool due to its strategic location at the mouth of the Indian Ocean and Red Sea. However, it had lost its attraction as a hub after South Yemen was overtaken by a pro-Soviet regime. As a result, the UAE emerged as a new hub for shipping and logistics and foreign ships paid $25,000 (which is equivalent to $49,224 today) for using Port Rashid in the 1970s.[5] The Dubai Port Authority (DPA) then proceeded to develop Jebel Ali Port (1985) and Jebel Ali Free Zone (1985). While neighboring Yemen was emerging from the shadow of civil wars, the Gulf countries established themselves as maritime hubs. By the early 1980s, on average, one ship passed through the Strait of Hormuz at a rate of every 12 minutes and Port Rashid was the largest harbor in the Gulf – the ports in the UAE carried a total of one million twenty-foot equivalent unit container cargo by 1991.[6] Although Yemen tried to open Aden port to Western ships and tourists and invite FDI to generate a revenue stream, and despite having untapped oil reserves worth $2.6 bn, it was already laden with $2.3 bn of debt and was unable to earn hard currency from oil reserves due to undercapacitated crude oil production and refinery capabilities.[7]

Gulf maritime economies were buoyant at the beginning of 1980s, and Dubai's status as a trading entrepot was more stabilized due to the upgrading of port infrastructures which were financed by handsome oil revenues. As early as 1982, two years after the diplomatic relations opened between the UAE and ROK, talks were held in Seoul between the President of the Korean Chamber of Commerce and Ahmed al-Otaiba, the Director-General of the Abu Dhabi Chamber of Commerce and Industry, to discuss strategies for strengthening bilateral trade. However, these prospects were soon to be eclipsed by the recession that followed the Iranian Revolution and Iran–Iraq War. Oil prices dip was pronounced between 1983 and 1986 as it dropped from $26/barrel in December 1985 to $7 per barrel in January 1986.[8] As a result, oil revenues dwindled from $8,732 mn in 1983 to $5,400 mn in 1986.[9] The debilitating impact of declining oil revenues was compounded by the ripple effects felt in the construction sector. As the import of cements which were central to the economic activities of the ports plunged, this proved to be damaging to the three major entrepot economies in the Gulf – of which Dammam (35.9%) had the largest share followed by Shuwaikh (23.5%) and Dubai (21.9%) – but with uneven effects.[10] This was only exacerbated by the excess port facilities that were dampening the prospects for growth and stability. This is only one of many examples, and by 1983, other sectors linked to the oil industry (e.g. machinery, timber, and other raw materials) were equally susceptible to economic slowdown. While there were steep declines in the imports passing through the Gulf ports, particularly in Shuwaikh, Dammam, and Jeddah, which fell between 26% and 46%, UAE's maritime economy enjoyed some degree of buffer from the decline in trade during the bust period.[11] However, as noted above, there were some disparities among the UAE ports: while Mina Zayed (Abu Dhabi), Mina Khalid (Sharjah), and Mina Saqr (Ras Al Khaimah) were in stagnation relative to the level of regional ports, the remarkable resilience of Port Rashid to war, revolution, and recessionary effects between 1978 and 1980 and throughout the 1980s is noted as an outlier, which is attributed to its agility to adapt its exports and reexports levels by servicing its economy to the Iranian market. Elsewhere, the ports of Mina Jebel Ali and Fujairah exemplified a nascent port showing growth spurt, albeit the size of growth for the latter is much more moderate than the former (0.34 mn as opposed to 3.26 mn tons of container port throughput in 1983 and 2.33 mn as opposed to 5.66 mn tons of container port throughput in 1986).[12]

On the eve of the Iraqi invasion of Kuwait, oil prices were also volatile. Dubai crude oil prices soared from $13.25 in June 1990 to $31.55 in October 1990, the highest record in four months.[13] Crude oil supply problems became even more acute since the share of the Middle East crude oil market is above 80%. Rumors about a forthcoming third oil shock gripped the Asian economies as there were heightened concerns over the rising crude oil prices. To facilitate access to crude oil supply, South Korean oil companies jumped on the bandwagon for oil exploration since the 1980s. By the early 1990s, South Korean oil companies were extracting crude oil from the concessions they won from three major overseas oil fields: North Yemen's Marib Basin (24.5% stakes were awarded to a consortium of four South Korean companies) and Indonesia's Sumatra and Egypt's Khalda petroleum fields.[14] Around that time, negotiations for petroleum explorations were also underway in Libya and Algeria. During the same period, South Korea was also awarded concessions for oil exploration in 11 oil fields, including the offshore Saleh oil field in Ras Al Khaimah, the UAE.

By the mid-1990s, South Korea and Japan were 100% dependent on petroleum imports (by comparison, Germany and Italy were 95% dependent, while European OECD countries were 60% dependent and the U.S. was 43% dependent).[15] As a consequence, the South Korean government prepared a number of contingency measures, including allocating public funds for price control and decreasing tariffs. One of the factors that kept the oil prices high was oil production cuts. Among the OPEC member states, Kuwait and the UAE were known for overproducing but in the run-up to the 1991 Gulf War, they agreed to the production quota to raise the oil prices. Crude imports are critical to the South Korean economy as it has been the engine to economic growth and industrialization since the Park Chung-hee era, and because it is a source of refinery feedstock. South Korea is one of the world's six largest oil refining countries, and as of 2018, the Korea Petroleum Association has claimed that South Korea joined the ranks of the top five oil refining capacities after the U.S., China, Russia, and India. In conjunction with the first five-year development plan (1962–1967), the Korean government established the first oil refinery in 1962 and expanded its oil refining capacity in the 1960s and

1970s to respond to growing energy demands by establishing four oil refining companies and five refineries. The oil refining capacity was linked to the HCI promotion policy in the 1970s, and the South Korea's oil refining industry became more stabilized as the country's industrialization took off in the following two decades. By 1990, the three Gulf countries of Oman (22.4%), the UAE (16.2%), and Saudi Arabia (13.0%) combinedly constituted for over half of ROK's refined oil exports.[16]

South Korea's oil dependence on the Middle East was thus subject to the geostrategic and geopolitical vulnerabilities in the region. While the U.S. and its allies were debating a military option shortly after the U.S. President George H.W. Bush was informed of the Iraqi invasion of Kuwait on August 2, 1990, George Bush the senior urged the allies to take part in military cost-sharing and foreign assistance targeting Jordan, Egypt, and Turkey, the three countries that were the hardest hit from the comprehensive sanctions on Iraq. For its part, South Korea spent KRW 8 bn for deploying medical service corps officers. The international coordination of economic assistance and burden-sharing, though largely seen as a continuum of the Carter Doctrine, was seen as a response to an international conflict that was multilateral in nature. For military cost-sharing, the U.S. requested $4 bn from Saudi Arabia, $3 bn from Kuwait, $1 bn from the UAE, $600 mn from West Germany, and unspecified amounts from South Korea.[17] Despite being geographically remote, there were hidden costs incurred for South Korea, which were safety concerns of the Korean residents in the region as well as the South Korean oil and shipping companies operating in the Strait of Hormuz and Bab el-Mandeb. Evacuation plans were drawn for the South Korean residents in Iraq and Kuwait (104 in total) and for the remaining 6,100 Koreans in Saudi Arabia, Bahrain, Qatar, the UAE, and Jordan and the Korean merchant marines and tankers stationed in Saudi Arabia and the UAE.[18]

The shifts in the international scene, even as somewhere as geographically distant as the Gulf, had repercussions on the security of the Korean Peninsula. The South Korean government raised its watch condition (WATCHCON) alert first to level three on January 13, 1991, and again to level two on January 17 to continue to keep a close eye on any potential shifts in North Korea's plans. As the war progressed and it became evident that military involvement was inevitable, the South Korean National Assembly provisionally passed a legislation on February 8, 1991 approving the deployment of five C-130 transport airplanes and 150 ROK Air Force (ROKAF) troops to Saudi Arabia and Al Ain, the UAE. Al Ain was considered the most suitable base for stationing the troops as it was beyond the remit of Iraqi Scud missile range and was logistically expedient for transporting South Koreans out of the war-affected zones.[19] South Korea's involvement in the region had been limited and primarily economic in character prior to the conflict.[20] Nevertheless, its involvement in the war increased South Korea's diplomatic and military contacts with Saudi Arabia and the UAE – these countries were treated as logistical repositories for Kuwait's post-war reconstruction scheme. While talks were underway on the post-war reconstruction costs and on reestablishing diplomatic relations with Iraq, ROK was the only Asian country contributing to all three areas of foreign assistance, ROKAF medical corps, and military air transport. Dispatching C-130 Hercules planes, which are adept in air transport, electronic warfare, and search and rescue missions and personnel transport virtually signaled ROK's entry into the coalition forces as the 29th country.[21] This had symbolic significance, since it was the only East Asian country to contribute troops to the coalition forces. Nevertheless, because military contributions were faced with staunch public resistance in South Korea, there were no further plans of deploying the ROK Army.

As a more in-depth empirical account will be given in Chapter 5, the cost-benefit analysis in a conflict-ridden context such as this is not only about incurred costs, as the lucrative spoils of war were also up for grabs among the Asian economies vying for post-war reconstruction contracts. This was no exception to the U.S. which sought to boost its arms sales. Although détente initially seemed to be the overriding zeitgeist that set the tone for the post-Cold War era, the euphoria was short-lived and the prospects for peace and security were hopelessly dashed. The U.S. military spending cuts were overturned and there was no mention of arms embargo during the U.S. Minister of Defense, James Baker's visit to the Middle East. Instead, militarism became the prevailing order of the regional security with the American military-industrial complex reaping the greatest benefits from the destructions of the war. By 1992, overseas arms sales consisted of 15% of the total American arms sales and further to this, experts forecasted that the U.S. overseas arms sales, particularly from Asia and the Middle East, would account for up to 25% of the total U.S. arms sales.[22] The U.S.–European competition in the defense industry fostered militarization in the region. In fact, both the American and European parties were encouraging arms sales to the Middle Eastern countries, and there was a sharp rise in the demands for the Patriot Missile Defense System, and to a lesser extent the M60 Patton and the F-16, F-15, F/A Super Hornet fighter jets.[23]

In addition to arms trade, the depressed markets of Kuwait, Saudi Arabia, and the UAE also showed signs of improvement in the post-war reconstruction period, as Saudi Arabia emerged as the first of the three Gulf states to pursue joint ventures with East Asian oil companies. The post-war reconstruction economies provided a fertile market for South Korean businesses as was the case for other East Asian economies. The average South Korean exports to the Middle East (e.g. Saudi Arabia, Oman, Kuwait, and the UAE) dropped by 20% in the duration of the Gulf War but there was a rebound effect as the exports doubled after the War (up to $2.8 bn) by February 1992.[24] Apprehension about the economy was lulled as the oil prices were stabilized during the 1993 cruise missile strikes on Iraq.

Both South Korea and the UAE have longstanding security and defense ties with the U.S. as key allies, and both countries are major clients of the U.S. arms trade. While the UAE, which had been participating in the

Saudi-led Arab coalition intervention in Yemen from March 2015 and 2019, is ranked as the seventh-largest importer of arms in the world. South Korea, which is also ranked ninth place in the same index, is equally hard pressed by the nuclear gridlock with North Korea in an ever-fragile peace retained since the armistice signed on July 27, 1953. The UAE was the first country in the world to purchase two THAAD systems as a result of the $3.48 bn arms deal inked with the U.S. in December 2011 and the THAAD system arrived in South Korea between March and September 2017. The U.S. extended the security umbrella to the ROK and the UAE by maintaining approximately 24,000 soldiers in the U.S. Forces (USFK) in South Korea since July 1957 and by stationing 3,500 U.S. troops in the Al Dhafra Air Base in Abu Dhabi. Cold War enmity had also been carried over to arms trade and the tensions with Russia and China were brought to the foreground. In April 1997, the U.S. pressurized the UAE and ROK into purchasing the Patriot missile defense system and warned both countries against purchasing the s-300 Russian air defense system adding that in such incident they would be banned from flying the U.S. fighter jets. Justification was made on the grounds of undermining the security of the U.S. fighter jets by increasing the chances of becoming a target of the Russian air defense system during joint military exercises with the U.S. While the Cold War bipolar rivalry was highlighted, THAAD dispute also arose between China and South Korea as the former protested against latter's decision to deploy the THAAD anti-missile system in September 2017.

The ROK–U.S. alliance has been under pressure under the Trump administration as the negotiations for burden-sharing broke down on November 26, 2019. The U.S.–UAE defense cooperation has also been characterized as asymmetric, with the U.S. unevenly benefiting from establishing military bases that serve its own agenda.[25] Despite the escalation of tensions in the Fujairah and Gulf of Oman tanker attacks in 2019 that reinforced dependency on the U.S. military presence in the region, the rebalancing act toward Asia and the U.S. retrenchment in the Middle East have undermined U.S. influence in the Middle East. As the state capacities of the Gulf states have improved significantly in the last two decades, there are also signs that the Gulf states are also venturing beyond traditional military alliances with the U.S. and looking to build ties with Russia and other major players. This is demonstrated through the convening of the Russian-Arab Cooperation Forum during the Russian Foreign Minister Sergei Lavrov and President Vladimir Putin's visit to Saudi Arabia and the UAE in March and October 2019. Putin's visit to Abu Dhabi in October culminated with a $1.3 bn deal in technology, health, and energy sectors. A month after Putin's visit, Russia seized the opportunity when purchasing the U.S. F-35 stealth fighter jet was not on the table and proposed to offer opportunities for potential clients such as the UAE, Turkey, and India to produce components for the Su-57 fighter jet. This was in a striking resemblance to the arms trade dilemma in the late 1990s noted above, and the UAE and Saudi Arabia were negotiating for the sale of Russian air defense system s-400, which broke down in November 2020.[26]

South Korea's strategic involvement in the Middle East is evidenced through its contributions to the coalition forces during the 1991 Gulf War and the 2003 Iraq War and the ROK–UAE military cooperation. With the exception of ROK's military dispatch to the Gulf of Oman and the Strait of Hormuz, ROK's security involvement in the Middle East was mostly through the U.S.-led multinational forces. The magnitude and gravity of transnational conflicts emanating from the MENA therefore tend to be much stronger than the reverse. For this reason, the GCC countries have utilized both defensive and offensive mechanisms for securing their borders against the penetration of external threats, especially from Iran and Yemen. These security interests have not only been constricted to the vicinity of the borders but also span the broader Asian and African continents – as demonstrated by the UAE Special Forces serving in the International Security Assistance Force (ISAF) in Afghanistan as the only Arab country – and extends as far as the Horn of Africa, as demonstrated through its presence in Somalia and the mediation efforts between Eritrea and Ethiopia. The gravity of political and security threats in the MENA has become more acute, particularly in the last two decades, following the Arab uprisings, political order in post-Saddam Iraq, and the civil war-turned-proxy war-embroiled Syria and the Yemeni civil war. Despite the shared desire to deter North Korea and Iran's nuclear proliferation among neighboring East Asian countries and the Gulf states, there has been a lack of initiatives calling for interregional and multilateral cooperation on this front.

A minor exception to this is the UAE's financial contributions to the Korean Peninsula Energy Development Organization (KEDO). The KEDO was founded by the U.S., South Korea, and Japan on March 15, 1995 to observe the U.S.–North Korean Agreed Framework which stipulates that Pyongyang freeze the facilities in the Yongbyon Nuclear Research Center and dismantle its nuclear program in exchange for financing and constructing two light-water reactors (LWR), 500,000 metric tons of heavy fuel oil as an alternative source of energy while ensuring that the international standards of nuclear safety are observed.[27] Prior to the inception of the organization, there was a consensus to build a Korean model-LWR despite North Korea's reservations. In responding to the Clinton administration's solicitation of finances for shipping 100,000 tons of oil to North Korea, the UAE joined 20 other countries in providing assistance to the KEDO as a non-member state.[28] The Korean-made LWR had an edge over its German, Russian, French, and American LWR counterparts for being cost-effective. However, KEDO's agenda hit a dead end in 2006 when the LWR construction was terminated after North Korea breached the agreed conditions which followed the accusation that Pyongyang was allegedly enriching uranium in a clandestine nuclear program in November 2002.

Economic cooperation which has been the conventional source of ROK–UAE bilateral ties are interlocked with the growing bilateral security ties. Reflecting Asia's economic strength, Ghaith Abdulla notes that there is a new tripartite division in the UAE's foreign policy in post-Zayed era, which looks to the West to ensure its security, to the Arab world to legitimize its identity, and toward East economically.[29] The leverage in business diplomacy was an outgrowth of the earlier industrialization efforts in heavy chemical industry drive led by Park Chung-hee in the 1970s, and though it faced a period of deep depression in the 1997 Asia-Pacific Financial Crisis (APC), it quickly regained momentum upon economic recovery. During the 1997 APC, the South Korean government privately initiated a "Big Deal" which refers to a series of negotiations held behind closed doors for business mergers and acquisitions among the top five South Korean conglomerates, Hyundai, Samsung, Daewoo, LG, and Korea Heavy Industries & Construction Company (KHICC). The Big Deal was an austerity policy introduced during the Kim Dae-jung administration which was designed to enhance confidence-building in the Korean economy and draw international support for "Sunshine policy."

The power plant industry was thriving even while South Korea was still emerging out of the 1997 APC. Exporting power plants in global markets by streamlining and integrating the operations of these companies was seen as an optimal decision considering that the annual electricity demands in the South Korean domestic market (3 mn KW) were only half of the production capacities of the KHICC and HHI combined (7.4 mn KW).[30] Between 1998 and 2000, KHICC announced the signing of a $700 mn power generation and seawater project with the Abu Dhabi Water and Electricity Authority and expanded its overseas market by opening field offices in Dubai (the UAE) and Taipei (Taiwan). SK Engineering & Construction also concluded a $60 mn contract with Abu Dhabi National Oil Company (ADNOC)'s construction project on sulfuric acid treatment facility in a refinery complex in Ruwais. By the early 2000s, Doosan Heavy Industries signed a $800 mn desalination plant construction contract with the UAE, and the power plant industry comprised more than half of Hyundai E&C's total revenue.[31]

By the early 2000s, the Middle East, including the UAE, emerged as a promising market for South Korea in the banking, automotive, defense, and construction sectors. Korea Aerospace Industries (KAI) and Lockheed Martin co-launched the first supersonic advanced trainer and light combat (T-50/A-50) Golden Eagle aircraft on August 30, 2005. Although it showcased the aircraft in Seoul Air Show 2005 and Dubai Air Show 2005, by 2009 the sales did not go through due to high costs and ROK lost the competition to Italy which sold 48 M-346s to the UAE. Nevertheless, South Korea is well-established in the automotive sector by ranking as the world's sixth-largest automobile producer and the world's fifth-largest automobile exporter. In the banking sector, Korea Exchange Bank (KEB) became the first Korean bank to open a branch in Dubai, as the 1970s–1980s construction boom was making a comeback to the Middle East in the early 2000s after it briefly spread to Southeast Asia in the 1990s. Notably, the emirate of Dubai emerged as the logistical and financial hub at the turn of the century, and was reputed for its openness and liberal outlook in business which has been a core strategy for future preparedness and economic diversification.[32]

As a commercial gateway in the region, Dubai promoted tourism by expanding and investing in tourist hotspots and leisurely amenities, but it has also been looking to attract highly skilled and competitive expatriates to meet its manpower needs, including through the ten-year golden visa introduced in 2019. In addition to the non-Emiratis predominantly hailing from South Asia (1 mn Indians and 350,000 Pakistanis), there was an estimate of 1,000 South Koreans in the UAE by mid-2004.[33] In conjunction with the expanding South Korean businesses in the UAE, South Korea held an exhibition that showcased products launched by Korean SMEs in Dubai in December 2003, which was attended by the UAE Minister of Economy, Fahim Al Qassimi. In an interview with a South Korean media outlet, Al Qassimi stressed the strategic importance of promoting joint ventures between South Korean and Emirati enterprises and to help Emirati businesses expand their markets in the Middle East, Russia, and Africa by building factories in Dubai.[34] In the same year, the UAE Deputy Prime Minister and Secretary of State for Foreign Affairs, Sheikh Hamdan Bin Zayed Al Nahyan echoed the importance of promoting bilateral economic cooperation and highlighting mutual areas of interests in science and technology, which took off in the mid-to-late 2010s.

The Dubai boom, business diplomacy, and security cooperation

At the turn of the century, South Korea was cautious but sanguine about the economic prospects. While South Korea prided itself on rapid industrialization, economic modernization, and democratization, it was also wary about the challenges in advancing national competitiveness by striking a fine balance between hard power (i.e. economic, military, and scientific tools) and soft power (i.e. diplomatic, informational, political attraction power). With these institutional and economic tools at their disposal, South Korea's overarching vision under Roh's collaborative government was aimed at working toward the establishment of a peace regime between the two Koreas, consolidating economic growth, and transforming itself into a welfare state. The last two objectives were considered vital for gaining the sociopolitical leverage necessary for achieving reunification. While South Korea was looking to promote democracy and good governance, it regarded other countries with a higher per capita GDP, such as Israel, Singapore, Bahrain, Kuwait, and the UAE, as exemplars of a modern state, despite the varying structural characteristics.

Roh Moo-hyun laid the groundwork for cementing and establishing economic and security cooperation in the second year of his term. The year 2004, in this regard, was a watershed year in the ROK–UAE bilateral relations. On December 10, a Samsung C&T-led consortium won a $880 mn contract alongside Belgium's BESIX and Dubai's Arabtec to build the world's tallest building, Burj Dubai (renamed to Burj Khalifa). Construction boom followed after soaring oil prices, which rose from $27.69 per barrel in 2003 to $37.66 per barrel in 2004 and again from $64.20 in 2007 to $91.48 in 2008 (in nominal price). In 2004 alone, the Arab oil producers accrued $300 bn from oil revenues.[35] The Burj Khalifa was the second major bid for skyscraper construction Samsung C&T won after being awarded the contract for building Malaysia's Tower 2 of Petronas Towers ten years earlier. Dubai gained publicity in South Korea partly not only because the contract for the world's tallest building was won by a South Korean-led consortium but also because of Dubai's reputation as a tourism hub. Nine days after the news came out regarding the deal, South Korean media outlets also reported on the passing of the UAE's founding President, Sheikh Zayed bin Sultan Al Nahyan.

With the rising oil prices revitalizing the economy and attracting capital, laborers, and resources to the UAE, Dubai's Emirates Airlines launched a direct flight between Seoul/Incheon and Dubai on May 1, 2005. The oil boom created new opportunities for infrastructure and public works projects, oil and gas exploration and power plant projects in the oil-producing states. In 2005, Hyundai E&C was awarded the largest contract with the Dubai Electricity & Water Authority, which amounted to $696 mn.[36] The UAE and ROK mutually benefited from the UAE's booming oil economy and the interdependent relationship between the two countries was underpinned by the process of globalization. Under the Roh administration, conditions of clientelistic state-business relations persisted and were promoted by the government. When Prime Minister Lee Hae-chan went on a tour to five Gulf countries (the UAE, Kuwait, Saudi Arabia, Qatar, and Oman) in November 2005 to promote "sales diplomacy," he figuratively referred to himself as the nation's sales representative for business and resource diplomacy. With a thriving manufacturing industry, ROK was riding the economic wave under the umbrella strategy of "sales diplomacy" to the extent that Samsung Group's revenue by the mid-2000s was comparable to the UAE's nominal GDP and Hyundai Motor Company's revenue corresponded to Vietnam's nominal GDP.[37] Although these figures imply that multinational corporations (MNCs) are key players in enhancing national economic competitiveness, South Korea's overdependency on MNCs has created economic imbalance. This is demonstrated by the revenues of the ten major South Korean conglomerates in 2018 which accounted for 44% of ROK's nominal revenue, which is more severe than Japan (24.6%) or the U.S. (11.8%).[38]

As South Korea increasingly became involved in Dubai's port, infrastructural, and power plant projects, Dubai Port International (DPI) acquired stakes in South Korea's Busan New Port, the second South Korean biggest port since 2004. Notably, DPI (present DP World) became the largest shareholder of Busan New Port on June 27, 2005. First, DPI acquired a

25% share in Busan New Port through CSX Transportation in 2004 and purchased further shares of 14.55% and became the largest shareholder by claiming 39.55% of the stake.[39] In response, the South Korean government spearheaded the policy of "Global Port Network" since 2006. This agenda was initially pursued with enthusiasm for the first two years as the government delineated a ten-step procedure. The government founded a global business division, International Logistics Council and International Logistics Fund, strengthened PPPs, and entrusted the private sector with the duty of conducting a market demand survey.[40] However, things took a downturn since the 2007–2008 Global Financial Crisis that mothballed the global port and terminal industry. The acquisition of port authority managements stirred controversies. Apart from the UAE's purchase in the shares of the Busan New Port in 2004, the U.S. treated DP World's attempt to purchase the port management businesses in six major U.S. seaports in 2006 as an issue of national security.

The UAE's logistics sector has prospered largely due to its expansionist strategies in port management. DPI, founded in 1999, offered an oversight function to the management of overseas port operations. In the same year, Saudi Arabia's South Container Terminal in Jeddah Islamic Port was DPI's first overseas port operation established in coordination with a local port authority. From thereon in, DPI expanded their overseas port operations to Djibouti Port (2000), India's Vizag Port (2002), and Romania's Constanza Port (2003). The UAE's port and logistics sector increased the efficiency of its operation and posted a 20% cargo growth in 2002 by founding the Ports, Customs and Free Zone Corporation through a merger between Federal Customs Authority and Jebel Ali Free Zone Authority in 2001. The renaissance of the overseas cargo market came after 2005 which enabled a series of overseas ports acquisitions with the establishment of Dubai Port World (DPW) as a merger between DPA and DPI. This was followed by the UAE's acquisition of P&O Maritime in the UK in 2006. While South Korea's port industry was alarmed at the rate and the extent to which the shares (80%) of its very own Busan New Port was sold to international port authorities, the DPA's port management and acquisition strategies served as an instructive case.

The Roh Moo-hyun administration aimed at killing two birds with one stone by promoting the twin policy of commercial diplomacy and security cooperation. Roh became the first South Korean president to visit the UAE in 2006. On May 13, 2006, Roh met with the UAE President Sheikh Khalifa bin Zayed Al Nahyan and became the third country to sign an agreement on joint oil stockpiling business. During his tour in Dubai, Roh marveled at the sight of skyscrapers and modernized landscape in Dubai and exclaimed, "This forest [Dubai] you created is truly a miracle…the green forest of Dubai, a beautiful city is a beautiful creation that will realize the precious value of mankind where creation and peace coexist."[41] Lee Myung-bak, who was a mayor of Seoul at the time of his visit to Dubai a year later, was equally impressed by the rapid rate of modernization in Dubai, which was dubbed the "Miracle of the desert." By 2007, it only took Dubai half the projected time to achieve what was set out in the ten-year vision and when Dubai achieved a growth rate of 13% in a five-year span (2000–2005), the Government of Dubai proceeded to launch the Dubai Strategic Plan 2015. Bolstered by the robust economic growth undergirded by hydrocarbon economy, UAE's International Petroleum Investment Company (IPIC) announced its plans to invest $2.2 bn in South Korea's Chungnam province in July 2007 to help expand the refinery of Hyundai Oilbank. The market share of Hyundai Steel exceeded 50% in the UAE by September 2008.[42] Moreover, this was paralleled by the rise in stock market investments among the GCC countries which increased by 80% from the previous year – the UAE invested $55.2 bn in the Korean stock market in 2007.[43] As this chapter discusses below, the UAE's geostrategic location and the strategic importance as a regional financial and commercial gateway also provided fertile grounds for cooperation in other fields including nuclear energy, security and defense, as well as health care and people-to-people connectivity.

But at the same time, the more the Korea's international commercial activities intensified, there were greater exposures to maritime security risks. Piracy in the Indian Ocean has emerged as a mutual security concern for both countries and the ROK–UAE bilateral relations extended into defense cooperation as South Korea's engagement with the UAE deepened toward the mid-2000s. In 2003, 2010, and 2011, South Korean freights, Dongwon and Samho Jewelry, and the Samho Dream supertanker, were captured by Somali pirates in the Indian Ocean and were rescued by ROK navy (ROKN) commandos Cheonghae unit. The South Korean government used backchannel negotiations for the release of the ships. A record ransom of $9.5 mn was paid for the release of the 2010 Samho Dream Supertanker in November 2010, which coincided with the seizure of the Singaporean ship, the Golden Blessing. The 2011 Operation Dawn of Gulf of Aden for Samho Jewelry entailed rescuing a Sri Lanka-bound commercial vessel mounted with chemicals that was departing from the UAE. The ROKN Cheonghae unit has been participating in the multinational antipiracy combined task force (CTF-150) in the Gulf of Aden, the Arabian Sea, and the Indian Ocean since March 2009 following the National Assembly's approval. Two months later, ROKN was also involved in a rescue mission for the first time for a North Korean vessel, Dabaksol. To date, Cheonghae unit dispatched a total of 8,478 ROKNS, rescued 21,895 cargo ships, and had been involved in 21 antipiracy operations.[44]

Somalia's piracy activities have been rampant, deeply affecting the freedom of passage and security of the UAE-flagged vessels since the 2010s. Piracy has been listed as one of the critical security issues affecting the UAE in addition to other chronic security threats posed by Iran's growing regional ambitions and the issue in Yemen. The UAE also took legal measures by sentencing ten Somali pirates that raided the UAE-flagged MV Arrilah-I to 25 years in prison in May 2012. Although the UAE signed military cooperation agreements with Somalia in 2014, this was terminated in following deteriorating relations between the Somali federal government when the Somali security forces seized $10 mn in cash from a UAE-registered civil aircraft at the Mogadishu Airport. In addition to piracy in the Gulf of Aden, South Korea was exposed to security issues with the abduction of pastors and missionaries in Afghanistan in 2004 and 2007. Ever since, instead of relying on the traditional methods of using backchannel negotiations in a trilateral negotiation structure, which consists of the Afghan government, tribes, and the Taliban militias, there was an increasing call to seek the help of the neighboring countries, including the UAE, Saudi Arabia, and Pakistan by forging close partnerships with them.

Moreover, the Somali pirates in the Gulf of Aden have been approached by North Korea as a potential client in illegal arms trade since 2015, including the sales of North Korea-made submarines (MS-29) equipped with a German engine (MTU-1800).[45] Ever since Pyongyang has been subjected to UN sanctions and unilateral U.S. sanctions, it has been relying on its bilateral trade with China to earn hard currency. While other sources of foreign currency also include loyalty payments and remittances from North Korean laborers overseas, Pyongyang has also stepped up on illegal arms trade to increase its foreign currency reserves. Unlike in the past when UN sanctions had a limited impact on the North Korean economy due to a buffer created by the laxed Chinese enforcement of sanctions, the introduction of UN sanctions (2321, 2371, 2375, 2397) since 2016 has had a crippling effect on the North Korean economy as North Korea's exports of minerals (especially coals), seafood, and the textile industry were grounded to a halt. In effect, the passage of these UNSC resolutions also banned issuing visas to North Korean workers. As a consequence, Pyongyang's bilateral trade with China sharply declined by 88.2% from $1.65 bn in 2017 to $195 mn in 2018.[46] Nevertheless, these sanctions were not sufficient measures to deter North Korea's illicit activities, and the resumption of nuclear activities came amid reports that North Korea had conducted a "very important test" at the Sohae Satellite launching site in December 2019.[47]

South Korea and the UAE share mutual security concerns regarding the Houthi rebels and nuclear proliferation. On July 29, 2015, a South Korean intelligence source confirmed that Houthi rebels in Yemen purchased 20 Scud missiles from North Korea – its clients also include Iran, Syria, and Palestine. The marriage of convenience between North Korea and Yemen is based on the former's need for hard currency and the latter's need for weaponries to combat political turmoil at home.[48] The trilateral strategic alliances between the ROK–UAE–KSA have been tacitly reinforced by illegal arms trade between Pyongyang and the Houthi rebels and the Houthi piracy in Red Sea. On November 18, 2019, South Korean vessels (Woongjin G-16 and T-1100) and a Saudi tugboat (Rabigh-3) were seized by the Houthi rebels and 16 sailors, including two Koreans were detained shortly after they were suspected of trespassing the territorial waters 15 miles west of Kamaran

Island in Yemen, and were released a day after the incident.[49] Therefore, South Korea also has stakes in the security of the Gulf of Aden, albeit to a much lesser extent than the UAE and Saudi Arabia. Within the broader umbrella of security and defense cooperation, ROKN special naval forces have been providing counterpiracy training to the UAE naval forces. Ten underwater demolition troops were deployed in addition to the 130 *Akh* (brother) special forces stationed in Al Ain for counterterrorism training.[50] In addition to the multinational coalition naval task force, CTF-150, ROKN Cheonghae unit has recently collaborated with the EU in the EU-led antipiracy joint military exercise in the Gulf of Aden between February and March 2017 and dispatched its destroyer, Choe Yeong.

Security and defense cooperation between ROK and the UAE were built on the basis of the former's rising energy demands and deepening commercial ties with the UAE at the turn of the century. During the second year of the Roh administration, ROK air force chief of staff went on a tour to the UAE, Malaysia, and Indonesia to discuss military exchange and defense cooperation with the military heads of these countries. The main objective for this visit was not only to boost arms sales for the South Korean defense industry but also to mobilize political backing for South Korea's plan to support the reconstruction and peace-building efforts in Iraq by deploying Zaytun division in the Kurdish governorate of Northern Iraq. Building on this visit, security cooperation was formalized 2.5 years later. Although the deployment of Akh (brother) unit did not commence until January 2011 following the approval of the National Assembly, the foundation for establishing security ties was laid in the ROK–UAE security cooperation pact signed during Roh's presidency in November 2006, which was two years after South Korea signed an agreement with Kuwait in November 2004. The security pact with both countries, Kuwait and the UAE, was signed around the time when Seoul was in need of a military support base for the Zaytun division deployed in Iraq, and the 130-Air force Daiman unit was based in Kuwait until both Zaytun and Daiman units withdrew in December 2008.[51] Though both agreements entail strengthening military exchanges and cooperation between the two parties and boosting arms exports, as will be discussed below, signing the security cooperation pact with the UAE is intimately tied to South Korea's commercial interests in exporting nuclear plants as well as furthering the interests of Seoul's business diplomacy at large.

Lee Myung-bak's resource diplomacy and the politics of nuclear energy cooperation

If Roh Moo-hyun laid the groundwork for building bilateral commercial and security ties when Dubai was entering a golden decade of urbanization and prosperity, the Lee Myung-bak administration cemented these ties and took them to new heights. Resource diplomacy was the raison d'etre of his presidency, but he also fostered military and defense cooperation as a means to advancing commercial interests. A year after his visit to Dubai as a mayor of Seoul, Lee Myung-bak became the president-elect on February 25, 2008. As a former businessman, Lee was keen on emulating Dubai's institutional governance and modernization paradigm – little at the time did he know that South Korea would later dispatch patent examiners to the UAE. Lee was inspired by the direct line of communication that the ruler of Dubai established with the businesspeople as well as the appointment of a non-UAE national in a ministerial position. Lee's appointees in the new cabinet thus consisted mostly of bureaucrats with professional background in finance and economics. The Prime Minister nominee, Han Seung-soo was a former economic advisor to Jordan, and David Eldon, the chairman of the national competitiveness enhancement committee, was a former chairman of the Dubai Financial Services Agency.

The "Dubai" influence had been shaped from Lee's frequent business trips to Dubai as a former CEO of Hyundai E&C, and Dubai's rapid transformation into a regional commercial hub was compatible with Lee's blueprint for executing the Saemangeum Seawall project and grand canal project.[52] The former had been dubbed "the Dubai of East Asia" which was originally a reclamation of rice fields dating back to Roh Tae-woo's election in 1982 and later transformed into an industrial land which was designed to encourage investments and commercial activities. It was also a pork-barreling project intended to garner votes from the Jeolla province.[53] In addition, the four major rivers restoration project, is a $19.6 bn project which was introduced in 2008 as a mega project intended to connect the four major rivers of Yeongsan, Geum, Nakdong, and Han.[54] Though supporters considered them as groundbreaking projects with economic potential, both projects stirred social and political controversies and faced insurmountable criticisms. The opposition mainly came from environmentalists (e.g. Birds Korea) and a mélange of civil societies (e.g. Citizens Alliance for Economic Justice, Green Union, Green Residents Solidarity) that were advocating for conservation of bird habitats as well as the general public that were opposed to exorbitant costs. On February 15, Lee met with Mohammed al-Shaibani, President of Dubai Investment Corporation (DIC) and both parties decided to create a $2 bn Korea–Dubai Fund to encourage DIC-affiliated companies to invest in the infrastructures in South Korea and suggested concluding a bilateral trade agreement. The ROK government also devised a plan to construct a Dubai-style port-business valley.

Leading up to the Global Financial Crisis of 2007–2008, the Government of Dubai also invested in science, technology, and innovation. Since becoming the first IT park free zone established in the Middle East in 2002, Dubai Techno Park was founded in the hopes of transforming Dubai into a hub of innovation and technology. With a corporate tax-free environment, a 100% foreign ownership of industrial units, repatriation of capital, and no restrictions in hiring foreign employees, Dubai Techno Park offered incentives for 20 South Korean businesses mulling over setting up their businesses. As South Korea's business ventures were established as a benchmark alongside those of Singapore, a memorandum was signed on October 10, 2008 between Korea's Daejeon Techno Park and Dubai Techno Park to promote cooperation in construction, biotechnology, environment, and medical technology. The Chairman of Korea Institute for Advancement of Technology symbolically framed this partnership as a marriage between "the miracle of the desert" and "the miracle on the Han River."[55] The launching of Dubai Techno Park captures the economic diversification efforts presided over by the Government of Dubai as a two-step process: (1) consolidating Dubai's status as a hub of commerce, tourism, and finance; (2) varying UAE's economic diversification strategies by transitioning from a commercial hub to an innovation hub and a knowledge-based economy by investing in the innovation priority sectors. At the national level, the UAE is also heavily invested in other innovation-driven initiatives including the development of satellites, namely DubaiSat-1, co-developed by Emirates Institute for Advanced Science and Technology and ROK's Satrec Initiative in 2009, and the first UAE-made satellite, KhalifaSat, which benefited from a knowledge transfer program in South Korea and was launched from Tanegashima Space Center, Japan on October 29, 2018. To promote space exploration and knowledge transfer, Mohammed bin Rashid Space Centre signed a memorandum of agreement with the Korea Aerospace Research Institute on March 6, 2017.

The seeds for innovation in the UAE have been sown since the late 2000s shortly after Dubai's economic modernization and urbanization drive had reached its zenith and became more stabilized. The heyday of Dubai's development is best captured by the peak of Dubai's construction boom in mid-2000s when Dubai was home to one-fourth of the world's cranes. Introducing a blueprint for innovation became more of a pressing concern especially after Dubai weathered the storms of the bust cycle and the 2007–2008 Global Financial Crisis – there were capital flights and quantitative easing was implemented to encourage interbank loans. It was not until mid-2009 that the economy started showing signs of recovery, and it was also then when the UAE commissioned 20 delegates for a briefing on investment opportunities in South Korea. After a hiatus in economic growth in the late 2000s, a decade later, the UAE under the direction of the Prime Minister's Office kickstarted the process of devising a comprehensive vision for innovation strategies. Under the broader vision of developmental and innovation roadmaps of the UAE Vision 2021 and UAE Centennial 2071, the UAE released a multitude of developmental roadmaps at the emirate-level which are comprehensive in scope – including space exploration, food and water security, renewable energy, artificial intelligence and environmental sustainability, and logistics and industrialization, health, tourism, and urban development strategies. The bilateral comprehensive cooperation created a synergistic effect which led to a surge in educational and scientific cooperation between the UAE and ROK, which culminated with the opening of a joint research center between Khalifa University and Korea Advanced Institute of Science and Technology in 2019.

The hallmark of Lee Myung-bak's presidency lies in Korea's first-ever nuclear energy export to the UAE. KEPCO and KHNP are the main entities that have been spearheading ROK's development of nuclear energy since 2009. As a newcomer to global nuclear energy exports, South Korea's decision to build nuclear power plant in the UAE on June 22, 2009 was a landmark agreement that enhanced its competitiveness in the global nuclear energy market. The UAE has been preparing to build a nuclear power plant since 2008, and it has been adhering to six pillars on developing nuclear energy that ensures transparency, nonproliferation and peaceful, safe, and secure domestic nuclear power program.[56] Korea's nuclear energy generation capacity ranks sixth in the world which accounts for more than 30% of electricity generation. At one point, it was even projected that nuclear energy would constitute over half of South Korea's source of electricity supply and that it has the world's highest capacity factor for nuclear power plants – above 90% since the 2000s.[57] The Korean consortium led by KEPCO was awarded a $20 bn contract to build four advanced power reactors (APR-1400) in Barakah, the UAE in December 2009, and South Korea became the fifth country to join the ranks of the major exporters of nuclear technology, according to the World Nuclear Association. By July 2009, South Korean consortium entered the second round of bidding alongside the contending bidders GE, Areva, and Hitachi.

However, prior to the nuclear agreement, there were concerns regarding the deficiency of a core indigenous nuclear power technology. Westinghouse Electric Corporation (WEC), a U.S. company that was eliminated in the first round of bidding, requested to participate in the production of nuclear reactor coolant pump (RCP) and nuclear power meter control system as part of the South Korean consortium given that the nuclear power plants built in South Korea adopted nuclear technology from WEC. Despite the earlier apprehensions that ROK would not have had acquired an adequate capacity for developing and exporting a homegrown nuclear technology, a Korean standard for nuclear power plants was established in 1995 and Doosan Heavy Industries developed indigenous key codes for designing nuclear power plants and for developing RCP and man–machine interface systems (MMIS). In addition, in South Korea, there were no reports of major accidents since the construction of Kori 1 nuclear power plant in 1978. The APR-1400 was certified by the European Utility Requirements in October 2017 and by the Nuclear Regulatory Commission on September 28, 2018. APR 1400 is an adaptation and an evolution of the Optimized Power Reactor (OPR-1000) Korean Standard Nuclear Power Plant design and WEC's System 80+ design. The first and only APR-1400 that is activated is Shin Kori 3 nuclear reactor in ROK which was completed in January 2016.[58] In South Korea, the first domestic nuclear energy development (Kori-1 nuclear power plant) was completed in 1978 with technical support from Westinghouse, and KHNP operates a total of 24 nuclear power plants.[59] The KEPCO-KHNP's vision for nuclear energy development was to meet electricity demands as well as to export a Korean-made nuclear power plant. The main objective was to develop a large-scale nuclear power plant with locally produced RCPs, nuclear power plant control, and measurement systems. Emerging markets for exporting Korean nuclear power plant technology were the UAE, Jordan, Turkey, China, Indonesia, Vietnam, and Morocco. Apart from nuclear energy, ROK was also steadily increasing renewable energy production vis-à-vis wind power, solar power, tidal power, clean coal, fuel cell, and hydraulic power.

Even though ROK only entered the global nuclear power market in the late 2000s, the development of nuclear energy program is historically rooted in the Rhee Syngman's presidency. As early as 1954, Walker Cisler (president of the present-day DTE Energy) shaped Rhee Syngman's view on nuclear energy as a potent and sustainable source of electricity supply. Prior to this, Cisler used to be a war materials producer for the U.S. Department of Defense during WWII and was an advisor to France and Western Europe for rebuilding Europe's power equipment. Rhee was compelled when Cisler pointed out that uranium could generate 12 mn kW of electricity which is more than two million times the electricity that could be generated with an equal amount of coal (4 kW). However, South Korea at the time of Cisler's visit was impoverished and dependent on U.S. aid with a meager per capita GDP of $27,900.[60] Therefore, Rhee created the Department of Nuclear Energy in 1956, promoted R&D, and awarded government-sponsored scholarships to invest in a cadre of scientists and enhance nuclear energy capacity, and the next year, South Korea acceded to the IAEA. Two years after Cisler's advice to Rhee, South Korea signed an agreement on the peaceful use of atomic energy with the U.S. during the Cold War era when nuclear energy cooperation was regarded as a form of aid to help contain the spread of communism. While South Korea also received technical support for nuclear energy development from Canada and France for heavy water-cooled reactors and light water-cooled reactors, the U.S. was at the backbone of nuclear technology assistance to South Korea. Inspired by Dwight D. Eisenhower's "Atom for peace" speech delivered to the UNGA on December 8, 1953, as part and parcel of the broader Cold War strategy of containment, a nuclear research program was also launched in close cooperation with the U.S. in 1955 for identical reasons.[61] South Korea's nuclear power plant export to the UAE bore fruition half a century after Rhee Syngman attended the groundbreaking ceremony held for South Korea's first experimental reactor, KEPCO, on July 14, 1959. The Park Chung-hee administration inherited Rhee Syngman's drive for nuclear energy and established the nuclear development committee on May 16, 1961, and the first Korean nuclear power plant (Kori-1) came online in 1978.

The inception of the populist Moon Jae-in administration on May 10, 2017 resulted in rolling back on pro-business policies executed by Lee Myung-bak. The nuclear phase-out policy was pledged during Moon's presidential campaign, and after 40 years of activation, Kori 1 nuclear power plant was permanently phased out as of June 18, 2017. The decision came amid the graft charges on nuclear power plant projects as well the safety implications of the Fukushima Daiichi nuclear accident on March 11, 2011. Among the five countries that decided to shut down the operation of nuclear reactors include Germany (Gundremmingen B), South Korea (Kori 1), Japan (Monju), Sweden (Oskarshamn 1), and Spain (Santa Maria De Garoña), Germany and South Korea were the two countries that phased out nuclear energy development based on governmental policy shift. The initial plan was to halt construction of the Shin Kori units 5 and 6 following Moon's election. However, because the public opinion swayed in favor (59.5%) of completing the construction of both units, the construction resumed, but Moon also made clear that there would be no plans for further construction of nuclear power plants during his term.[62] For the past 40 years it was activated, the total energy supply amounted to 150,000 GW, which is roughly equivalent to 34 times of Busan's energy consumption.[63] Despite the KHNP's recommendation to renew the operation of the nuclear power plant based on the 70–80-year safety timeframe, the Kori nuclear power plant closed down after the license was renewed for another ten years following the expiry of the initial contract period of 30 years. Environmental activists and civil societies, on the other hand, were in favor of the shutdown. The disintegration of the Kori nuclear power plant is expected to take 20 years to complete and the projected cost is $543.8 mn.[64] Though the construction of UAE's Barakah nuclear plant contract was awarded to South Korea, the UAE has been keen on broadening and diversifying partnerships in international nuclear energy cooperation. As a result of the policy shift, among other explanations, South Korea was unable to monopolize the LTMSA contract for Barakah nuclear power plant. Due to the nuclear phase-out policy by the Moon administration, the much-needed resources for supporting the development of nuclear energy were siphoned off. The development of nuclear energy reactor components was stalled and the funds for nuclear power R&D dried up which also induced a brain drain of scientists and nuclear physicists. In nuclear power export, KEPCO also lost the preferred bidder status for acquiring Toshiba's NuGen nuclear project in Britain in July 2018.

The UAE signed a nuclear energy cooperation agreement with France on January 15, 2008, a year prior to the signing of the nuclear energy cooperation agreement with Korea on June 22, 2009. During the French President Nicolas Sarkozy's visit to the Gulf states in January 2008, a military agreement establishing the first French base in the GCC was also signed alongside the nuclear agreement, which follows the 1995 defense agreement signed between the two parties on establishing a military base for the French air force and the navy and infantry forces that were to take effect in 2009. Although France's Total, together with Suez, and the state-owned enterprise in nuclear energy were gearing up to develop two third-generation nuclear reactors in the UAE, the contract was awarded to South Korea in the final round of the

UAE civil nuclear bid.[65] The nuclear bid won by the KEPCO-led consortium in December 2009, however, was virtually diminished to a subcontract by mid-2019 from a long-term maintenance agreement (LMTA) to a long-term maintenance services agreement (LTMSA) as a result of the nuclear phase-out policy. Instead, Team Korea, which is a consortium responsible for the construction of the fourth unit of Barakah nuclear power plant, signed a LTMSA. To date, while Nawah Energy Company contracted operating support services agreement (OSSA) and long-term engineering agreement (LTEA) to South Korea's KHNP and KEPCO and LTMSA to KHNP and KEPCO-KPS, long-term support agreement (LTSA) was awarded to France's EDF and the total contract period was also reduced from 10–15 years to five years. Instead of securing a monopoly LMTA contract, Nawah Energy Company opted for a pluralistic bidding process to subcontractors since the nuclear phase-out policy was deemed to carry risks. These changes, however, also indicate that the UAE is taking a similar path to ROK's nuclear energy development since Team Korea is playing a similar role to the U.S.'s WEC in the 1970s, which served as an important channel for the transfer of nuclear technologies to South Korea.

The civil nuclear bid won by the KEPCO-led consortium reinvigorated the construction market almost immediately after the recovery from the 2008–2009 global financial crisis and eased the entry of Korean companies into the UAE market. According to the International Contractors Association of Korea, the UAE was the largest market for construction contracts in 2009 and 2010.[66] GS E&C, Samsung Engineering, Daewoo E&C, & SK E&C won contracts amounting to $10 bn for the expansion of the Ruwais oil refinery in March 2010 and Hyundai E&C and KEPCO were each awarded a $900 mn and a $1.5 bn contract as the main contractors for the construction of Borouge petrochemical plant and thermal power plant in Abu Dhabi in October. Further to this, there was a paradigmatic shift in South Korea's defense industry from pursuing conventional methods of weapons manufacturing purely for defense purposes to proactively seeking the expansion of arms exports such as T-50 supersonic advanced trainers, K-9 self-propelled howitzers, K-11 rifles, and submarines, through a close coordination between the government agencies, namely the Ministry of Knowledge Economy (renamed to the Ministry of Trade, Industry and Energy), MND, Export-Import Bank of Korea, and KOTRA. Devising a holistic national strategy involving diplomatic, defense, and industrial efforts was vital to augment the South Korean arms industry, as well as to promote PPPs and civil–military relations.[67] The export of nuclear power plants to the UAE and the development of aluminum alloys served these purposes.

The ROK MND and the ROK Ministry of Knowledge Economy's desire to boost arms exports coincided with the deployment of 130 ROK Special Forces (Akh unit) for a 4–6 months rotational stationing in the UAE from December 2010. This was the first time South Korea dispatched troops to a non-conflict country, becoming the 11th country to sign a security cooperation agreement with the UAE.[68] The mission of the Akh unit included providing training for the UAE Special Forces and conducting joint military exercise, as well as to protect South Korean nationals in the UAE in case of emergency. However, the approval from the National Assembly did not come easily as controversies were stirred among the Democratic Party lawmakers who opposed overseas military deployments other than for the UN peacekeeping operations citing on the grounds of mixing commercial with strategic interests. What politicians were not aware at the time, however, is that the signing of the first security cooperation pact predates the award of the nuclear power deal and other major commercial contracts and was initially signed during Roh Moo-hyun's presidency. Since the ROK MND conducted a mock counterterror drill during the UAE Crown Prince and Deputy Supreme Commander of the UAE Armed Forces, Sheikh Mohammed bin Zayed Al Nahyan's visit to South Korea in May 2010, bilateral military exchanges with the UAE have been robust and memoranda on military cooperation were signed on information exchange, logistics, military science and technology, and defense across several occasions, and over the course of three administrations.

The ROK–UAE security ties are regarded as one of the many facets – both as direct and indirect means – which has yielded palpable diplomatic and commercial outcomes. This is best demonstrated through the elevation of bilateral diplomatic relations to special strategic partnership and the comprehensive scope of MOUs signed during and after Moon Jae-in's visit to the UAE in March 2018. Other milestones also include agreements signed in March 2011 and March 2015 with Abu Dhabi Investment Authority (ADIA) and Investment Corporation of Dubai for joint investment opportunities in the UAE, South Korea, and elsewhere. As the world's third-largest sovereign wealth fund, ADIA also acquired the State Tower Namsan for $485.7 mn in 2015 but has put it up for sale in August 2018. Moreover, strengthening bilateral strategic ties is also inevitable in light of the increasing exposures of South Koreans to piracy and abduction by the Islamist rebels in the MENA; the opposite could also be said to be true. On May 21, 2019, President Moon expressed his gratitude to the Crown Prince of Abu Dhabi, Sheikh Mohammed bin Zayed Al Nahyan for UAE's efforts in releasing a South Korean citizen detained in Libya.

In the same month preceding the signing of the joint investment agreement with ADIA in March 2011, Korea National Oil Corporation (KNOC) signed a memorandum with ADNOC for securing an exclusive right for securing 1 bn barrels of oil with an additional stockpile of 6 mn barrels of oil; heads of terms were also signed for developing three onshore and offshore oil fields. This was considered a groundbreaking agreement since it conferred South Korea's access to the UAE oil reserves of which 40% was previously reserved exclusively for the U.S., UK, France, and Japan from the 1930s and 1940s over a 30-year period. Although South Korea has had a long history of winning contracts for construction and power plant industries, the nuclear power deal signed in December 2009 offered a major boost to other commercial sectors.

Energy security cooperation with the UAE was critical to ensure an interrupted flow of oil as a buffer against supply shortages that could result from U.S. sanctions against Iran. South Korea received assurances about continued energy supply from the UAE. Despite the widespread criticisms on corruption charges against the civil servants and businessmen involved in deals and contracts, South Korean companies were also able to secure more contracts following the signing of MOUs over the years. In March 2012, a year after concluding the MoU, KNOC and the GS Energy-led consortium won a 30-year concession with ADNOC for the first time in South Korea's history for developing three unexplored oil fields. By July 2019, KNOC and GS Energy also became the first Korean companies to extract $6.2 bn of crude oil for 24 years from Haliba oil field. In May 2015, GS Energy acquired a 3% oil production from ADNOC and secured the right to produce and sell crude oil for 40 years. These concessions demonstrate that diplomatic and commercial efforts take time to materialize – in some cases, over the three presidencies.

ROK's soft power projection in Korean Wave (*Hallyu*), educational exchange, and health care cooperation

Cultural diplomacy was a defining feature of the Park Geun-hye administration. Park's efforts were in diversifying South Korea's bilateral cooperation with the UAE to include food, agriculture, and culture while she inherited the legacies of resource diplomacy and security and defense cooperation from the two predecessors. Though the roots of *Hallyu* long predates Park's presidency, South Korea's soft power projection was facilitated by improvements in institutional capacity and abetted by a combination of endogenous and exogenous factors – hallyu in the Gulf reached its pinnacle in the early 2010s. A year after signing the MoU, Korean Cultural Center opened in Abu Dhabi in March 2016. Korea–Arab Society (KAS), a state-sponsored organization aimed at fostering exchanges between South Korea and member states of Arab League, was established in 2008. Though hallyu in the Gulf states, especially in Saudi Arabia, the UAE, and Iran initially spread through TV dramas and K-pop, as exemplified by the millions of views on YouTube for Psy's Gangnam Style and the airing of Korean drama series, Winter Sonata, in Abu Dhabi TV in 2004, the scope of hallyu is not only confined to pop culture but also broadly includes K-beauty (i.e. cosmetic products), export of halal foods, sports, health care, and educational exchange.[69]

Healthcare cooperation is at the backbone of ROK–UAE bilateral relations and is linked to medical tourism in Korea. Healthcare MOUs were initially signed during Lee's presidency – first in March 2011 between the UAE Ministry of Health, Abu Dhabi Health Authority, and Dubai Health Authority and the second in January 2014 with Sharjah Health Authority. In the last decade, South Korea has had a huge success in exporting medical treatment and administration and health IT and in promoting medical tourism. In 2014, Seoul National University Hospital signed a five-year $1 tn contract with the Sheikh Khalifa Specialty Hospital (SKSH) outbidding its contenders in the U.S., UK, and Germany. The Medical Office of the Ministry of Presidential Affairs gave the highest rating to the SKSH for quality service and care and health IT. In 2015, Catholic University Seoul St. Mary's Hospital opened a Korean health examination center which was modeled after its own as the first comprehensive medical examination center that opened in Korea. The key attributes to success in healthcare partnerships include advanced and cutting-edge medical treatment, cultural awareness, and efficiency.

In recent years, there has been a rise in the exports of Korean products, including skin care products and halal food. Korean cosmetic brand, The Face Shop and Etude House opened several branches in Dubai and Abu Dhabi since 2007. The sales of Korean products have received a boost through the popularity of hallyu as well as through President Park's visit to the UAE in March 2015. The South Korean government has been sponsoring halal certification and halal-related consulting fees since 2012, and Korea Agro-Fisheries & Food Corporation opened their field office in Abu Dhabi six months after President Park's visit. The UAE's halal food market is strategically important considering that halal food constitute 20% of the global food market. In addition, the rising profile of South Korea's soft power projection and hallyu has also created opportunities for educational exchanges. KAS solicited applications for an exchange program from youths in South Korea and the Arab League member states since 2009. And on July 26, 2010, 48 students from the Institute of Applied Technology in the UAE visited South Korea on a short-term visit to study Korea's nuclear power. People-to-people connectivity has been fostered through the inauguration of King Sejong Institute for Korean Language at Zayed University, which was opened in association with Chungnam National University in October 2010 for the purpose of equipping diplomats and students in Korean language and culture. Moreover, presently there are nine active Korean clubs in universities across the UAE. Sports diplomacy has also been a medium for fostering educational exchanges, especially in Taekwondo, and to a lesser degree in table tennis. Sheikha Maitha bint Mohammed bin Rashid Al Maktoum, who won a silver medal in Karate in the 2006 Doha Asian Games, played as a wild card in the 2008 Beijing Olympics in Taekwondo, while Chung Cheong University sent delegates via world peace volunteer corps in November 2004 to promote Taekwondo and sports diplomacy. In table tennis, the UAE national table tennis team arrived in South Korea as early as August 1999 for an off-season training alongside Saudi Arabian and Qatari national table tennis teams that arrived in the same year.

Conclusion

The history of ROK–UAE bilateral relations has been contingent on state capacities, boom-bust cycle, and the ebb and flow of regional geopolitics. Although bilateral relations took off only two decade and a half later when Roh Moo-hyun became the first South Korean president to visit the UAE on May 13, 2006, longstanding history of economic involvement in the construction and power plant industries since the 1970s predates formal diplomatic relations between the two countries. Though the underlying structural characteristics and the rate of development between "the Miracle of the desert" and "the Miracle of the Han River" are vastly different, both models have inspired one another in urban planning and institutional governance. While energy security cooperation remains highly relevant and is at the backbone of bilateral relations, the scope and depth of bilateral relations have transcended beyond the traditional parameters of economic and commercial ties to include security and defense, nuclear energy, and healthcare cooperation. A survey of the 40 years of diplomatic history between ROK and the UAE suggests that the scope of cooperation in the ROK–UAE relations is the most diversified among ROK's diplomatic relations in the Middle East, especially due to agreements in security and healthcare partnerships. In a relatively short span of time, the ROK–UAE relations have evolved from a dependent relationship to a mutually interdependent relationship. This could be explained by South Korea's history of industrialization in the earlier decades when the demands for energy were fueled by Park Chung-hee's policy of HCI drive. However, as state-building in the UAE progressed and stabilized over time, UAE's drive for economic diversification, sustainability, and future-preparedness generated new demands in innovation priority sectors, adding breadth and depth to bilateral relations.

The deepening commercial ties between the two countries also imply that cooperation in the economic and strategic domains is not mutually exclusive. Since becoming a middle power, South Korea's material capabilities have increased commensurate to its institutional capacity and political significance. As such, South Korea's increased commercial presence in the Indian Ocean and the Gulf of Aden has unwittingly increased its exposures to maritime security threats (i.e. hijacking and piracy). While South Korea is predisposed to embrace multilateralism and the preservation of international order and peace as a middle power, it is the world's sixth largest arms importer in the world and the seventh largest military in the world. Military and defense capabilities are critical assets to South Korea given the precarious geopolitical configurations in the Korean Peninsula since the Korean War. While South Korea has not been a direct party to any major conflicts, it has deployed forces to Afghanistan ISAF, alongside the UAE, as well as to the Gulf of Aden. In the past, it had also contributed medical and military resources to the 1991 Gulf War and participated in the U.S.-led multinational force as part of the 2003 Iraq War. These military experiences on the ground have indirectly

Security cooperation with the UAE 129

drawn South Korea into the orbit of Middle East conflict zones, and though the stakes may not be as high as the countries that are directly party to the conflicts, South Korea's continued dependency on Middle Eastern crude oil implies that it is a mutual interest to ensure peace and stability in West Asia. What is noteworthy is that the UAE is the only country in the world that South Korea deploys its special forces for military training purposes. Thus, the case of UAE–ROK relations suggests that commercial and strategic interests in diplomatic relations are closely intertwined and as strategic relations expand over time, the stakes for the latter are bound to increase proportional to that of the former.

In the course of the bilateral diplomatic history, the groundwork for establishing the strategic and economic ties was laid during the Roh Moo-hyun and Lee Myung-bak administrations. From bureaucratic and domestic perspectives, defense cooperation agreement and nuclear energy agreement were controversial decisions. However, from a diplomatic standpoint, it was a necessary step in the right direction. In stark contrast to the pro-business approach taken by the Lee Myung-bak administration, the Moon Jae-in administration overturned the policies implemented by his predecessor. While the nuclear phase-out policy is a cause that is championed by civil groups and environmental activists, the abrupt decision that was a reversal of what was embodied in the nuclear power deal was alarming to the nuclear energy community and the business community, and it undercut the prospects for exporting South Korea's nuclear energy technology abroad. The inconsistencies exhibited in the policies of the two administrations reflect the classic weakness of foreign policy implementation in democracies which take a long time to develop. This is problematic as the volition for a long-term vision and policy coherence is critical for policy decisions to bear fruition. Park Geun-hye administration's health care, halal foods and cultural exchanges and connectivity reflect the efforts to complement hard power with soft power.

Notes

1 World Bank Group, "World Bank Group and Republic of Korea: 60 years of partnership," n.d., http://pubdocs.worldbank.org/en/754261483515257926/Korea-Timeline.pdf.
2 Stephen Haggard, Byung-kook Kim & Chung-in Moon, "The transition to export-led growth in South Korea: 1954–1966," *The Journal of Asian Studies* 50, no. 4 (1991), 868.
3 Mohamed Elhage, S. Nuri Erbas, Mitra Farahbaksh, Mangal Goswami & Holger Floeremeier, "The United Arab Emirates: Selected issues & statistical appendix," *International Monetary Fund*, June 17, 2005, 16.
4 The World Bank, "Gross domestic product 2018," September 19, 2018, https://databank.worldbank.org/data/download/GDP.pdf; US Energy Information Administration (EIA), "What countries are the top producers and consumers of oil?" n.d., www.eia.gov/tools/faqs/faq.php?id=709&t=6; Energy Information

Administration, "United Arab Emirates: International Energy Data and Analysis," 5, May 18, 2015, www.eia.gov/international/content/analysis/countries_long/united_arab_emirates/uae.pdf.
5 Huh Sung-soon, "South Yemen removes Lenin Statue and Red Stars," *Chosun Ilbo*, June 8, 1990, 4.
6 Kim Chan-ho, "The UAE government's support in Dubai Port World (DP World)'s growth process," *Korea Maritime Institute*, July 2009, 176.
7 Anne M. Hughes, "The future of Gulf ports," *Geography*, 64 (1) (1979), 54.
8 A. R. Walker, "Recessional and Gulf War impacts on port development and shipping in the Gulf States in the 1980s," *GeoJournal* 18 (3) (1989), 274.
9 UAE Central Bank Monthly Statistical Bulletin, June 1986.
10 Hughes, "The future of Gulf ports," 55.
11 Walker, "Recessional and Gulf War impacts on port development," 275.
12 Walker, "Recessional and Gulf War impacts on port development," 277.
13 Index Mundi, "Crude Oil (Petroleum): Dubai Fateh monthly price – US dollars per barrel," n.d., www.indexmundi.com/commodities/?commodity=crude-oil-dubai&months=360.
14 Na Jong-ho, "The status of foreign oil explorations," *Chosun Ilbo*, August 2, 1990, 7.
15 John H. Lichtblau, "Oil imports and national security: Is there still a connection?" *The Energy Journal* 15 (1994), 337.
16 Korea Petroleum Association, "The oil refining capacity," 2018, http://engn.petroleum.or.kr/sub03/02.php; Na Jong-ho, "South Korea-Kuwait trade," *Chosun Ilbo*, August 3, 1990, 7.
17 Chosun-Ilbo, "The U.S. demand cost-sharing in the Persian Gulf," August 31, 1990, 1.
18 Na Jong-ho & Kim Seung-young, "Gas masks distributed to all neighboring countries," January 12, 1991, *Chosun Ilbo*, 3.
19 Kim Chang-soo, "Deployment preparations underway," *Chosun Ilbo*, February 11, 1991, 11.
20 Brian Bridges, "South Korea and the Gulf crisis," *The Pacific Review* 5 (2) (1992), 143.
21 See Timrek Heisler, "C-130 Hercules: Background, sustainment, modernization, issues for Congress," June 24, 2014, *Congressional Research Service*, 6.
22 Kim Seung-yong, "Soaring overseas sales of the US advanced weapons," *Chosun Ilbo*, October 15, 1992, 14.
23 The Congress of the United States Congressional Budget Office, "Limiting conventional arms exports to the Middle East," September 1992, 15–59.
24 Hankyung, "Exports for domestic markets on an exponential rise after the Gulf War," April 12, 1991.
25 Leah Sherwood, "Risk diversification and the United Arab Emirates' foreign policy," in Khalid S. Almezaini & Jean-Marc Rickli (Eds.), *The Small Gulf States: Foreign and Security Policies before and after the Arab Spring* (Abingdon, Oxon: Routledge, 2017), 148–152.
26 Boyko Nikolov, "Russia is offering UAE to produce components for Su-57 fighter jet," *BulgarianMilitary.com*, November 20, 2019, https://bulgarianmilitary.com/2019/11/20/russia-is-offering-uae-to-produce-components-for-su-57-fighter-jet/.
27 Korea Peninsula Energy Development Organization, "About us: Our history," n.d., www.kedo.org/au_history.asp.

28 U.S. Congress House Committee on International Relations Subcommittee on Economic Policy and Trade, *North Korean Military and Nuclear Proliferation Threat: Evaluation of the US-DPRK Agreed Framework* (Washington DC: US Government Printing Office, 1995), 134.
29 Ghaith Abdulla, *The Making of UAE Foreign Policy: A Dynamic Process Model* (Abu Dhabi, UAE: The Emirates Center for Strategic Studies and Research, 2014), 26.
30 Lee Tae-ho, "The government-led "Big Deal" of the five major conglomerates and the obstructed plans of Samsung Motors and LG Semiconductors," *Hankyung*, March 29, 2019, A21.
31 Choi Woo-suk, "Conditions are ripe for plant exports in the Middle East," *Chosun Ilbo*, May 2, 2002, 18.
32 Kwon Hyung Lee et al., *The Logistics Hub Strategies of GCC Countries and Korea's Strategies for Enhancing Cooperation with Saudi Arabia and the UAE* [in Korean] (Seoul: Korea Institute for Economic Policy, 2015), 144.
33 Ibid.
34 Choi Woo-suk, "The pearl of the Middle East: Dubai, UAE," *Chosun Ilbo*, February 2, 2004, B7.
35 Tim McMahon, "Historical crude oil prices (Table): Oil prices 1946-present," *InflationData.com*, 2019, https://inflationdata.com/articles/inflation-adjusted-prices/historical-crude-oil-prices-table/; Lee Kyung-eun, "Number of funds have increased 15 times in five years…global financial companies in a cutthroat competition in the Arab oil producing states," *Chosun Ilbo*, May 17, 2005, B1.
36 Kim Sung-gon, "Hyundai Engineering & Construction wins power plant construction award," *Seoul News*, May 31, 2005.
37 Sun Woo-jung, "Global company power surpasses national power," *Chosun Ilbo*, July 23, 2005, A18.
38 Hankyung, "Revenues for Samsung Electronics and Hyundai Motor Company combined accounts for 20%…deepened dependence on big business," September 5, 2018, B2.
39 Korea Port Engineering Corporation, "Capture Busan new port management rights: Capital contest between Dubai and Singapore," July 7, 2005.
40 Kim, "The UAE government's support in Dubai Port World," 174–175.
41 Sung Ki-hong & Kim Bum-hyun, "President Roh: I was shocked about Dubai," *Yonhap News*, May 15, 2006.
42 Lee Kyung-ha, "IPIC, Hyundai Oilbank invests KRW 210tn in advanced facilities," *Energy & Environment News*, July 19, 2007.
43 Hong Won-sang, "Middle East producers to increase domestic stock market investment," *Chosun Ilbo*, September 27, 2007, B1.
44 Johanna Loock, "10th Anniversary of South Korea's overseas anti-piracy mission," Maritime Security Review, March 26, 2019, www.marsecreview.com/2019/03/10th-anniversary-of-south-koreas-overseas-anti-piracy-mission/
45 Channel A, "North Korea strives to bypass sanctions by trying to export submarines to Somali pirates," *News Clip*, 6:39, July 19, 2018, www.ichannela.com/news/main/news_detailPage.do?publishId=00000010366.
46 Kevin Gray, "Sanctions on North Korea are counterproductive," *Just Security*, November 26, 2019, www.justsecurity.org/67473/sanctions-on-north-korea-are-counterproductive/.

47 Devan Cole & Zachary Cohen, "Trump warns Kim could lose a 'special relationship' after North Korea claims 'important' test at missile site," *CNN Politics*, December 9, 2019, https://edition.cnn.com/2019/12/08/politics/north-korea-donald-trump-test-kim-jong-un/index.html.
48 Samuel Ramani, "North Korea's balancing act in the Persian Gulf," *Huffington Post*, August 17, 2015, www.huffpost.com/entry/north-koreas-balancing-ac_b_7995688.
49 ROK Embassy to UAE, "Notice regarding the seizure of Korean vessels off the coast of Yemen," November 20, 2019, https://overseas.mofa.go.kr/ae-ko/brd/m_11117/view.do?seq=1342004.
50 Carol Huang, "South Korean anti-piracy experts to train UAE," *The National*, June 28, 2011, www.thenationalnews.com/uae/south-korean-anti-piracy-experts-to-train-uae-1.440111.
51 Kuwait News Agency (KUNA), "Last S. Korean troops to head for Iraq on Sept. 25," September 23, 2008, www.kuna.net.kw/ArticleDetails.aspx?id=1939865&language=en.
52 Matthew Carrol & Peter Spreejens, "HE Lee Myung-bak, President of the Republic of Korea – Guest Speaker," *The Business Year*, 2012, 19–20.
53 Tae-Soo Song, Min-Suk Yang & Chong Su Kim, "The Saemangeum Reclamation Project and Politics of Regionalism in South Korea," *Ocean & Coastal Management* 102, part B (2014), 594–603.
54 Eunsook Yang, "South Korean government under the former CEO, President Lee Myung-bak," *UNSCI Discussion Papers*, no. 18 (2008), 127–132.
55 Chung Chul-hwan, "Dubai to implant Korean ventures in the desert: Sheikh Mohammed takes cutting edge technology with new growth model," *Chosun Ilbo*, April 28, 2008, A2.
56 Lee Jun-ho & Kim Beom-jun, *The Study on Legislation and Policy of the Development of Nuclear Energy in UAE* [in Korean] (Seoul: Korea Legislative Research Institute, 2010), 14-16.
57 Sungyeol Choi & Il Soon Hwang, "Nonproliferation drivers from civil nuclear power: South Korea's external constraints and internal beneficiaries," in Karthika Sasikumar (Ed.) *Organizational Cultures and the Management of Nuclear Technology: Political and Military Sociology Annual Review* (New York, NY: Routledge, 2012), 89–92.
58 Sonal Patel & Darrell Proctor, "NRC certifies South Korea's APR1400 nuclear reactor design for US use," *Power Magazine*, May 1, 2019.
59 Korea Hydro & Nuclear Power, "National quality management award: Status manual case study," 2016, 2.
60 Kim Sung-hyun, "70 Years of history and the New Korea (1945–2015): The first groundbreaking ceremony of first nuclear reactor, and Korea became a source of nuclear exports," *Chosun Ilbo*, July 2, 2015, A10.
61 Choi & Hwang, "Nonproliferation drivers from Civil Nuclear Power," 90–91.
62 World Nuclear Association, "World Nuclear Performance Report 2018," August 2018, 5; 15.
63 Ibid.
64 Koh Jae-man, "South Korea's first nuclear power plant Kori unit 1 resigns after 40 years…permanent suspension at 12:00 on 19th," *Maeil Economy*, June 18, 2017, A6.

65 Emmanuel Jarry, "France, UAE sign military and nuclear agreements," *Reuters*, January 15, 2008, www.reuters.com/article/us-france-sarkozy-gulf/france-uae-sign-military-and-nuclear-agreements-idUSL1517472620080116.
66 Oh Yoon-hee, "24 Contracts in Saudi Arabia this year, 48% of total overseas," *Chosun Ilbo*, May 27, 2011, B5.
67 Lee Sung-hoon, "We need to tear down the barrier between civil-military relations to develop $1.6 trillion defense industry," *Chosun Ilbo*, March 9, 2010, A4.
68 ROK Ministry of National Defense, *Defense White Paper 2018* (Seoul: ROK Ministry of National Defense, 2018), 195–196.
69 Mohamed Elaskary, "The Korean Wave in the Middle East: Past and present," *Journal of Open Innovation* 4 (51) (2018), 7.

References

Abdulla, Ghaith. *The Making of UAE Foreign Policy: A Dynamic Process Model* (Abu Dhabi, UAE: The Emirates Center for Strategic Studies and Research, 2014).
Bridges, Brian. "South Korea and the Gulf crisis," *The Pacific Review* 5 (2) (1992), 141–148.
Carrol, Matthew and Peter Spreejens. "HE Lee Myung-bak, President of the Republic of Korea – Guest Speaker," *The Business Year*, 2012.
Channel A. "North Korea strives to bypass sanctions by trying to export submarines to Somali pirates," *News Clip*, 6:39, July 19, 2018, www.ichannela.com/news/main/news_detailPage.do?publishId=00000010366.
Choi, Sungyeol and Il Soon Hwang. "Nonproliferation drivers from civil nuclear power: South Korea's external constraints and internal beneficiaries," in Karthika Sasikumar (Ed.) *Organizational Cultures and the Management of Nuclear Technology: Political and Military Sociology Annual Review* (New York, NY: Routledge, 2012), 85–102.
Choi, Woo-suk. "Conditions are ripe for plant exports in the Middle East," *Chosun Ilbo*, May 2, 2002, 18.
Choi, Woo-suk. "The pearl of the Middle East: Dubai, UAE," *Chosun Ilbo*, February 2, 2004, B7.
Choi, Won-suk. "Kia Motors' thriving business in China and the Middle East," April 21, 2009, *Chosun Ilbo*, B2.
Chosun-Ilbo. "The U.S. demand cost-sharing in the Persian Gulf," August 31, 1990, 1.
Chung, Chul-hwan. "Dubai to implant Korean ventures in the desert: Sheikh Mohammed takes cutting edge technology with new growth model," *Chosun Ilbo*, April 28, 2008, A2.
Cole, Devan and Zachary Cohen. "Trump warns Kim could lose a 'special relationship' after North Korea claims 'important' test at missile site," *CNN Politics*, December 9, 2019, https://edition.cnn.com/2019/12/08/politics/north-korea-donald-trump-test-kim-jong-un/index.html.
The Congress of the United States Congressional Budget Office. "Limiting conventional arms exports to the Middle East," September 1992.
Elaskary, Mohamed. "The Korean Wave in the Middle East: Past and present," *Journal of Open Innovation* 4 (51) (2018), 1–16.

Elhage, Mohamed S. Nuri Erbas, Mitra Farahbaksh, Mangal Goswami and Holger Floeremeier. "The United Arab Emirates: Selected issues & statistical appendix, *International Monetary Fund,* June 17, 2005.

Gray, Kevin. "Sanctions on North Korea are counterproductive," *Just Security,* November 26, 2019, www.justsecurity.org/67473/sanctions-on-north-korea-are-counterproductive/.

Haggard, Stephen, Byung-kook Kim and Chung-in Moon. "The transition to export-led growth in South Korea: 1954-1966, *The Journal of Asian Studies* 50 (4) (1991), 850–873.

Han, Jae-hyun. "International oil prices: Prices vary depending on the Dubai, WTI and Brent Crude origins," *Chosun Ilbo,* August 22, 2002, B12.

Hankyung. "Exports for domestic markets on an exponential rise after the Gulf War," April 12, 1991.

Hankyung. "Revenues for Samsung Electronics and Hyundai Motor Company combined accounts for 20%...deepened dependence on big business," September 5, 2018, B2.

Heisler, Timrek. "C-130 Hercules: Background, sustainment, modernization, issues for congress, June 24, 2014, *Congressional Research Service.*

Hong, Won-sang. "Middle East producers to increase domestic stock market investment," *Chosun Ilbo,* September 27, 2007, B1.

Huang, Carol. "South Korean anti-piracy experts to train UAE," *The National,* June 28, 2011, www.thenationalnews.com/uae/south-korean-anti-piracy-experts-to-train-uae-1.440111.

Hughes, Anne M. "The future of Gulf ports," *Geography* 64 (1) (1979), 54–56.

Huh, Sung-soon. "South Yemen removes Lenin Statue and Red Stars," *Chosun Ilbo,* June 8, 1990, 4.

Index Mundi. "Crude oil (Petroleum): Dubai Fateh monthly price – US dollars per barrel," n.d., www.indexmundi.com/commodities/?commodity=crude-oil-dubai&months=360.

Jarry, Emmanuel. "France, UAE sign military and nuclear agreements," *Reuters,* January 15, 2008, www.reuters.com/article/us-france-sarkozy-gulf/france-uae-sign-military-and-nuclear-agreements-idUSL1517472620080116.

Kim, Chang-soo, "Deployment preparations underway," *Chosun Ilbo,* February 11, 1991, 11.

Kim, Chan-ho. "The UAE government's support in Dubai Port World (DP World)'s growth process," *Korea Maritime Institute,* July 2009.

Kim, Heung-chong. 2002 International commodity market outlooks, *Korea Institute for International Economic Policy,* December 2001.

Kim, Seung-yong. "Soaring overseas sales of the US advanced weapons," *Chosun Ilbo,* October 15, 1992, 14.

Kim, Sung-gon. "Hyundai Engineering & Construction wins power plant construction award," *Seoul News,* May 31, 2005.

Kim, Sung-hyun. "70 Years of history and the New Korea (1945–2015): The first groundbreaking ceremony of first nuclear reactor, and Korea became a source of nuclear exports," *Chosun Ilbo,* July 2, 2015, A10.

Koh, Jae-man. "South Korea's first nuclear power plant Kori unit 1 resigns after 40 years…permanent suspension at 12:00 on 19th," *Maeil Economy,* June 18, 2017, A6.

Korea Hydro & Nuclear Power. "National quality management award: Status manual case study," 2016.

Korea Peninsula Energy Development Organization. "About us: Our history," n.d., www.kedo.org/au_history.asp.

Korea Petroleum Association. "The oil refining capacity," 2018, http://engn.petroleum.or.kr/sub03/02.php.

Korea Port Engineering Corporation. "Capture Busan new port management rights: Capital contest between Dubai and Singapore," July 7, 2005.

Kuwait News Agency (KUNA). "Last S. Korean troops to head for Iraq on Sept. 25," September 23, 2008, www.kuna.net.kw/ArticleDetails.aspx?id=1939865&language=en.

Lee, Jun-ho and Beom-jun Kim. *The Study on Legislation and Policy of the Development of Nuclear Energy in UAE* [in Korean] (Seoul: Korea Legislative Research Institute, 2010).

Lee, Kwon Hyung, Son Sung-hyun, Park Jae-eun and Jang Yun-hee. *The Logistics Hub Strategies of GCC Countries and Korea's Strategies for Enhancing Cooperation with Saudi Arabia and the UAE* [in Korean] (Seoul: Korea Institute for Economic Policy, 2015).

Lee, Kyung-eun. "Number of funds have increased 15 times in five years…global financial companies in a cutthroat competition in the Arab oil producing states," *Chosun Ilbo*, May 17, 2005, B1.

Lee, Kyung-ha. "IPIC, Hyundai Oilbank invests KRW 210tn in advanced facilities," *Energy & Environment News*, July 19, 2007.

Lee, Sung-hoon. "We need to tear down the barrier between civil-military relations to develop $1.6 trillion defense industry," *Chosun Ilbo*, March 9, 2010, A4.

Lee, Tae-ho. "The government-led "Big Deal" of the five major conglomerates and the obstructed plans of Samsung Motors and LG Semiconductors," *Hankyung*, March 29, 2019, A21.

Lichtblau, John H. "Oil imports and national security: Is there still a connection? *The Energy Journal* 15 (1994), 329–346.

Loock, Johanna. "10th anniversary of South Korea's overseas anti-Piracy mission," Maritime Security Review, March 26, 2019, www.marsecreview.com/2019/03/10th-anniversary-of-south-koreas-overseas-anti-piracy-mission/.

McMahon, Tim. "Historical crude oil prices (Table): Oil prices 1946-present," *InflationData.com*, 2019, https://inflationdata.com/articles/inflation-adjusted-prices/historical-crude-oil-prices-table/.

Na, Jong-ho. "The status of foreign oil explorations," *Chosun Ilbo*, August 2, 1990, 7.

Na, Jong-ho. "South Korea-Kuwait trade," *Chosun Ilbo*, August 3, 1990, 7.

Na, Jong-ho and Seung-young Kim. "Gas masks distributed to all neighboring countries," January 12, 1991, *Chosun Ilbo*, 3.

Nikolov, Boyko. "Russia is offering UAE to produce components for Su-57 fighter jet," *BulgarianMilitary.com*, November 20, 2019, https://bulgarianmilitary.com/2019/11/20/russia-is-offering-uae-to-produce-components-for-su-57-fighter-jet/.

Oh, Yoon-hee. "24 Contracts in Saudi Arabia this year, 48% of total overseas," *Chosun Ilbo*, May 27, 2011, B5.

Patel, Sonal and Darrell Proctor. "NRC certifies South Korea's APR1400 nuclear reactor design for US use," *Power Magazine*, May 1, 2019.

Ramani, Samuel. "North Korea's balancing act in the Persian Gulf," *Huffington Post*, August 17, 2015, www.huffpost.com/entry/north-koreas-balancing-ac_b_7995688.

ROK Embassy to UAE. "Notice regarding the seizure of Korean vessels off the coast of Yemen," November 20, 2019, https://overseas.mofa.go.kr/ae-ko/brd/m_11117/view.do?seq=1342004.

ROK Ministry of National Defense. *Defense White Paper 2018* (Seoul: ROK Ministry of National Defense, 2018).

Sherwood, Leah. "Risk diversification and the United Arab Emirates' foreign policy," in Khalid S. Almezaini and Jean-Marc Rickli (Eds.), *The Small Gulf States: Foreign and Security Policies before and after the Arab Spring* (Abingdon, Oxon: Routledge, 2017), 144–167.

Song, Tae-Soo, Min-Suk Yang and Chong Su Kim. "The Saemangeum Reclamation Project and politics of regionalism in South Korea," *Ocean & Coastal Management* 102 (part B) (2014): 594–603.

Sun, Woo-jung, "Global company power surpasses national power," *Chosun Ilbo*, July 23, 2005, A18.

Sung, Ki-hong and Bum-hyun Kim. "President Roh: I was shocked about Dubai," *Yonhap News*, May 15, 2006.

UAE Central Bank. "UAE Central Bank monthly statistical bulletin," June 1986.

US Congress House Committee on International Relations Subcommittee on Economic Policy and Trade. *North Korean Military and Nuclear Proliferation Threat: Evaluation of the US-DPRK Agreed Framework* (Washington DC: US Government Printing Office, 1995).

US Energy Information Administration (EIA). "What countries are the top producers and consumers of oil?" n.d., www.eia.gov/tools/faqs/faq.php?id=709&t=6.

US Energy Information Administration. "United Arab Emirates: International energy data and analysis," 5, May 18, 2015, www.eia.gov/international/content/analysis/countries_long/united_arab_emirates/uae.pdf.

Walker, A. R. "Recessional and Gulf War impacts on port development and shipping in the Gulf States in the 1980s, *GeoJournal* 18 (3) (1989), 273–284.

World Bank. "World Bank Group and Republic of Korea: 60 years of partnership," n.d., http://pubdocs.worldbank.org/en/754261483515257926/Korea-Timeline.pdf.

World Bank. "Gross domestic product 2018," September 19, 2018, https://databank.worldbank.org/data/download/GDP.pdf.

World Nuclear Association. "World Nuclear Performance Report 2018," August 2018.

Yang, Eunsook. "South Korean government under the former CEO, President Lee Myung-bak," *UNSCI Discussion Papers*, no. 18 (2008).

5 Business and security implications after the Gulf wars and post-ISIS Iraq

Introduction

South Korea's diplomatic relations with Iraq date back to June 26, 1981 when the Iraqi Consulate was established in Seoul. Prior to signing the agreement for establishing the Iraqi Consulate in April, Iraq had been a key supplier of crude oil and emerged as a promising market for South Korean construction companies. The 1973 oil embargo dealt a blow to the oil importing countries, including South Korea, which was prompted to devise a contingency plan, such as founding the Mapo Oil Reserve Base in 1978 to make up for the shortage of energy supply. Despite the abundant energy resources in Iraq, the country's frequent exposures to geopolitical risks have led to stunted economic growth and political instability. Over time, South Korea's relations with Iraq have been caught in political crossfire between the Iraqi Federal Government and the Kurdistan Regional Government (KRG).

This chapter explores how South Korea's foreign policy identity as a middle power has been shaped by the country's commercial interests in Iraq since the Iran–Iraq War and the 1991 Gulf War and South Korea's alliance commitment to the U.S. More specifically, it examines the commercial and strategic implications of South Korea's military contributions to the 1991 Gulf War and the 2003 Iraq War and offers a survey of South Korea's energy security policy in Iraq.

The economic and strategic implications of the first two Gulf wars

On the eve of the Iran–Iraq War, there was an estimate of 739 Korean construction workers based in Basra who decided to flee from Iraq to Kuwait via Safwan border crossing. On the other side of the border, South Korea's Hyundai E&C in Kuwait was preparing for logistical support to transport Korean construction workers crossing the border from Iraq, but the plan was aborted as Kuwait, which hosted 17 Korean companies, banned the entry of foreigners into its soil.[1] As a consequence, Korean workers who were held in Iraq and Kuwait were transferred to field offices in neighboring countries

DOI: 10.4324/9781003092100-5

in the Middle East, including Saudi Arabia. The agility to which Korean construction companies were able to transfer its workers within the region attests to the extensive network of South Korean companies that entered the Middle Eastern construction market.

As South Korea's economic footprints expanded in the region, there were clear trade-offs between commercial interests and geopolitical volatility; it increased its geoeconomic stakes in the region and unwittingly jeopardized the security of South Korean expatriates, including in the geopolitical flashpoint between Iraq and Iran. On May 23, 1982, Kurdistan Democratic Party (KDP)'s European office announced that two South Koreans were abducted by Kurdish Iraqi guerrilla fighters. It also took two French citizens hostage and demanded that the Iraqi government release detained Kurdish activists. Due to restricted access to Iraqi Kurdistan, the ROK Ministry of Foreign Affairs sought to negotiate for the release of two hostages through multi-track diplomacy. In addition to hostage crisis, South Korean nationals were increasingly becoming exposed to oil tanker attacks, including in an attack by Iraqi planes on an Iranian oil field off the coast of Kharg Island in 1985, which claimed the lives of two Korean sailors on board. Joint militaristic and diplomatic interventions, political savviness, and cultural awareness have become vital as piracy incidents, abductions of foreign nationals, and oil tanker seizures became more commonplace.

The ROK Ministry of Foreign Affairs and Ministry of Employment and Labor proposed phased plans for evacuating its nationals for ten Korean construction companies by the mid-1980s as the number of Koreans in Iraq and Iran combined reached 15,000. Korean residents in Iraq were by and large concentrated in Baghdad and Basra – with an estimate of 8,000 and 1,000 laborers, respectively.[2] Despite precarious geopolitics, by the mid-1980s, Iraq emerged as the second most promising market for the construction sector in the Middle East after Saudi Arabia. At the same time, South Korea was vying for competition in the Iraqi construction sector against Chinese companies in civil construction and engineering, which was reputed for cost-effectiveness by tendering bids at the lowest price.

As part of post-war reconstruction efforts, Iraq constructed a grand canal between Tigris and Euphrates rivers by confiscating heavy machineries worth billions of dollars from foreign construction companies operating in Iraq. Although Korean construction companies initially had to evacuate its staff from field offices in Iran and Iraq, post-war reconstruction Iraq also created fertile ground for post-war reconstruction projects in the construction sector. In August 1988, shortly after the ceasefire, Korea Institute of Economics and Technology estimated that construction tenders from Iran and Iraq combined would amount to $15–$17 bn. In addition to construction project orders, South Korea's exports to Iraq also received a boost, with trade revenues worth $5.3 bn.[3] However, despite the sanguine outlook, as a whole, Seoul was only able to clinch less than 1% of all contracts as the post-war reconstruction market in Iraq was dominated by American companies.[4]

The aftermath of the Iran–Iraq War had severe economic repercussions, including the militarization of the economy, stagnant growth in the energy, industrial, and agricultural sectors, inflation, and privatization inertia.[5] After the eight-year Iran–Iraq War turned out to be fruitless, Saddam Hussein looked to divert the public attention away from the economic and political failings of the Baath regime by embarking on a new foreign adventure. Reclaiming oil-rich Kuwait as Iraq's lost province became the main catalyst for assembling a Republican Guard division of 10,000 men and 300 tanks north of Kuwait on July 15, 1990, which later increased to a deployment of 140,000 Iraqi soldiers and 1,800 tanks.[6] In response to Iraq's invasion of Kuwait on August 2, 1990, the U.S. Congress passed a bill authorizing the use of force against Iraqi aggression on Kuwait on January 14, 1991.[7]

During the 1991 Gulf War, the South Korean Embassy in Baghdad remained operating with one staff. Hyundai E&C, which had $1.3 bn worth of accounts receivable from construction projects, also stayed behind.[8] As a result, after the initial review by the UN Compensation Commission, a subsidiary organ of the UN established in 1991, the ROK Ministry of Foreign Affairs offered Hyundai E&C over $5 mn in war compensation.[9] Considering its commercial stakes and given the presence of 1,300 Koreans in Iraq and Kuwait, Seoul withheld from taking a position apart from declaring that it is opposed to the use of force. South Korea's Ministry of Foreign Affairs spokesperson took a softer approach toward Iraq and released a press statement on August 2, 1990 encouraging Iraq to resolve the conflict peacefully and urged the Iraqi forces to retreat from Kuwait at the earliest possible date. Iraq deliberately took the foreigners hostage as a way of diverting attention away from the looming prospects of an arms embargo. Although the U.S. spearheaded the efforts to coalesce its allies to impose an arms embargo, it faced opposition from France and Russia. By September 1990, the permanent members of the UN Security Council convened a meeting to resolve an air blockade of all civilian cargo and freight aircrafts to and from Iraq and occupied Kuwait.

Seoul was cautiously observing the developments on the ground before deciding on what course of action to take. It was mulling over the decision to deploy troops for the U.S.-led coalition forces. According to declassified documents released by the ROK Ministry of Foreign Affairs in March 2021, the U.S. had pressurized South Korea into supporting the Gulf War in response to Roh Tae-woo's Nordpolitik, claiming that South Korea sought closer ties with Russia at the expense of Korea–U.S. relations.[10] In anticipation that Iraq's position would be undermined by Saddam Hussein's foreign policy miscalculations and the international imposition of sanctions, Seoul finally caved in to U.S. pressure and endorsed sanctions against Iraq as a non-UN member state. The UNSC held a plenary meeting on August 25, 1990 and passed the UNSC resolution 665 (1990) on approving the use of military force against Iraq's invasion of Kuwait. The resolution served the purpose of justifying U.S. military intervention in Iraq and sanctioning against Iraq. Not long thereafter, former U.S. Assistant Secretary of State for East Asian and Pacific Affairs Richard Solomon pushed Seoul to make military contributions. Citing security reasons, Seoul was reluctant to dispatch troops. The effectiveness of military interventions and the rationale for contributing troops had been called into question during the Vietnam War; yet military expenditures during the 1991 Gulf War were estimated to outweigh that of Korean War. The total number of troops and military equipment that went into three weeks of Gulf War was equivalent to three months of military expenditure during the Korean War.[11]

As the first war in the post-Cold War period, George H.W. Bush's administration was deploying the largest military force since the Vietnam War. To avoid direct military involvement, Seoul suggested that it would at best offer military supplies and equipment in a form of "symbolic support."[12] South Korea's emphasis on "symbolic support" is attributed to the lucrative construction contracts won in Iraq. Due to its commercial interests, Seoul reluctantly offered morale support for the U.S.-led coalition in the Gulf War. In the meantime, America's APAC allies Japan and Australia vowed to increase their financial and military contributions. ROK and Japan, however, were largely criticized by *Washington Post* for initially dragging their feet in exacting sanctions on Iraq and for refusing to become directly involved in military interventions. Seoul's moral obligations for supporting the U.S. were invoked on the basis of the history of the UN Command dispatching troops to the Korean War. However, the South Korean government was also facing foreign policy dilemmas and was reluctant to become involved in politically sensitive issues.

In a House Foreign Affairs Committee hearing held on September 20, 1990, the Democrats and subcommittee chairman Stephen Solarz and Ohio representative Thomas Luken both claimed that its allies, including South Korea, should do more to shoulder the burden of the costs of the war as beneficiaries of U.S.-led UN Command and U.S. military contributions. However, the U.S. officials also acknowledged that South Korea was the first country to offer logistical support for the U.S. in the 1991 Gulf War.[13] The ROK Ministry of Defense deployed 150 military medical personnel to northeastern Saudi Arabia, following the approval from the National Assembly. In addition to exacting sanctions, Washington also requested military aid from Seoul following Iraq's occupation of Kuwait. The type of military aid, however, was not munitions for wartime operations, but was basic supplies such as military uniforms, military boots, medicines, and gas masks in the event that conflict intensifies.[14] Initially, Korean residents in Kuwait assembled in clusters of families by settling in temporary makeshift shelters as they took instructions from the ROK Embassy.

South Korea's participation in the 1991 Gulf War was primarily viewed as an alliance commitment to the U.S. A survey conducted by the Ministry of Information and Communication via Gallup Korea in February 1992 reveals that 59.1% of the respondents were in favor of pledging an additional financial assistance of $280 mn and sending five additional military transport aircrafts to the Gulf War. The largest proportion of respondents (41.1%) identified national interests as the primary reason for supporting the deployment of multinational forces. Moreover, 34.4% of the survey respondents also viewed ROK–U.S. ties positively.[15] South Korean construction companies embarked on large-scale post-reconstruction projects in Kuwait from May 1991. Apart from commercial interests, Seoul reciprocated to the military contribution of the UN forces during the Korean War by dispatching troops to UN multinational forces in the Gulf War. However, civil society organizations, including a coalition of 24 women's civil society organizations such as Korean Church Women's Association, released a statement protesting the dispatch of Korean citizens and using tax to support the expenses for the Gulf War. In particular, concerns were raised about financing the costs of the war that did not enjoy widespread support from Korean citizens. These civil societies organized a debate on South Korea's military dispatch to the 1991 Gulf War which was attended by U.S. Ambassador Donald Gregg, Iraqi Deputy Ambassador Burhan Ghazal, and ROK Defense Minister Lee Jong-gu.

The prospects for protracted conflicts in the Middle East affected oil supply, the safety of Korean workers in the region, and the route of cargo ship passing through the economic corridor from Seoul to Tripoli and other vessels and oil tankers sailing toward the Strait of Hormuz. Abductions took place during the 1991 Gulf War, as Hyundai E&C employee Kim yong-ho, a Korean worker in Kuwait City, who was mistaken for a Thai worker was taken hostage with 100 other Thai workers by the Iraqi military command while two other Korean employees from the same company went missing.[16] On August 4, the ROK Ministry of Foreign Affairs held a meeting with Iraqi Deputy Ambassador to South Korea Burhan Ghazal and expressed concerns regarding escalating geopolitical tensions in the Middle East and the safety of three Korean workers who were abducted by Iraqi soldiers. Ghazal confirmed that the Iraqi Revolutionary Command Council planned to withdraw Iraqi troops from Kuwait the next day. In the following year, five Korean construction workers from Hyundai E&C who were crossing the Iran–Iraq border during the Gulf War were abducted by Kurdish rebels after being held in Kirkuk. Since South Korea does not have diplomatic relations with Syria, the ROK Ministry of Foreign Affairs sent a diplomatic note to the Iranian, Turkish, and Jordanian Ministries of Foreign Affairs calling for an immediate release of the detained construction workers.

Since the early 1990s, South Korea's trade with Iraq and Kuwait shared similar characteristics such as the volume of imports exceeding exports from both countries, with crude oil and petroleum products accounting for over 90% of total imports. The 1991 Gulf War was an alarming development for resource-poor South Korea as it is dependent on the Middle East for crude oil supply. By 1990, Iraq and Kuwait combined comprised of 11.8% of the total import volume.[17] Taken as a whole, Iraq and Kuwait were minor trading partners for South Korea, yet they remained strategically important sources of oil suppliers for Seoul's energy security. Though the trade volume was relatively less, South Korea's exports to the Middle East were much more diversified in comparison to what it imported from Middle Eastern markets. To illustrate, South Korea exported $82 mn worth of textiles, rubber, and steel products and imported $125 mn of crude oil from Iraq. The volume of South Korea's crude oil imports from Iraq in terms of the absolute volume of trade recovered in the early 2010s following the Global Financial Crisis of 2007–2008; the rate of oil imports dropped again between 2014 and 2017 at the peak of the military operation against Islamic State and rose again in 2018.[18]

As the 1991 Gulf War became imminent, the Ministry of Construction formed a Special Committee on the Gulf Crisis presided over by Lee Huikyung, the then Minister of Economic Planning. Korean construction companies were facing financial pressures and were short of KW 70.9 bn in operating fund.[19] The financial pressure was fueled by the surge in oil prices and economic sanctions imposed on Iraq. According to the Bank of Korea, By 1990, Iraq and Kuwait combined owed $120 mn of debt to South Korea.[20] Seoul's bond issued to these countries is by and large export receivables while its debts to Iraq are local currencies and securities it purchased from Iraq.[21] The economic repercussions of the Gulf War were also manifested through South Korea's decline in exports to 8 of 11 trading partners in the region including Iraq and Kuwait and to a lesser extent, Saudi Arabia. South Korea was barred from trading with Iraq due to economic sanctions while its trade with Saudi Arabia's private sector contracted due to factors associated with war such as shortage of foreign exchange and increased risk in maritime transportation in the UAE, Egypt, Bahrain, Jordan, and Yemen. By contrast, South Korea's volume of trade with Lebanon, Syria, and Oman was projected to be on the rise due to the rise in purchasing power concomitant with the increased oil production and rising demands for daily necessities and military supplies.[22]

In August 1990, South Korea's total number of overseas construction contracts from Iraq was between $500 mn and $600 mn.[23] To ensure continued access to LNG and to diversify the supply of energy importers for the impending Gulf crisis, South Korea also established economic partnership with Indonesia and jointly invested in Indonesia's gas field in Madura, which turned out to be Seoul's first overseas gas development. In addition to Middle Eastern markets, Indonesia supplied 4.2% of South Korea's crude oil imports by September 1990.[24] By 1993, the Gulf War and the foiled coup attempt against Muammar Qaddafi in Libya dampened the prospects for the construction sector in the MENA.

The sight of the war was gruesome; at Saddam Hussein's command an Iraqi Brigadier General was executed in public square facing the Kuwait Ministry of Interior after being charged for looting. Given the heavy-handedness of Saddam Hussein Baath regime, there was little to suspect about the fall of the Iraqi forces at the time. Apart from the militaristic dimension, Baathist rhetoric and symbols served as a mechanism for ensuring the survival of the regime as well as fostering a collective solidarity and as a rallying cry for supporting the three conflicts.[25] In the 1991 Gulf War, banks closed down and abductions, looting, and shooting ensued. Iraqi soldiers went from house to house inspecting Kuwaiti citizens. As the conflict progressed, South Korean residents in Kuwait fled the country by taking an overland route to Amman. While many were relieved that they were able to return safely back to South Korea, others were lamenting over property damage or having left the country empty-handed – and still others demanded compensation for property loss.

The UNSC embargo imposed between August 1990 and April 1991 against Iraq was destructive insofar as imposing a ban on all trade, including an oil embargo, arms embargo, freezing of Iraqi government's financial assets abroad, and suspension of international flights.[26] South Korea was equally apprehensive about an imminent oil shock. In light of this, the National Assembly's council held a hearing where analysts made forecasts of oil prices that were predicted to surge up to $50-60 dollars per barrel in the possible scenario of an all-out war.[27] In the meantime, the Ministry of Power and Resources (currently renamed as the Ministry of Knowledge Economy) prepared a contingency plan to tighten restrictions on oil consumption targeting both industrial users and consumers in South Korea, including an agenda to curb power supply. Ten ship building companies in South Korea such as Hanjin Shipping, Honam Tanker, Yugong Shipping, and Beomyang Merchant Marine were likewise scrambling for a solution as they were directly impacted by volatile oil prices in securing fuel for ships. Moreover, trade deficits following the Gulf War were estimated to be around $1–$1.5 bn.[28] Accordingly, the Ministry of Finance provided support by giving an extension for the processing of export bills to Iraq and Kuwait, established an emergency hotline with Korean banks, and created emergency funds.

In the post-Gulf War period, South Korea's import of conventional weapons increased by 46% from 1994 to 1995 against the backdrop of the rise in military expenditure in China and the broader APAC. Arms imports in the Middle East accounted for 23% of the global arms trade by 1995 when arms embargo was imposed on Iraq.[29] The then U.S. Secretary of Defense Les Aspin also reviewed the defense cost-sharing agreements for hosting American troops and commended South Korea for having the highest share of defense costs among the U.S. allies throughout the Gulf War.[30] By April 1993, Seoul had a record share of 78% of burden-sharing costs for the U.S. military presence in the Korean Peninsula. Seoul's military cost-sharing had steadily increased throughout the progression of the Gulf War between 1991 and 1993, with burden-sharing costs constituting up to 73% in 1991, 76% in 1992, and 78% in 1993.[31]

Tensions reignited in January 1993 with the launch of cruise missile strikes on Iraq by the U.S., Britain, and France in retaliation to Saddam Hussein's violation of UNSC resolutions. The charges included Saddam Hussein directing the Iraqi Intelligence Service's assassination attempt on former U.S. President George H.W. Bush and the Emir of Kuwait; sponsoring and sheltering terrorist organizations such as Mujahedin-eKhalq (MEK), Palestine Liberation Front, and Abu Nidal Organization and family members of terrorists (i.e. suicide and homicide bombers); offering training to Iraqi and non-Iraqi terrorists in Salman Pak, a clandestine terrorist training camp.[32] Saddam Hussein also declared *Jihad* [holy war] against the multinational forces that launched an air raid on Iraq's no-fly zone and Saudi Arabia during the Gulf War in a live broadcast on CNN and later again in a statement released during the 2003 U.S. invasion of Iraq.[33]

During a meeting hosted by The Korea Society in New York, the then Assistant Secretary of State for East Asian and Pacific affairs Richard Solomon pointed out that North Korea is a major weapons supplier to Iraq and insinuated that North Korea had also been cooperating with Russia for the provision of Iraq's chemical and biological weapons.[34] Despite the geographic remoteness of Iraq, the possibility of Pyongyang's provocation was raised presuming that it would take advantage of the U.S. security vacuum on the Korean Peninsula with the outbreak of the Gulf War. With the rise of détente, there was a decline in U.S. military spending and Seoul and Washington downsized the scale of joint U.S.–ROK Team Spirit military exercise from 200,000 to 180,000 in 1991. The Iraqi government objected to Seoul's deployment of military medical unit but maintained cordial relations with Seoul in other arenas. Seoul dispatched five C-130 Hercules transport aircraft, 150 support agent and additional military equipment such as helmets, clothing, barbed wire, automobile, batteries, tires, and emergency food rations in February 1991.

In spite of the ambivalent relationship between South Korea and Iraq when it came to strategic interests, South Korea continued to adopt a pragmatic policy toward Iraq by expanding commercial partnerships. Commercial ties were fostered by closely coordinating between the Ministry of Foreign Affairs, Ministry of Trade and Industry, Korea Federation of Textile Industries, and KOTRA and by convening meetings with Iraqi government and business counterparts. The South Korean business delegation also petitioned to the Iraqi government to remove South Korea from Iraq's list of unfriendly countries. By 1999, South Korea was neither included in Iraq's list of friendly nor unfriendly countries list, but it aimed to be re-designated as a friendly country in hopes of boosting commercial ties. Though South Korea was initially ranked as the 11th friendly trading partner to Iraq, it was taken off the "friendly country" list due to a number of political reasons, including participating in the 1991 Gulf War and publicly backing the joint U.S. and British air raids in Iraq in December 1998. Though sanctions had not been completely lifted by then, Iraq's oil-for-food program was established by the UN in 1995 which allowed for Iraq to legally trade oil in exchange for food and humanitarian relief to the Iraqi people. The controversial oil-for-food program was exploited by Saddam Hussein and his officials who were benefited from the kickbacks induced by artificially deflated prices of Iraqi oil as well as dispensing oil vouchers in the form of bribery to global leaders in the UN.[35]

Business arrangements were temporarily brought to a halt by President Clinton's order on an airstrike on Iraq, referred to by the code name

Operation Desert Fox, from December 16 to December 19, 1998. In a press conference on the eve of the airstrike, former U.S. Secretary of State Madeleine Albright declared that the U.S. had received strong backing from allies, including South Korea, Japan, Canada, and the EU. As the U.S. launched a bombing campaign on Iraq, the ROK Ministry of Oceans and Fisheries prepared contingency measures for South Korea-flagged ships that were en-route to Iraq. Even during the brief airstrike on Iraq, it was presumed that the U.S. attack would create a deterrence effect for North Korea at the same time as creating a security vacuum in East Asia. On the other hand, Seoul was relatively resilient to the economic impact of the airstrike, including surges in oil prices and trade deficits which were considered to be minimal as Seoul's exports to Iraq annually amounted to $1 mn a year and the global share of Iraqi crude oil was only 1%.[36] As international oil prices stabilized at the turn of the century, there were sanguine projections about a revitalized construction sector in the Middle East and the possibility of rolling out massive scale reconstruction projects in Iraq. Yet at the same time, there were also concerns regarding structural and political impediments such as fiscal insolvency and disputes over account receivables in war-torn Iraq. As commercial activities of Korean companies were significantly hampered by prolonged conflicts and economic sanctions against Iraq, automaker Daewoo Motors launched an automotive manufacturing plant in Hanoi in 2001 and exported 500 buses to Iraq via a third country to circumvent sanctions. As the UN-imposed sanctions relief became imminent, the state-funded KOTRA's Baghdad field office reopened in October 1999 after being closed down for eight years while economic sanctions were put in place. By early 2000s, automakers and electronics companies such as LG Electronics and Hyundai, Kia, and Daewoo were preparing to resume exports to Iraq via their production facilities in Egypt and were considering opening a field office in Baghdad shortly after Egypt and Iraq signed an FTA agreement.

The Baghdad–Pyongyang security nexus

Historically, Iraq's relations with North Korea date back to 1968 but ties were briefly cut in 1980 with the inception of Iran–Iraq War and were re-established in 2008. In April 1976, North Korean Vice Premier Kong Jin Tae also visited Iraq and met with President Ahmed Hassan al-Bakr on a four-day visit and showed great interest in reconstruction projects and offering support for social development.[37] Regardless of the differential treatment between the Iraqi and North Korean regimes, they were symbolically bound up with the branding of rogue states and subject to antagonistic U.S. foreign policy. The George W. Bush administration took a different approach toward the two states as the former was perceived as a greater threat than the latter, which was not based on nuclear capabilities, but based on historical, political, and strategic grounds.[38]

146 *Security implications after the Gulf wars*

In November 1997, the ROK Ministry of Foreign Affairs spokesperson condemned Iraq's rogue behavior and reiterated its position of endorsing UNSC Resolution 1137 (1997) and Security Council Chairman's statement no. 45 and no. 59 which called on Iraq to implement the UNSC resolutions after tensions escalated with disarmament crisis.[39] In response, North Korea blasted South Korea for backing the U.S. airstrike on Iraq in December 1998, and as reported through the state-run Korean Central Television (KCTV), they perceived the assault on Iraq as a threat to their very own nuclear program. Two South Korean nuclear inspectors joined the IAEA nuclear inspection team in Iraq in 1998. Prior to the nuclear inspection activities in Iraq, South Korean nuclear scientists had joined the UN Special Commission for the inspection of WMDs. With the Iraqi arms inspection put in place, there was a plunge in international oil prices, which fell to the lowest levels in 46 months since Iraq signed the nuclear arms inspection agreement.

In addition to nuclear capabilities, Iraq also gained reputation as one of the world's top ten countries with cyber warfare capabilities alongside Russia and China. Contrary to what had been known at the time, the Iraqi air defense system was vulnerable to disruption through cyber-attacks from the U.S.-led coalition during the launch of Operation Desert Storm.[40] After the Gulf War, Baghdad and Pyongyang's rogue behaviors were under the radar. As Iraq was subjected to IAEA's nuclear inspection in 1998, the U.S. Navy transferred 18 F-15E fighter jets and two AC-130 Gunship aircraft to Iraq to prepare for a possible armed assault in the event that Baghdad objected to the activities of the UN nuclear inspectors in Iraq. Iraq and North Korea had been first designated as state sponsors of international terrorism by the U.S. State Department in 1979 and 1988, respectively. Iraq was listed as state sponsor of terrorism between 1979 and 1982 and was back on the list between 1990 and 2004.[41] In 2001, former U.S. Secretary of Defense William Cohen singled out Iran, Iraq, and North Korea as the three biggest threats to the U.S. Further to this, Iraq and North Korea were also featured as among the most repressive and 11 worst-rated countries list in Freedom House's Freedom in the World Index 2000–2001.[42]

Though economic sanctions are regarded as a chief instrument of coercive diplomacy and a popular means for reining in on rogue regimes, the efficacy of economic sanctions continued to generate heated debates. South Korean civil society organizations engaged robust discussions on the provision of food aid and humanitarian relief and advocated for agricultural cooperation between global North-South relations.[43] Further to this, by 1999 former U.S. Secretary of Defense William Perry declared U.S. administration's policy toward North Korea a failure. Perry noted that the biggest concern for the U.S. policy circles was neither Iraq nor Kosovo, but North Korea and advised diplomatic engagement rather than following a policy of disengagement or deterrence.[44] Debates surrounding the efficacy of sanctions carried on into the Bush administration. Bush's hawkish foreign policy posture was perceived by some analysts as complementary to the Clinton administration's "weak approach" to Iraq. The Democrat senator Thomas Daschle suggested that while North Korea, Iran, and Iraq jointly constituted a threat to the U.S., they are fundamentally different actors. But rather than commenting directly about the nuclear capabilities or rogue behavior, one of the main reasons that a different strategy was suggested toward Pyongyang was largely due to its proximity to U.S. allies, namely South Korea and Japan. However, the cursory assessment was given before North Korea launched its first nuclear test in 2006 and before it withdrew from the NPT in 2003. Former U.S. Secretary of State Colin Powell, on the other hand, posited that Iraq was the greatest threat among rogue regimes as unlike North Korea and Iran, as it was unwilling to engage in dialogue.[45]

While analogies were commonly drawn between and on the treatment of rogue regimes, the Clinton administration pursued sharply contrasting strategies toward Iraq and North Korea. In order to put an end to the North Korea missile program, the Clinton administration offered food aid and regular satellite launches and sought a political solution through diplomatic channels, albeit with limited success.[46] By contrast, the Clinton administration's dual containment policy on Iraq and Iran was predicated on three methods for containing the influence of "backlash states," a term coined by former national security advisor Anthony Lake – isolation, pressure, diplomatic and economic measures.[47] The U.S. containment of Iraq was arguably more potent and vigorous than that of Iran. The U.S. enforced no-fly zones over Iraq and the key provisions of UNSC Resolution 715 (1991) entailed monitoring Iraq's WMD programs. Baghdad and Pyongyang were not only collectively referred to as rogue states for developing weapons of mass destruction but claims on ballistic missile cooperation between the two countries in 2006 found that Iraq was funding the construction of a Scud missile manufacturing plant in Sudan for its own use with North Koreans building and running the plant.[48] In 1997, Pyongyang was manufacturing 150 Scud-C missiles and selling them to Iraq, Egypt, and Syria. South Korea, on the other hand, signed an additional protocol safeguards agreement with the IAEA in June 1999 which subjected the country's nuclear facilities to stringent regulations.

In the post-Cold War period, Iraq and North Korea figured prominently in the two-war framework. Deterrence was the underlying logic of the two-war framework, for which the U.S. tried to deter attacks on its allies while engaging in a major combat. The size of the U.S. Army was reduced by 15% under the Clinton administration's two-war framework which applied to Iraq and North Korea. As an alternative to the two-war framework was the 1-4-2-1 framework which was predicated on defending the homeland while maintaining a strong presence in the regional theaters of Europe, the Gulf, northeast Asia, and the Pacific rim.[49] By featuring the rogue regimes in the "Axis of Evil" speech, President Bush effectively sabotaged Kim Dae-jung's Sunshine policy toward Pyongyang. The U.S. under the Bush administration was faced with the dual challenge of pacifying Iraq and disarming North

Korea by cooperating with Beijing and negotiating with Pyongyang. The failure of the Bush administration to control Iraq and disarm North Korea in the aftermath of the 2003 Iraq War and the collapsed six-party talks marked the demise of American global hegemony in the early 21st century.[50]

The 2003 Iraq War and the dispatch of Seohee, Jema, and Zaytun units

In October 2002, the Congress authorized military action against Iraq and George W. Bush prepared the U.S. for another war with Iraq. The 2003 Iraq War, however, was arguably one of the most controversial foreign policy decisions in recent history.[51] Amid pressures to contribute troops to the U.S.-led multinational force, South Korea tried to play up the image of contributing to humanitarian and post-war reconstruction efforts through the dispatch of 1,180 noncombatant troops for Seohee and Jema units that were stationed for a year in southern Iraq between April 2003 and 2004.[52] While the 1991 Gulf War is frequently juxtaposed with the 2003 Iraq War, the latter fundamentally differs from the former in that it lacked legitimacy and international consensus and elicited negative public opinion for military intervention. Former weapons inspectors found that Saddam Hussein had no WMD capability – at least not one that was deemed threatening to the U.S.[53] The strategic importance accorded to Iraq as the world's second-largest oil reserve, a key source of oil supply outside the U.S., and the interconnection between petro-military-industrial complex were the main drivers behind the U.S. invasion of Iraq.[54] Reflecting the widespread international anti-war sentiment, Korean–Iraqi anti-war peace organizations and 15,000 peace activists were engaged in large-scale anti-war demonstrations in Baghdad and across seven cities in South Korea in March 2003. These peace activists were vehemently opposed to the war and declared, "If we cannot stop the war in Iraq, we cannot stop the war on the Korean peninsula."[55]

Since the start of the war, security alert was raised to high alert in September 2004. Both South Korean and American officials were alerted about intelligence on a possible terrorist attack from Al-Qaeda in retaliation to South Korea's troop deployment to Iraq. Upon receiving requests from Washington to send additional troops, the South Korean government confirmed in June 2004 that it was dispatching additional troops to northern Iraq. As a result, South Korea dispatched 18,000-strong Zaytun unit to Erbil and 1,300-strong Daiman unit to Kuwait between April 2004 to December 2008. From 2004 and 2008, South Korea became the third-largest country with foreign military contingent in Iraq. This put additional pressures on South Korea, where there was a lack of cultural awareness about the Iraqi political climate and the Iraqi demographics which consists of the Sunni Iraqis, Shia Iraqis, and Iraqi Kurds.[56]

In spite of the banner of "collaborative governance," Roh's foreign policy also created a sharp divide between public opinion and foreign policy. The

Roh Moo-hyun administration strategically backed the Bush administration's hawkish foreign policy posture which justified a preemptive attack on Iraq against the proliferation of WMDs – which flew in the face of the rising anti-war sentiment. These decisions were Roh's strategic calculus to use the 2003 Iraq War as a bargaining chip for negotiating on the North Korean issue. In an interview given to Newsweek in March 2003, Roh stressed that North Korea should be treated as a negotiator rather than a criminal.[57] However, in supporting its rogue regime counterpart in the Middle East, Pyongyang censured Seoul for "playing with fire[58]" and for taking sides with the U.S. While Pyongyang's response had been more rhetorical in nature, since regime security is at stake, from Pyongyang's perspective, they had all the reasons to lash out against Washington's decision to lure South Korea into the cause of toppling the Saddam Hussein regime. Any actions that were taken against rogue regimes, especially involving the U.S., were considered as a direct threat to North Korea. In fact, in March 2003, South Korea's former Prime Minister Goh Kun warned that the 2003 Iraq War might spark renewed tensions on the Korean Peninsula. At the same time, speculations were also raised about the possibility of North Korea's resumption of nuclear activities and military aggressions. Based on transactional diplomacy, Bush reciprocated to Roh's support thrown behind the war efforts by reaffirming U.S. commitment to supporting peace on the Korean Peninsula by promoting dialogue and diplomatic efforts.[59] In line with Roh's public backing of the 2003 Iraq War, the Roh administration deployed an additional 3,000 troops to Iraq in April 2004. While public opinion was divided along party lines and civil societies were opposed to the decision, as was the case with successive administrations such decisions were defended on the grounds of protecting national interests. It was projected that additional deployment of troops would indirectly bolster South Korea's economic prospects by generating revenues by facilitating the entry of Korean companies into the post-war reconstruction market in Iraq as well as strengthening South Korea's alliance with the U.S.

Amid the 2003 Iraq War, a poll conducted by AP-Ipsos found mixed results among 1,000 participants in nine countries around the world, including Germany, France, UK, Canada, Italy, Spain, Mexico, South Korea, and the U.S. The survey results suggested that populations from Mexico, Spain and South Korea were particularly pessimistic to the outlook of Iraq in the post-Saddam era, whereas over half of Americans and Britons responded that Iraq is better off after Saddam Hussein was deposed from power.[60] These polarized results came in spite of the U.S. toppling Saddam Hussein early on during the invasion. The progression of the war implied that the conflict was far from over, implying that earlier expectations of a quick, decisive U.S. victory, which was limited to military and political victory, were overhyped. The early military defeat did not help mitigate the underlying issue of political fragmentation (i.e. sectarianism) of the society and Iraq, as was the case with Syria, quickly became a breeding ground for terrorist activities, namely the Islamic State of Iraq and Syria (ISIS).

150 *Security implications after the Gulf wars*

The 2003 Iraq War did not produce any tangible benefits apart from the political gains from deposing Saddam Hussein. The fact that George W. Bush and Tony Blair's claims that Iraq possessed WMDs turned out to be a hoax was also a major reason behind the backlash faced by South Korean public. As a consequence, South Korea and Italy were among the first countries to announce troop drawdown from Iraq. South Korea announced that it would draw down roughly half of its troops by 2007. At the time, it was also estimated that six other countries would either reduce or pull out their troops entirely by late 2006.

South Korea was also concerned about the implications of growing antiwar sentiment in the Middle East on its national image. Although South Korea was not a party to the 2003 Iraq War, it was perceived as a major participant in the war by virtue of its longstanding alliance with the U.S.[61] Nevertheless, Zaytun unit's contribution to humanitarian and security efforts in Northern Iraq was well-received by the then Erbil governor Nawzad Hadi Mawlood who had officially requested the South Korean government to redeploy on behalf of the Erbil governorate and Kurdistan Regional Government.[62] In order to enhance South Korea's national image and to bolster public diplomacy in the Middle East, President Roh commissioned four ministers, from the Ministries of Foreign Affairs, Defense, Trade, Industry and Energy, and Construction and Transportation to the region in 2004, including to Saudi Arabia and Egypt. To promote humanitarian initiatives, Korean hospital also opened in 2010 in Erbil, where Zaytun unit was stationed.

As the war waged on, South Koreans in Iraq became targets in a string of criminal and terrorist threats. Abductions, shooting spree, robbery, and theft became prevalent in conjunction with anti-U.S. insurgency in Iraq. A South Korean diplomat was also kidnapped and threatened to leave Iraq in October 2003, and two months later, two Koreans were killed, and two other nationals injured in Saddam Hussein's hometown, Tikrit, which was another incident involving four employees of a subcontractor for a transmission line construction for the U.S. military. Moreover, U.S. security vacuum resurfaced as a concern as the U.S. troops stationed in South Korea and Germany were transferred to Iraq. By June 2003, the U.S. announced that it would withdraw 12,500 troops from South Korea. However, the public opinion had turned against the hosting of U.S. troops and they were on different wavelengths on foreign policy issues, namely on American foreign policy on the 2003 Iraq War and North Korea. This follows the anti-U.S. sentiment which had taken on new heights following the Yangju highway incident and the candlelight vigil held for two Korean middle school students who were killed by the U.S. armored vehicle in 2002.[63]

Roh's announcement on dispatching non-troops to Iraq in support of the U.S.-led coalition was met with public backlash. Amid raging protests against the U.S. invasion of Iraq, the Grand National Assembly twice deferred voting on a legislation on noncombatant troop deployment to Iraq. What fueled these protests was the prevailing sentiment of antimilitarism that carried over from the previous year following the tragic death of two South Korean teenagers who were ran over by the U.S. military vehicle. The legislation for the deployment of noncombatant troops was approved, which was the second time South Korea dispatched noncombatant troops to Iraq after it contributed $500 mn of air transport and field hospital in the 1991 Gulf War.[64] On top of that, the U.S. continued to request military contributions among its allies, and South Korea was also to contribute up to 10,000 military troops to Iraq. Although South Korea was not given much of a leeway at that point, public opinion from a local daily newspaper *Joongang Ilbo* predicted that over 58% of South Koreans would support troop dispatch to Iraq provided that it was UN-mandated.[65]

As the U.S. allies were debating sending their troops, each country was looking to their own national interests and priorities. The Roh administration prioritized resuming six-party talks with North Korea. South Korea finalized its decision to send an additional 3,000 troops at a time when Kim Sun-il, a South Korean citizen based in Iraq, was abducted. The Al-Qaeda linked militants which abducted the South Korean civilian contractor for a Korean supplier to the U.S. military gave a 24-hour ultimatum demanding that the South Korean government withdraw its troops from Iraq. What was even more agitating was the fact that the same militant group had executed a U.S. civilian in the previous month for the same reasons. While the South Korean government, alongside other U.S. allies, emphasized that their troops would contribute to reconstructing and establishing peace in Iraq, Roh could not escape the growing criticisms from the public, especially after the kidnapped civilian contractor was beheaded. Kim Sun-il's beheading was a high-profile case and sent shockwaves domestically and internationally, which fueled further anti-U.S. sentiment. Following the execution, 5,000 South Koreans rallied in front of the U.S. Embassy in Seoul as a protest against the war in Iraq.

Speculations were rife about an Iraqi-based terrorist organization which operated a division named "*Nidham Kouri*" that specifically targeted South Koreans.[66] In October 2004, Al-Qaeda also published a series of threats warning South Korea against their military presence in Iraq. For the first time, the head of Al-Qaeda Ayman al-Zawahiri released an audio tape through Al Jazeera on October 2, 2004 calling on the Muslim world to launch a preemptive attack against the U.S. and their allies, including South Korea, which was mentioned twice in his speech alongside U.S., Britain, and Japan.[67] Earlier, in July, an intercepted email written by Abd Al-Razzaq, an Al-Qaeda-linked terrorist suspect, revealed that he was planning to board a flight to South Korea. Later in October, Southeast Asia-based al-Qaeda linked group Martyr Hammoud al-Masri Battalion published a declaration issuing threats to the South Korean government on an Arabic language website al-Muntada.[68] In the following year, two South Koreans were taken hostage by a Jihadist group based in Iraq, which gave a 72-hour ultimatum for troop withdrawal and threatened to execute the hostages; the Zaytun unit in Erbil was also hit by a rocket attack for the very first time since its deployment. Terrorist attacks on South Korean nationals were seldom, but the strings of terrorist attacks became more prevalent after the 2003 Iraq War, including a terrorist attack claimed by Al-Qaeda targeting a South Korean national in Yemen in 2009. Almost a decade later, Iraqi gunmen attacked the Akkas gas field, operated by Korea Gas Corporation (KOGAS) Akkas B.V., a subsidiary of KOGAS, which left two Iraqis dead.

The security in Kurdish autonomous regions, Erbil, Sulaymaniyah, Duhok, and Kirkuk Governorate, a disputed territory claimed by Turkmens, Arabs, and Kurds, and where Zaytun unit was stationed, generated widespread fears over a possible outbreak of civil war incited by rallies calling for Kurdish independence and ongoing conflicts with Turkey. Though not officially backed by the KRG, the two major political parties in the autonomous Kurdistan region KDP and the Patriotic Union of Kurdistan were suspected of using social movements as a leverage for the elections scheduled for January 2005. The Zaytun unit tried to establish amicable relations with the KRG by supplying humanitarian aid to the conflict-prone region and reaffirmed Zaytun unit's mission to promote peace and support post-reconstruction activities in Iraq. The latter was also an important strategy for playing down South Korea's image as a chief ally of the U.S. at a time when anti-U.S. sentiment was at the highest level following the U.S. invasion of Iraq. According to the OECD and World Bank, Iraq was the largest recipient of South Korea's humanitarian aid during the post-war reconstruction efforts in the 2000s.[69] In 2004, President Roh visited the Zaytun unit in Erbil to boost the morale of the troops stationed there. While endorsing South Korea's dispatch of Zaytun unit, former KRG President Masoud Barzani and former KRG regional minister of municipalities Nazaneen Muhammad Wusu advised South Korean troops to refrain from interfering in Iraq's internal affairs but to focus on improving security ties and providing medical support. South Korea continued to forge close ties with the KRG by agreeing to operate a joint working-level committee to help support South Korean troops deployed in Erbil. In close coordination with KRG, both parties discussed security and defense cooperation including on establishing a garrison, improving access to airports, troop deployment, and supply of military supplies. In return, KRG agreed to send Peshmerga Civil Defense Forces to support the activities of Zaytun unit, as the latter agreed to provide training for the Kurdish police and civil defense units until it pulled out from Iraq four years later.[70]

South Korea's commercial interests in post-war reconstruction Iraq

Following the 2003 U.S. invasion of Iraq, post-war reconstruction efforts in Iraq not only entailed getting its economy back on track but also necessitated a broader and comprehensive structural shift in institutional reforms for ensuring sustained peace and stability. While Obama had announced the plans to pull out 50,000 U.S. troops from Iraq by August 2010 it was also presumed that the formation of a new Iraqi government would request for a reserve of U.S. troops to remain to help transfer the authority to a local government and ease government transition. There was a great concern regarding the potential for Iraq to backslide into civil war if there were to be a security vacuum. While South Korea and Iraq's commercial ties were burgeoning after the 2003 Iraq War, bilateral ties beyond economic cooperation were largely inhibited due to prolonged political instability, and travel bans were imposed on Iraq and Syria since August 2007 and August 2011 due to security concerns. After the U.S. troop withdrawal since December 2011, Iraq was infiltrated by ISIS and other terrorist organizations while Syria has been mired in a dragged-out civil war-turned-proxy war.

Since the Iraqi economy was unstable in the post-reconstruction period, South Korean government pledged a $6 mn grant to the Iraqi ministry of municipalities and public works to support the purchase of heavy machineries and construction equipment.[71] On the commercial front, South Korean construction companies laid their eyes on post-war reconstruction projects in Iraq. In January 2004, Seoul received a green light from Washington to proceed with post-war reconstruction projects in Iraq by joining the Core Group, which was comprised of South Korea, the U.S., Japan, the EU, the UAE, Spain, UK, and Canada, among others. KOTRA, the ROK Ministry of Foreign Affair's arm for official development assistance (ODA), Korea International Cooperation Agency (KOICA), and Korea International Trade Association jointly spearheaded efforts to bolster economic cooperation with Iraq. KOICA organized a high-profile event in 2004 that was attended by high-ranking Kurdish officials in Erbil, where Zaytun unit was dispatched, as a way of boosting bilateral relations with the Kurdistan Regional Government. The Roh administration endeavored to develop further ties in economic cooperation by agreeing to participate in International Compact, which is a joint initiative between the UN and the Iraqi and U.S. governments for bringing intracontinental donors to propel political, economic, and social development in Iraq.[72] In addition, for the first time South Korea hosted and convened an interregional forum in 2010 that was attended by 13 state-owned Asian oil companies from the top ten energy importing economies and oil-producing countries such as Kazakhstan, Uzbekistan, Turkmenistan, Iraq, Thailand, and Vietnam.

Around four dozen South Koreans based in Erbil were involved in the provision of military supplies and the construction of garrison facilities. Although Iraq was economically unstable and was unable to pay $1bn it owed to Hyundai E&C, the latter inked a $220 mn contract for a post-war reconstruction project in 2004.[73] However, international bidding which was held for the first time since the Baathist government nationalized oil companies was negotiated under unfavorable conditions due to a large gap in service fees. Service contracts also deterred international oil companies from participating in oil and gas field development projects in Iraq. Business deals were hamstrung by Iraq's fiscal crunch and the absence of a legal framework

154 *Security implications after the Gulf wars*

and the tensions between the Iraqi central government and the Kurdistan Regional Government in northern Iraq.

Domestically, sectarianism which is rampant in Iraqi society has stymied Iraq's economic development. The Iraqi government's attempts to regulate the oil industry and distribute revenues along social cleavages among Sunnis and Shiites and the Kurdish population in the north floundered as the Kurdish community demanded a greater share of their entitlement to the oil fields in the autonomous region. The management of oil revenues was directly linked to sectarianism as the oil reserves were predominantly concentrated in the Kurdish-majority north and Shiite-majority south. To resolve political wrangling over the control of oil revenues, the Iraqi government was resolute in that no contracts would be validated unless a new national oil law is passed by the Iraqi parliament. Iraq's Ministry of Oil spokesperson Assem Jihad reiterated this position by stressing that "there was a clear warning to these companies that they will be blacklisted and excluded from any future cooperation with the [oil] ministry."[74] South Korea's SK Energy and KNOC were among the dozen parties that signed an oil contract with the Kurdish north that was deemed illegal.

By mid-2000s, Iraq was the sixth largest supplier of crude oil to South Korea and a decade later, Iraq emerged as the top five crude oil exporters to Seoul.[75] In April 2009, two South Korean companies in the oil refining industry, SK Energy and the state-run Korean KNOC-led consortium, initially signed a memorandum with Kurdistan Regional Government for developing 2 bn barrels of oil field in the Iraqi Kurdistan region, namely the Bazian oil refinery and three other oil fields in northern Iraq but was annulled on February 22, 2008. The cancellation of oil fields projects in northern Iraq also clouded the prospects for developing the Basra oil field in southern Iraq, which was part of the deal for signing a memorandum on social overhead capital (SOC) agreement between former Iraqi President Jalal Talabani and South Korean President Lee Myung-bak during a summit held in Seoul in 2009. As a consequence, the Iraqi federal government suspended crude oil exports to SK Energy, one of the companies in the KNOC-led consortium. The consortium was later blacklisted from tendering their bid on Iraqi oil projects due to the claim that the deal was deemed "illegal" for it was unauthorized by the Iraqi central government.[76] The incident spawned criticisms on the lack of political tact and cultural awareness of Seoul's resource diplomacy. In addition, in 2015, STX heavy industries called off a $406.8 mn contract to build a gas pipeline in Iraq due to protracted conflict and violence in Anbar province, which was laid siege by the Islamic state extremists.

After the Kurdish oil deal saga, South Korea was able to sign a $3.55 bn agreement with Iraq during the Lee Myung-bak administration in exchange for $2 bn of crude oil from Basra, which is also said to account for 70% of oil production in Iraq.[77] As a former businessman, President Lee was especially keen on expanding South Korea's commercial interests in post-reconstruction

Iraq and wider Middle East. In particular, Lee had strategically laid his eyes on the $550 mn new generators project and a $84 mn oil refinery project.[78] In February 2009, former Iraqi President Jalal Talabani became the first Iraqi president to visit South Korea since the two countries established diplomatic ties in 1989, and he thanked South Korea for Zaytun unit's contributions to Iraq's reconstruction process during his four-day visit to Seoul. He also met with South Korean business representatives in a meeting hosted by the Korea Chamber of Commerce and Industry to discuss business opportunities in the post-war reconstruction period. On a separate development, South Korea also signed an agreement on airport operating systems with the semi-autonomous Kurdish region in northern Iraq.

South Korea's commercial deal with Iraq blossomed since former Iraqi President Jalal Talabani's historic visit to Seoul in 2009. In a move to facilitate Iraq's reconstruction efforts, it opened its oil fields for foreign investment for the first time in 40 years. And by December, South Korea's state-run KOGAS became one of the four foreign oil companies to have concluded a deal to develop Iraq's Badra oil field, in which it had a 30% stake in the project.[79] During his visit to Korea in April 2011 at the invitation of President Lee Myung-bak, which was also the first visit outside of a Middle Eastern country, Iraq's Prime Minister Nouri al-Maliki met with Korean businessmen and visited industrial companies in Korea and signed the Korea–Iraq Economic and Energy Cooperation Agreement to promote bilateral trade and investment opportunities. While praising al-Maliki's political leadership and democratic government, Lee offered to impart South Korea's experience in economic industrialization and asked for the support of the Iraqi government in facilitating the participation of Korean companies in post-war reconstruction projects in Iraq. Maliki, who was awarded an honorary doctorate in political science from Korea University during his visit, stressed the importance of strengthening ROK–Iraqi bilateral ties especially in the education and energy sectors. Maliki also proposed South Korea's participation in future infrastructure projects, including a 100,000-unit planned city in Basmayah, Iraq, which is modeled after Genoa, Italy.[80] In addition, KOGAS also signed a 20-year deal to develop the Akkas and Mansuriya gas field with the Iraqi oil ministry in April 2011 after Kazakhstan's KazMunaiGaz pulled out from the agreement in May 2010. The gas development agreement was signed in exchange for embarking on the 100,000-unit housing project.[81]

Thus, indiscreet actions that follow from blindly prioritizing commercial interests in the region came at a cost. South Korean businesses have been vulnerable to political disputes in the region. Caught in a political wrangling between Iraq and Kuwait over the Mubarak Al-Kabeer Port, in 2010 an Iraqi Shiite militia Kata'ib Hezbollah issued a warning to a South Korean consortium participating in the construction of Mubarak Al-Kabeer Port project on Boubyan Island, which was projected to be one of the largest in the region. Iraq called on Kuwait to stall the project claiming that it would interfere with its shipping lanes. Despite the volatile security condition, South Korean companies signed an agreement with Iraq's Electricity Minister Raad Shalal to build 50 energy plants across Iraq from 2012. Contracts were worth $ 3.125 bn each with the construction of an increment of 25 energy plants in each phase.[82] Apart from the Kurdistan region in northern Iraq, Hyundai also won a $218.9 mn contract to construct a 500 megawatt Al Quds power station in Baghdad.

While there was a general consensus in recognizing the need for prioritizing resource diplomacy, the Lee administration's energy security policy was contested by various media outlets for a lack of long-term strategy. While acknowledging the need for a proactive government policy to support Korean companies in the market, former South Korean Ambassadors to Iraq and Kazakhstan pointed out that despite South Korea's position as the world's seventh-largest importer of crude oil, the Lee administration's resource diplomacy has largely been devoid of a strategic blueprint and roadmap for pursuing a long-term energy security policy. Lee Myung-bak's position of supporting the renewal of Zaytun unit's dispatch to Erbil was primarily driven by his interests in promoting South Korea's resource diplomacy. In fact, it was suggested that the hyped-up promotion of resource diplomacy by government bureaucracies such as the Blue House, Prime Minister's Office, Ministry of Foreign Affairs, and Ministry of Knowledge Economy has had an adverse impact on resource diplomacy by raising the prices of the oil fields.[83]

In 2011, South Korea acquired 400,000 barrels of crude oil in return for KOGAS's participation in the Zubair oil field development project in Iraq. However, more than a decade later, the legacy of Lee Myung-bak's resource diplomacy still lives on which is evidenced by KNOC's debt accumulation of KRW 7 tn by 2019. By 2020, KNOC pushed the deficit to KRW 27 tn. Collectively, four major state-owned companies, including KNOC, KOGAS, KORES, and KHNP accumulated KRW 90 tn of debt in the same year. Compared to the start of the Moon administration in 2017, the debt has risen to KRW 10 tn with less than 30% return on investment since 2008.[84] During the state audit in 2014, the losses incurred from resource diplomacy amounted to KRW 300 bn and hydrocarbon explorations in seven of the ten oilfields that the Lee administration invested failed to yield tangible results after investing over KRW 1 tn.[85] South Korea's oil and gas exploration led by state-owned companies between 2013 and 2014 had also been concentrated in the Iraqi Kurdistan region, namely the five major oilfields, Sangaw North, Sangaw South, Qush Tappa, Hawler, and Barzian oil fields. However, by 2016, KNOC pulled out of Sangaw and Barzian oil fields – and two years later terminated contracts with all other oil fields but one by citing lack of profitability and oil and gas fields that failed to produce. Moreover, the last remaining oilfield project was barely producing – at 10% of total capacity. The cost was colossal, as KNOC lost KRW 635.2 bn that it invested into the SOC of the Iraqi Kurdistan region. KNOC's debt ratio soared above 2200%

by 2019, which also compelled them to sell foreign assets.[86] In some respects the Lee administration's resource diplomacy has helped reorient the focus and prioritize commercial diplomacy. But with mounting debts, resource diplomacy has largely been considered a failure, and devoid of a viable energy security strategy.

The failure of resource diplomacy is partially attributed to structural factors. That is, the volatile won-dollar exchange rate posed considerable challenges for South Korean general trading companies stemming from financial issues, which equally applied to public oil companies such as KNOC. Likewise, negotiations led by the Prime Minister's Office for package deal in 2009 with the Iraqi, Azerbaijani, and Nigerian counterparts, which enabled South Korean companies to trade in Korean won, also collapsed. From a bureaucratic-organizational perspective, President Lee and the cabinet members of his administration, including Lee's brother and former MP Lee Sang-deuk, former Undersecretary of Knowledge Economy Park Young-jun, Deputy Prime Minister for Economic Affairs Choi Kyoung-hwan and Minister of Trade, Industry and Energy Yoon Sang-jik were identified as key political figures in spearheading the resource diplomacy at the helm of the Lee administration. What was problematic was the allegations that were revealed during the state audit conducted by the Ministry of Trade, Industry and Energy that KOGAS made illegal investments in the Iraqi oilfields while violating the Construction Industry Act which involved Lee's brother and former undersecretary Park.[87] It was suspected that both officials jointly coordinated to pass the legislation amendment in the parliament.

Regardless, resource diplomacy with Iraq was abetted by former Iraqi Foreign Minister Hoshyar Zebari's visit to Seoul in February 2012. An MOU was signed for fostering diplomatic and political cooperation between the two countries which entail tackling political discussions on bilateral and international issues, promoting technological transfer and exchange of exchange of expertise, capacity-building, and reconstruction and political training courses. Though the memorandum was titled diplomatic and political cooperation, there was limited disclosure about what areas and issues the two countries sought cooperation in these domains. Instead, al-Iraqiyya channel, which is an Iraq-based satellite channel that was created shortly after the overthrow of Saddam Hussein, revealed that primary area of emphasis was investments.[88] During the then South Korean Minister of Trade, Industry and Energy Lee Hee-bum's visit to Baghdad in April 2011, former Iraqi Prime Minister Nouri al-Maliki reiterated the importance of promoting infrastructural development in Iraq and in education, oil refineries, and electricity and power. The Iraqi delegates vowed that they would carry a list of projects linked to the development of Iraq's infrastructure to encourage the participation of South Korean companies ahead of their visit to Seoul in the following week.[89]

During al-Maliki's visit to Seoul in the same month, investment and energy security were the focal point of bilateral economic cooperation, and South Korean business delegates were also invited to attend the meetings. As a result of the high-level exchanges held between Iraqi PM Nouri al-Maliki's government and the Lee Myung-bak administration, South Korea became one of the first countries to secure access to 250,000 barrels of Iraqi oil per day – which is equivalent to 10% of South Korea's daily crude oil imports – in the case of emergency.[90] As a member of International Energy Agency since 2002, all member states, including South Korea, are required to have an emergency oil reserve for 90 days' worth of energy consumption. After the agreement signed with Iraq on energy cooperation, Iraq has agreed to store four million barrels of oil in South Korea and open an office in Seoul for commercial exports of oil.[91] In addition, Iraq and the wider Middle East emerged as a growing market for the construction sector in the 2010s. In hopes of availing of the opportunities offered by "the second Middle East boom," a series of roundtables among policymakers and academics were held throughout the first half of 2012. The Ministry of Land, Transport and Maritime Affairs established a joint committee between South Korea and Iraq and discussed opportunities for Korean construction companies to participate in post-war reconstruction projects, water management, and sewage projects, the Baghdad metro project, railway, port and oilfield development projects, and housing projects. To put an end to the housing crisis in Iraq, South Korea's Hanwha Engineering & Construction and Iraq's National Investment Commission signed a deal to build 100,000 housing units in Iraq, which is part of a 1 mn housing unit project underway across major Iraqi governorates.

Between 2013 and 2014, Iraq accounted for 9.3% of South Korea's source of crude oil imports and overseas construction projects in the early to mid-2010s doubled while construction deals increased from 6.2% in 2011 to 25% by mid-2014. There was an estimate of 80 Korean companies in Iraq and 1,300 Korean residents in Iraq.[92] To bolster economic cooperation between the two parties, high-level meetings were frequently held at the invitation of the South Korean government. In 2017, former Minister of Land, Infrastructure and Transport Kang Ho-in met with Iraqi Foreign Minister Ibrahim al-Jaafari to discuss possibilities for collaborations in post-ISIS economic reconstruction efforts in Iraq after the recapture of Mosul by the Iraqi forces. The meeting was held against the Iraqi government's announcement of setting up post-war reconstruction projects worth $275 bn in conjunction with the inauguration of the second economic development plan (2013–2017). Minister Kang suggested that Korea's experience in the post-war economic development could offer a role model for Iraq's post-war reconstruction efforts – such as in infrastructure, health, and finance. Minister al-Jaafari expressed his gratitude for the contributions of South Korean companies to post-war reconstruction projects, namely the Karbala refinery project and Bismayah New City project. Both parties sought to strengthen commercial ties by procuring funds from

Security implications after the Gulf wars 159

the World Bank and by resuming the Korea–Iraq joint committee which was suspended since it was last convened in Seoul.

Given that South Korea's bilateral relations with Iraq were mainly driven by energy security concerns, it also cultivated ties with the KRG in northern Iraq. The Deputy Director-General for the African and Middle Eastern Affairs Bureau of the ROK Ministry of Foreign Affairs met with the KRG counterpart Minister Falah Mustafa Bakir in December 2012 during his visit to Erbil. South Korea's relations with KRG were equally important due to the presence of Korean Consulate and Korea International Cooperation Agency (KOICA) in the Kurdistan regional governorate and the stationing of South Korea's Zaytun unit in Erbil between 2004 and 2008. Both parties discussed Iraq's political tensions at the time, and while former foreign minister of the KRG was not content with power-sharing between the KRG and the Iraqi federal government, Bakir nevertheless expressed relief at Saddam Hussein's fall, declaring that "the days of authoritarianism is over and we [Iraq] will not accept a return to dictatorship."[93] Although cultural cooperation remained marginal in South Korea's relations with Iraq, in June 2016, former Iraqi President Fuad Masum sent a letter ahead of the 40th session of UNESCO's World Heritage Committee asking for South Korea's support for inscribing Iraq's Marshlands on UNESCO's world heritage list, to which President Park Geun-hye and former head of the MENA Department at the ROK Ministry of Foreign Affairs Kwon Hee-suk pledged to offer full support.[94]

In addition to economic cooperation facilitated by public–private business delegations and high-level meetings arranged between the two countries, President Lee Myung-bak also wrote a letter to the Iraqi federal government to foster cooperation in the defense industry. High-level ministerial level talks were held between Baghdad and Seoul as Iraqi Defense Minister Abdul-Qader Mohammed Jassim al-Mifarji visited South Korea in January 2009 and attended a military parade held by the ROK MND. President Lee was also keen on promoting arms trade by exporting T-50 trainer jets manufactured in South Korea. In December 2013, Iraq became the MND's first customer that signed a $1.1 bn deal for purchasing South Korea's 24 FA-50 light combat aircrafts, which was co-developed by Korea Aerospace Industries and Lockheed Martin, designed for military training and medium combat.[95] Previously, T-50 variants were sold to Indonesia, Turkey, Peru, the Philippines, and Thailand. Iraq had relied on Soviet-manufactured arms in the past, but after the fall of Saddam Hussein, it looked elsewhere to diversify arms imports, including from Lockheed Martin.[96] South Korea's arms sales to the Middle East had been disproportionately concentrated in a handful of countries in the region, namely Turkey, Iraq, Egypt, Jordan, and Saudi Arabia. Iraq, in particular, was the second largest market for South Korean arms sales after Turkey, between 2016 and 2017, in which South Korea sold a total of 430 munitions. South Korea's customers for arms sales increased from seven countries between 2010 and 2014 to 17 countries between 2015 and 2019. The Middle East has been a small market for South Korean arms sales relative to the APAC which accounted for 50% of total arms exports, and Europe, which accounted for 24% of total arms exports. By comparison, the Middle East accounted for 17% of the total arms exports.[97] Following on from arms sales, the two countries held high-level exchanges at the ministerial level as former Iraqi Defense Minister Khaled al-Obeidi visited Seoul and met with former South Korean Defense Minister Han Min-goo to discuss military cooperation, especially in training and logistical support of the Armed Forces.[98] As Iraq sought to fortify its defense industry with the departure of U.S. troops from Iraq in December 2011, it held its first defense industry exhibition at the International Defense Exhibition in Baghdad, which was also attended by Korean defense companies.

The Islamic State of Iraq and Syria

South Korea's economic and security cooperation in Iraq was fraught with political risks especially as militants in the ISIS gained foothold in northern Iraq and Syria in 2014, with daunting security implications. Given the security risks in Mosul and Anbar province stemming from ISIS occupation, KOGAS announced in 2015 that it would suspend further investments in Iraq until the situation stabilizes. There were also unnerving reports that the ISIS was targeting military facilities and South Korean nationals for terrorist attacks. In June 2016, South Korea's National Intelligence Service revealed that ISIS called on Jihad against the "crusaders," denoting the countries and their citizens that contributed to the military interventions carried out by the U.S.-led coalition force in Syria and Iraq between 2018 and 2019. Information was collected on 77 airbases and personal information of 21 civilians through a group of hackers known as United Cyber Caliphate. In spite of the non-combatant nature of South Korea's humanitarian aid, South Korea was included among the 60 countries that were specifically targeted by IS through a video recording released through Dabiq, an online magazine published by ISIS that promotes radicalization. Before his death, Abu Bakr al-Baghdadi, the leader of ISIS, went insofar as blackmailing the detonation of Seoul. Moreover, two South Korean nationals who had attempted to join the ISIS were revoked of their citizenship, and a video footage was also released showing an ISIS member demonstrating South Korean martial art Taekwondo. The footage raised the speculation that more South Korean nationalities may have enlisted to join the Sunni jihadist group. Unbeknownst to the South Korean government, there were also supporters and members of ISIS among Southeast Asian and Central Asian laborers working in South Korea.[99] For this reason, the South Korean government has been deleting accounts suspected of belonging to the Islamic State and increasing concerns were voiced about the importance of raising awareness about the ISIS and Islamist organizations and for developing sound counterterrorism measures against extremism and radicalization.

By June 2014, it was reported that South Korea's dependence on Iraqi oil had subsided when previously Iraq was South Korea's top three supplier of crude oil imports. Instead of perceiving it as a worrisome trend, Seoul considered it as an opportunity to wean off its energy dependence on a country that was increasingly exposed to escalating political instability, largely in part due to the presence of the ISIS in the country. By the first quarter of 2014, the total prices of South Korea's Iraqi crude oil purchase declined by 31.1% from the same period in the previous year and the total crude oil imports for Iraqi oil was down by 7.3% from 9.3% in the previous year. South Korea had lesser dependence on purchasing Iraqi crude oil relative to other suppliers in the market.[100] As a result, Iraq became South Korea's fifth largest source of crude oil imports. As is the case today with reimposing strict sanctions against Iran, South Korea has traditionally turned to other suppliers in the Middle East to diversify energy imports such as Saudi Arabia, Kuwait, the UAE, and Qatar in the event of political instability.

South Korea continued to offer support for Iraq's reconstruction efforts in liberated areas by contributing troops to the U.S.-led international coalition.[101] South Korea's Middle East policy has been more or less in sync with the U.S. position toward the region. In a press briefing in September 2014, the ROK Ministry of Foreign Affairs spokesperson stated that South Korea was in favor of former U.S. President Barack Obama's plan for airstrikes to defeat the ISIS and earmarked $1.2 mn for humanitarian assistance.[102] In the same year, the Yazidi women and children were enslaved and killed in northern Iraq while being abducted and facing death threats and being forced to proselytize to Islam. The U.S.-led coalition had been targeting Raqqa, which was the self-declared capital of the Islamic caliphate, and Mosul, which is the second-largest city in Iraq for air strikes. In the following year, the Kurdish Peshmerga forces and Iraqi elite Special Forces Golden Division, together with a handful of Sunni Arab tribesmen led the efforts in retaking major infrastructures in the country including the Baiji oil refinery, Sinjar, and a major road connecting Syria and Iraq. However, while the Iraqi special forces and Peshmerga forces made advances in reclaiming lost territories from the militants; in Syria, the Islamic State militants have been gaining more territory in Aleppo. By 2016, while the U.S. continued to offer protection and artillery support and train 5,000 Iraqi armed forces to conquer the city of Mosul, ISIS fired rockets targeting the U.S. base while it continued to coordinate with Iraqi troops and Peshmerga forces. In addition to providing infrastructural and humanitarian assistance to Iraq, former South Korean Ambassador to Iraq expressed South Korea's support for Iraq's war against terrorism and offered moral and diplomatic support to the Iraqi government and the Iraqi Armed Forces on the occasion of liberating the Iraqi city of Fallujah from Daesh's control.[103] In May 2016, the ROK Ministry of Foreign Affairs condemned terrorist attacks in Baghdad, which resulted in 80 casualties and 110 injuries, and pledged to support Iraq in helping eradicate terrorism. Seoul offered $4 mn for humanitarian aid to UNDP's Funding Facility for Stabilization in October 2017 to help rebuild Iraq, including Mosul, which was retaken by the Iraqi forces since it was first conquered by the Islamic State militants in 2014. A month later, Iraq was also affected by an earthquake which struck the Iran–Iraq border.

In tandem with President Park Geun-hye's blueprint for spurring the growth engine through "the second Middle East boom," South Korea continued to provide humanitarian aid to Iraq and both countries continued to foster bilateral economic, health, and educational cooperation. In addition to stressing the conventional area of cooperation centered on commercial ties, further talks were also held about ensuring the safety of Korean companies and residents working in Iraq as well as discussing South Korea's support in Iraq's state-building efforts. From the Iraqi side, former Iraqi Foreign Minister Ibrahim al-Jaafari proposed introducing visa waiver program for diplomats and public servants. During the ministerial meeting held between the two countries, political developments in the two countries were also discussed, including North Korea's nuclear program and security in Iraq and wider Middle East.[104] Though discussions on key geopolitical issues were dealt with at ministerial-level meetings, there lacked a common political vision between the two countries as Iraq virtually emerged as a theater for proxy battleground between Iran and the U.S. since the post-2003 Iraq War.

In September 2014, South Korea expressed its support for the U.S. decision to use countermeasures to repel the Islamic State. In addition to extending $1.2 mn of humanitarian aid to help combat terrorism, Seoul was also considering expanding humanitarian assistance to northern Iraq which was equally affected by humanitarian crisis. However, the South Korean government made it clear that neither the U.S. made a request to South Korea to offer military support nor that it intends to offer one since the Obama administration resumed military strike following a two year-and-a-half hiatus and U.S. military withdrawal from Iraq. Former UN Secretary General Ban Ki-moon also rallied support behind the U.S. decision to launch an airstrike against the Islamic state and encouraged South Korea to join the international community in supporting counterterrorism efforts. The South Korean government took great interest in international community's effort to combat terrorism considering the commercial stakes in Iraq and 1,000 South Korean residents in Iraq. In the first speech delivered at the 69th session of the UNGA, President Park Geun-hye emphasized the importance of coordinating an international response to combating ISIS and reiterated South Korea's commitment toward that effort through information sharing, border control, countering violent extremism, and providing law enforcement. Park also reiterated that Seoul was ready to expand ODA support to developing countries and offer humanitarian aid to countries laid siege by the ISIS.[105]

While South Korea pledged $1.2 mn in aid to refugees in Syria and Iraq in 2014, Seoul was alarmed by the news that a South Korean national was allegedly enlisted by Islamic state in the same year, which was testified by a Saudi teenager Hamad al-Tamimi, who was also recruited by the Islamic state. According to the CIA, there was an estimate of 15,000 foreigners recruited by the Islamic state in Syria.[106] This was an act of retaliation from the Islamist militants in response to the U.S. announcing that it would launch an airstrike in Syria. Further to this, a picture of an Islamic state militant firing a K2C rifle manufactured in South Korea was circulated in June 2015. The rifle, which was exported to Iraqi special forces, was presumed to have been acquired by ISIS militants by confiscating arsenals and military vehicles of the Iraqi Armed Forces.[107]

Though not directly party to geopolitics in the Middle Eastern regional security complex, much like Iraq, South Korea has been caught in a proxy war between Iran and the U.S. South Korean businesses and residents in Iran and Iraq have been frequently exposed to political risks in the region, including Iran's missile strikes on Iraqi military bases that were housing U.S. troops, an attack that was launched in retaliation to the U.S. assassination of former Commander of Quds Force, Qasem Soleimani. While there were no American or Iraqi casualties, South Koreans working in the Iranian provinces of Khuzestan, Sistan and Baluchestan, Hormozgan, and Bushehr were told to evacuate the country, and the South Korean government also advised South Korean businesses against issuing travel and work visas to Iraq and Iran. Kata'ib Hezbollah, which comprises 40 militias, is part of the popular mobilization forces, a state-sponsored umbrella organization that is supported by Iran. While Trump had previously declared in January 2019 that the ISIS had been defeated and announced U.S. troop drawdown to half, to 3,000 forces, in September 2020, Iraq continues to grapple with the reeling political and economic situation after the ISIS and amid ongoing protests. As Iraq has increasingly been drawn into Iranian sphere of influence, South Korea's bilateral relations with Iraq will inevitably be bound up with the future trajectory of U.S.–Iran relations which is largely dependent on the final outcome of the Iran nuclear deal renegotiation that is currently underway.

Conclusion

This chapter has shown that South Korea's bilateral relations with Iraq have been largely hampered by Iraq's internal ethnic and sectarian divisions and America's neoconservative foreign policy under the Bush administration. In addition to the intractable issue of sectarianism and ethnic violence and internal fragmentation, it has been challenging for South Korea to straddle between its commercial and political interests between Iraq and the U.S. Though South Korea has generally preferred to stay out of regional conflicts, South Korea had to pay a great price for its alliance commitment to the U.S. as the third largest military contributor to the 2003 Iraq War by becoming increasingly exposed to security risks in Iraq and the wider MENA.

The Kim Sun-il incident sent shockwaves in South Korea and among Korean companies operating in the region as it became evident that South Korea was no longer perceived as a neutral country. Despite Iraq's strategic importance to South Korea as the world's second-largest oil producer (as of 2021), South Korea's resource diplomacy had virtually collapsed as it was caught in a tug of war between the Iraqi federal government and the KRG. For a time, South Korea was able to rhetorically play up its contributions to Iraq's post-war reconstruction efforts to further its commercial interests in the country as well as neutralize its national image and reputation which was damaged by the rising anti-war sentiment following the 2003 Iraq War. For the most part, ROK–Iraq relations have been arrested by geopolitical instability in Iraq as it has been increasingly rendered a theater for proxy wars between the U.S. and Iran based on the geopolitical developments in the aftermath of the 2003 Iraq War.

Notes

1. Park Gap-chul, "Quasi-War posture in Kuwait…prohibition of entry of foreigners, disruption of the withdrawal of Koreans from Iraq," *Chosun Ilbo*, October 2, 1980, 1.
2. Chosun-Ilbo, "A phased withdrawal plan for evacuating 15,000 Korean workers in Iraq and Iran," February 19, 1984, 1.
3. Wall Street Journal, "South Korea estimates Iran-Iraq building orders: Special to the Wall Street Journal," August 11, 1988, 1.
4. Hankyung, "The scale of construction contracts for Korean companies in the post-Gulf war period," April 21, 2003.
5. Abbas Alnasrawi, "Iraq: Economic sanctions and consequences, 1990–2000," *Third World Quarterly* 22 (2) (2001): 206.
6. Anthony Tucker-Jones, *The Gulf War: Operation Desert Storm 1990–1991* (Barnsley: Pen & Sword Military, 2014), 13.
7. U.S. Government Publishing Office, "Public Law 102-1 102d Congress: Joint Resolution," January 14, 1991.
8. Yonhap News Agency, "Baghdad Trade Center opens next month," September 20, 1999.
9. Hankyung, "Hyundai E&C receives KRW 37.2bn in compensation for the Gulf War," January 28, 2001.
10. YTN, "North Korea threatens to withdraw delegation over diplomatic relations established between Korea and the Soviet Union," *News Clip*, 02:15, March 29, 2021, www.ytn.co.kr/_ln/0101_202103291714441271.
11. Yonhap News Agency, "Formalizing requests for boosting support from allies," August 31, 1990.
12. Yonhap News Agency, "U.S. request to South Korea for strengthening support of the Gulf War," August 22, 1990.
13. Yonhap News Agency, "Solomon not to consider requesting South Korea to dispatch troops to the Middle East," September 20, 1990.
14. Yonhap News Agency, "The U.S. requests military supplies from Korea," August 18, 1990.

15 Yonhap News Agency, "High approval rate for additional support to the Gulf," February 4, 1991.
16 Yonhap News Agency, "One Korean worker detained in Iraq," August 3, 1990.
17 Yonhap News Agency, "The impact of the Middle East conflict on the domestic economy," August 3, 1990.
18 Trading Economics, "South Korea imports from Iraq," n.d., https://tradingeconomics.com/south-korea/imports/Iraq.
19 Yonhap News Agency, "70.7bn won to enter the construction market," October 17, 1990.
20 Yonhap News Agency, "Iraq-Kuwait owes $120mn to South Korea," November 29, 1990.
21 Yonhap News Agency, "Korea's Iraq-Kuwait bond issued are $134mn," August 5, 1990.
22 Yonhap News Agency, "Exports to eight countries in the region are disrupted by Gulf War," August 21, 1990.
23 Yonhap News Agency, "Interview with high-ranking diplomatic, security, and economic officials," August 8, 1990.
24 Yonhap News Agency, "The 12th Korea-Indonesia Resource Cooperation Committee established," September 7, 1990.
25 Ibrahim al-Marashi, "Lessons learned: Civil-military relations during the Iran-Iraq War and their influence on the 1991 Gulf War and 2003 Iraq War," in Nigel Ashton & Bryan Gibson (Eds.) *The Iran-Iraq War: New International Perspectives* (New York, NY: Routledge, 2013), 18.
26 Alnasrawi, "Iraq: Economic sanctions and consequences," 208.
27 Yonhap News Agency, "Government introduces contingency planning in preparation of the Gulf War," January 11, 1991.
28 Yonhap News Agency, "$1bn in exports disrupted by collapse," January 10, 1991.
29 SIPRI, "Military expenditure by country as percentage of government spending, 1988–2019," 2020, www.sipri.org/databases/milex.
30 Steven Lee Myers, "Clinton proposes a budget increase for the military," *The New York Times*, A1-1.
31 Yonhap News Agency, "Korea shares 78% of world-class defense costs," April 22, 1993.
32 The White House, "Saddam Hussein's support for international terrorism," n.d., https://georgewbush-whitehouse.archives.gov/infocus/iraq/decade/sect5.html.
33 Christopher J. Lamb & Irving Lachow, "Reforming Pentagon decision-making," *Joint Force Quarterly* 43 (4) (2006), 69; PBS News Hour, "Statement from Saddam Hussein calls for Jihad," April 1, 2003, www.pbs.org/newshour/nation/middle_east-jan-june03-saddam_04-91.
34 Yonhap News Agency, "Solomon thanks the Korean government for their support to the U.S. for the Persian Gulf War," January 18, 1991.
35 Committee on Energy and Commerce, "The United Nations oil-for-food program: Saddam Hussein's use of oil allocations to undermine sanctions and the United Nations Security Council," *Committee on Energy and Commerce House of Representatives*, (Washington, DC: U.S. Government Printing Office, 2005), 6–16.
36 Yonhap News Agency, "Economic and security impact of Iraqi airstrike," December 17, 1998.
37 ROK Ministry of Foreign Affairs, "Republic of Korea diplomatic documents release," 1976, 1023.

38 Chun Kyung-man, "Security implications on the Korean Peninsula after the Iraq War [in Korean]," *Defense Policy Research* (64) (2004), 29–31.
39 Yonhap News Agency, "Statement released by the Ministry of Foreign Affairs on Iraq," November 19, 1997.
40 William S. Davis & John Benamati, *E-commerce Basics: Technology Foundations and E-Business Applications* (London: Pearson, 2003), 18; U.S. Government Publishing Office, "Operation Desert Storm: Evaluation of the air campaign," Letter Report, June 12, 1997, GAO/NSIAD-970-134.
41 U.S. Department of State, "Patterns of Global Terrorism 2002," April 2003, 79; Congressional Research Service, "State sponsors of acts of international terrorism – legislative parameters: In brief," https://fas.org/sgp/crs/terror/R43835.pdf, 8.
42 Freedom House, *Freedom in the World: The Annual Survey of Political Rights and Civil Liberties: 2000–2001* (New York, NY: Freedom House, 2001), 8.
43 Administration and Enforcement of U.S. Export Control Programs, "Hearings before the Subcommittee on Oversight of the Committee on Ways and Means House of Representatives One Hundred Second Congress: First session serial 102-72," April 18; May 1, 1991, 357; Yonhap News Agency, "Korean NGOs urge the lifting of economic sanctions against North Korea," May 4, 1999.
44 For more on this, see "U.S. policy toward North Korea I: Perry review," *House Hearing*, 106 Congress (Washington DC: U.S. Government Printing Office, 2000).
45 Joseph Tse-Hei Lee, Harry Cliadakis & Anne Cliadakis, "Iraq, North Korea, and the End of American Global Hegemony," *Indian Journal of Asian Affairs* 19 (1) (2006), 6.
46 Sebastian Harnisch, "U.S.-North Korean relations under the Bush administration," *Asian Survey* XLII (6) (2002), 862–863.
47 Seyed Mohsen Mirhosseini, "Evolution of dual containment policy in the Persian Gulf," *Sociology and Anthropology* 2 (3) (2014), 107–108.
48 Barbara Starr, "North Korea helping with Scuds?" *ABC News*, January 7, 2006, https://abcnews.go.com/International/story?id=82923&page=1.
49 Michael O'Hanlon, *Defense Strategy for the Post-Saddam Era* (Washington, DC.: Brookings Institution Press, 2005), 95–98.
50 Lee, Cliadakis & Cliadakis "Iraq, North Korea, and the end of American global hegemony," 17; 20.
51 See Chun Kyung-man, "Analysis of the decision-making process for sending additional troops to Iraq [in Korean]," *Korean Military* (19) (2004), 184–217.
52 ROK Ministry of National Defense, "Status of overseas contingent units in the Middle East," December 31, 2019.
53 Raymond Hinnebusch, "The US invasion of Iraq: Explanations and implications," *Critique: Critical Middle Eastern Studies* 16 (3) (2007), 209–210.
54 Michael Cox & Doug Stokes, *U.S. Foreign Policy* (Abingdon, UK: Oxford University Press, 2008), 392.
55 Hankyoreh, "Iraqi invasion should be stopped to prevent the crisis on the Korean Peninsula," March 11, 2003.
56 Hong Sun-nam, "An analysis of the implications of Korea's Middle East dispatch on South Korea-Middle East relations: A political and diplomatic analysis [in Korean]," *Korea Middle East Studies Association* 25 (1), (2004), 25; Park Chan-gi, "The Middle East after the 2003 Iraq War and South Korea's countermeasures [in Korean]," National Security and Strategy 4 (3) (2004), 193–200.

57 Pressian, "North Korea is not a criminal, but a negotiator <Newsweek Press Conference,> The U.S. should refrain from excessive adventurism," February 24, 2003.
58 Ibid.
59 Pressian, "Roh-Bush: Peaceful solution sought for North Korea's nuclear development and in seeking active cooperation in Invasion of Iraq," March 14, 2003.
60 AP, "Poll: Americans say Iraq now better off; those surveyed in France, Germany, Mexico, Spain and South Korea say Iraq is worse off since the US invasion in March 2003," March 9, 2006, D5.
61 In-Seop Lee, Hong-Sik Yu, Neung-Woo Kim, Yong-Su Youn, Se-Won Chang & Sung-Yon Hwang, "Effects of the dispatch of Korean troops to Iraq on image of Korea," *Mediterranean Studies* 8 (2) (2006), 177.
62 Yonhap News Agency, "Interview with Erbil governor," March 11, 2007.
63 Kim Seong-han, "Military dispatch to Iraq and the ROK-U.S. Alliance," *Strategy 21: KIMS* 6 (2) (2003), 111.
64 Toronto Star, "South Korea again delays sending army team to Iraq; protesters oppose helping US with war; many want American soldiers to go home," March 29, 2003, A25.
65 Barbara Demick, "Seoul may send 10,000 troops to Iraq; Roh has made no decision, but observers say a South Korean deployment could be repaid by US flexibility vis-à-vis North Korea," *Los Angeles Times*, September 17, 2003, A8.
66 Yonhap News Agency, "Spying on the activities of a terrorist group, 'God's Lion' targeting Koreans," August 3, 2004.
67 SBS News, "Al Zawahiri: Attack Korea too," October 2, 2004, *News Clip*, 1:15, https://news.sbs.co.kr/news/endPage.do?news_id=N0311670212&srm=comment.
68 The Jamestown Foundation, "Al-Qaeda threatens Korea," May 9, 2005, Vol. 1 No.6, https://jamestown.org/program/al-qaeda-threatens-korea/.
69 Axel Marx & Jadir Soares, "South Korea's transition from recipient to DAC donor: Assessing Korea's development cooperation policy," *International Development Policy* 4 (2) (2013), 107–142.
70 Yonhap News Agency, "Korea-Kurdish joint working level committee established," June 3, 2004.
71 Al Bawaba, "South Korea donates US $6mn of equipment, machines to Iraq," March 20, 2005, 1.
72 Catherine Glière, *EU Security and Defence: Core Documents 2008*, Vol. 9 (Pretoria: Institute for Security Studies, 2009), 193–202.
73 Ibid.
74 Sinan Salaheddin, "Iraq threatens to stop crude exports to South Korea over Kurdish oil deal," *Whitehorse Daily Star*, December 28, 2007, 17.
75 Ibid; U.S. Energy Information Administration, "South Korea," July 16, 2018, www.eia.gov/international/analysis/country/KOR.
76 Asia News Monitor, "South Korea/Iraq: Two S. Korean firms fail screening for Iraqi oil deal," April 3, 2009.
77 Construction Week, "South Korea, Iraq agree on $3.55 billion deal to rebuild Iraq," February 26, 2009, www.constructionweekonline.com/article-4520-s-korea-and-iraq-sign-355bn-oil-for-development-deal.
78 Ibid.
79 Asia News Monitor, "South Korean gas firm wins deal to develop Iraqi oil field," December 14, 2009.

80 Tareq Amin, "Prime Minister Maliki discussed in South Korea building of housing city in Iraq, similar to Italy's Genoa," *Iraqi News*, May 12, 2011.
81 Kuwait News Agency, "Iraq signs final deal with South Korea's KOGAS for gas field," October 14, 2011.
82 Al Bawaba, "Iraq, Republic of Korea: Iraq hires South Korean group of companies for energy plants," April 9, 2011.
83 MBN, "South Korean Ambassador to Iraq: The price of resource diplomacy is rising," April 23, 2008, www.mbn.co.kr/news/politics/340032.
84 Ahn Jong-ho, "State-owned energy companies in crisis," *Daehan Economy*, April 6, 2021, www.dnews.co.kr/uhtml/view.jsp?idxno=202104051424483830378.
85 Seongtae Park, "A diplomatic catastrophe of the Lee administration," *JTBC*, October 24, 2014, https://news.jtbc.joins.com/article/article.aspx?news_id=NB10615873.
86 MBC, "MB received direct report on Kurdish oilfields," May 20, 2018, 00:46:56, https://imnews.imbc.com/replay/straight/4613231_28993.html.
87 Kim Gyeong-taek, "Who led resource diplomacy and who are the five members?" *Kookmin-Ilbo*, November 16, 2014, http://news.kmib.co.kr/article/view.asp?arcid=0008862174&code=61111111&cp=nv.
88 BBC Monitoring Middle East, "Iraq, South Korea sign deal on diplomatic, political cooperation; roundup," February 17, 2012.
89 Aswat al-Iraq, "Iraq's PM plans to visit South Korea to discuss several infrastructure projects," April 20, 2011.
90 Reuters, "South Korea to get at least 250,000 bpd in emergency crude from Iraq," April 28, 2011, www.reuters.com/article/oil-korea-iraq-idCNL3E7FS0CC20110428.
91 Min-jeong Lee, "Iraq to store strategic oil in South Korea," *The Wall Street Journal*, September 11, 2013, www.wsj.com/articles/SB10001424127887324549004579069062851115976.
92 Koo Chae-un, "The implications of geopolitical risks in Iraq," *Asia Economy*, June 18, 2014, http://view.asiae.co.kr/news/view.htm?idxno=2014061804220707112.
93 MENA Report London, "Iraq, Republic of Korea: Kurdistan Region and South Korea reiterate broadening relations," December 29, 2012.
94 National Iraqi News Agency, "Iraq calls on South Korea to support inclusion its marshes file on the World Heritage list," June 20, 2016.
95 Asia News Monitor, "South Korea/Iraq: Lee sends personal letter to Iraqi leaders calling for defense industry cooperation," January 31, 2013; Reuters, "South Korea's KAI sells fighter jets worth $1.1bn to Iraq," December 12, 2013.
96 BBC Monitoring Asia Pacific, "South Korea to export 24 FA-50 light attackers to Iraq," December 12, 2013.
97 SIPRI, "SIPRI arms transfers database," 2020, http://armstrade.sipri.org/armstrade/html/export_values.php; SIPRI, "SIPRI Fact Sheet: Trends in International Arms Transfers, 2019," March 2020, www.sipri.org/sites/default/files/2020-03/fs_2003_at_2019.pdf.
98 National Iraqi News Agency, "Defense Minister heads to South Korea to discuss military cooperation and support aspects of Seoul for Iraq." December 13, 2014.
99 YTN, "Indonesian arrested for his involvement in IS: What is South Korea's counterterrorism policy?" November 18, 2015, *News Clip*, 9:07, www.ytn.co.kr/_ln/0101_201511181851380228.
100 Kim Eun-jung, "South Korea less dependent on Iraq crude oil imports," *Yonhap News Agency*, June 26, 2014.

101 National Iraqi News Agency, "Iraq/South Korea/reconstruction of liberated areas," March 19, 2015.
102 BBC Monitoring Asia Pacific, "South Korea supports US plan for airstrikes in Syria, Iraq," September 11, 2014.
103 National Iraqi News Agency, "South Korea reaffirms its support for Iraq in its war against terrorism," June 28, 2016.
104 BBC Monitoring Asia Pacific, "South Korea asks Iraq to better protect its firms, people," January 18, 2017.
105 Lee Jong-seo, "Keynote speech at the UN General Assembly for the first time since President Park Geun-hye took office," October 6, 2014, *Newsmaker*, www.newsmaker.or.kr/news/articleView.html?idxno=5753.
106 Yonhap News TV, "The recruitment of a Korean IS member," September 13, 2014, www.ytn.co.kr/_ln/0104_201409131141472143.
107 Herald Economy, "IS warriors using 'Korean rifle K-2'?" June 18, 2015, http://biz.heraldcorp.com/view.php?ud=20150618000885.

References

Administration and Enforcement of U.S. Export Control Programs. "Hearings before the Subcommittee on Oversight of the Committee on Ways and Means House of Representatives One Hundred Second Congress: First session serial 102-72."

Ahn, Jong-ho. "State-owned energy companies in crisis," *Daehan Economy*, April 6, 2021, www.dnews.co.kr/uhtml/view.jsp?idxno=202104051424483830378.

Amin, Tareq. "Prime Minister Maliki discussed in South Korea building of housing city in Iraq, similar to Italy's Genoa," *Iraqi News*, May 12, 2011.

Al Jazeera. "South Korea ends Iraq mission," December 22, 2008, https://en.trend.az/world/other/1375758.html.

Alnasrawi, Abbas. "Iraq: Economic sanctions and consequences, 1990-2000," *Third World Quarterly* 22 (2) (2001), 205-218.

AP. "Poll: Americans say Iraq now better off; those surveyed in France, Germany, Mexico, Spain and South Korea say Iraq is worse off since the US invasion in March 2003," March 9, 2006, D5.

Asia News Monitor. "South Korea/Iraq: Two S. Korean firms fail screening for Iraqi oil deal," April 3, 2009.

Asia News Monitor. "South Korean gas firm wins deal to develop Iraqi oil field," December 14, 2009.

Asia News Monitor. "South Korea/Iraq: Lee sends personal letter to Iraqi leaders calling for defense industry cooperation," January 31, 2013; Reuters, "South Korea's KAI sells fighter jets worth $1.1bn to Iraq," December 12, 2013.

Aswat al-Iraq. "Iraq's PM plans to visit South Korea to discuss several infrastructure projects," April 20, 2011.

Al Bawaba. "South Korea donates US $6mn of equipment, machines to Iraq," March 20, 2005, 1.

Al Bawaba. "Iraq, Republic of Korea: Iraq hires South Korean group of companies for energy plants," April 9, 2011.

BBC Monitoring Asia Pacific. "South Korea to export 24 FA-50 light attackers to Iraq," December 12, 2013.

BBC Monitoring Asia Pacific. "South Korea supports US plan for airstrikes in Syria, Iraq," September 11, 2014.
BBC Monitoring Asia Pacific. "South Korea asks Iraq to better protect its firms, people," January 18, 2017.
BBC Monitoring Middle East. "Iraq, South Korea sign deal on diplomatic, political cooperation; roundup," February 17, 2012.
Bridges, Brian. "Korea and the Gulf crisis," in Susan Pares (Ed.), *Korea: The Past and the Present* (Kent: Global Oriental, 2008), 225–231.
Bryan Gibson (Eds.), *The Iran-Iraq War: New International Perspectives* (New York, NY: Routledge, 2013), 15–32.
Chosun-Ilbo. "A phased withdrawal plan for evacuating 15,000 Korean workers in Iraq and Iran," February 19, 1984, 1.
Chun, Kyung-man. "Security implications on the Korean Peninsula after the Iraq War [in Korean]," *Defense Policy Research* (64) (2004a), 29–57.
Chun, Kyung-man. "Analysis of the decision-making process for sending additional troops to Iraq [in Korean]," *Korean Military* (19) (2004b), 184–217.
Committee on Energy and Commerce. "The United Nations oil-for-food program: Saddam Hussein's use of oil allocations to undermine sanctions and the United Nations Security Council, *Committee on Energy and Commerce House of Representatives* (Washington, DC: U.S. Government Printing Office, 2005).
Congressional Research Service. "State sponsors of acts of international terrorism – legislative parameters: In brief," https://fas.org/sgp/crs/terror/R43835.pdf.
Construction Week. "South Korea, Iraq agree on $3.55 billion deal to rebuild Iraq," February 26, 2009, www.constructionweekonline.com/article-4520-s-korea-and-iraq-sign-355bn-oil-for-development-deal.
CNN. "Oil prices fall after ultimatum," March 18, 2003, https://edition.cnn.com/2003/BUSINESS/03/18/oil.prices.reut/index.html.
Cox, Michael and Doug Stokes. *U.S. Foreign Policy* (Abingdon, UK: Oxford University Press, 2008).
Davis, William S. and John Benamati. *E-commerce Basics: Technology Foundations and E-Business Applications* (London: Pearson, 2003).
Demick, Barbara. "Seoul may send 10,000 troops to Iraq; Roh has made no decision, but observers say a South Korean deployment could be repaid by US flexibility vis-à-vis North Korea," *Los Angeles Times*, September 17, 2003, A8.
Elizabeth, Laura. "Early end to Iraq War could hurt South Korea," *Wall Street Journal*, March 27, 2003, C14.
Feldman, Noah. "A very long engagement: It took 35 years for democracy to take hold in South Korea, and US troops could be in Iraq just as long," *The Wall Street Journal*, August 27, 2010, www.wsj.com/articles/SB10001424052748703632304575451863370935240.
Freedom House. *Freedom in the World: The Annual Survey of Political Rights and Civil Liberties: 2000-2001* (New York, NY: Freedom House, 2001).
Glière, Catherine. *EU Security and Defence: Core Documents 2008, Vol. 9* (Pretoria: Institute for Security Studies, 2009).
Hankyoreh. "Iraqi invasion should be stopped to prevent the crisis on the Korean Peninsula," March 11, 2003.
Hankyung. "Hyundai E&C receives KRW 37.2bn in compensation for the Gulf war," January 28, 2001.

Hankyung. "The scale of construction contracts for Korean companies in the post-Gulf war period," April 21, 2003.
Harnisch, Sebastian. "U.S.-North Korean relations under the Bush administration," *Asian Survey* XLII (6) (2002), 856–882.
Hinnebusch, Raymond. "The US invasion of Iraq: Explanations and implications," *Critique: Critical Middle Eastern Studies* 16 (3) (2007), 209–228.
Herald Economy. "IS warriors using 'Korean rifle K-2'?" June 18, 2015, http://biz.heraldcorp.com/view.php?ud=20150618000885.
Hong, Sun-nam. "An analysis of the implications of Korea's Middle East dispatch on South Korea-Middle East relations: A political and diplomatic analysis [in Korean]," *Korea Middle East Studies Association* 25 (1) (2004), 1–32.
Iglauer, Philip. "Iraq seeks stronger Korea ties," January 16, 2021, *The Korea Herald*, www.koreaherald.com/view.php?ud=20140126000153.
Kim, Eun-jung. "South Korea less dependent on Iraq crude oil imports," *Yonhap News Agency*, June 26, 2014.
Kim, Gyeong-taek. "Who led resource diplomacy and who are the five members?" *Kookmin-Ilbo*, November 16, 2014, http://news.kmib.co.kr/article/view.asp?arcid=0008862174&code=61111111&cp=nv.
Kim, Seong-han. "Military dispatch to Iraq and the ROK-U.S. alliance," *Strategy 21: KIMS* 6 (2) (2003), 106–130.
Kirk, Don. "North Korea warns South on backing U.S. in Iraq," *International Herald Tribune*, March 22, 2003, 6.
Koo, Chae-un. "The implications of geopolitical risks in Iraq," *Asia Economy*, June 18, 2014, http://view.asiae.co.kr/news/view.htm?idxno=2014061804220707112.
Kuwait News Agency. "Iraq signs final deal with South Korea's KOGAS for gas field," October 14, 2011.
Lamb, Christopher J. and Irving Lachow. "Reforming Pentagon decision-making," *Joint Force Quarterly* 43 (4) (2006), 68–71.
Lee, In-Seop, Hong-Sik Yu, Neung-Woo Kim, Yong-Su Youn, Se-Won Chang and Sung-Yon Hwang. "Effects of the dispatch of Korean troops to Iraq on image of Korea [In Korean]," *Mediterranean Studies* 8 (2) (2006), 169–199.
Lee, Joseph Tse-Hei, Harry Cliadakis and Anne Cliadakis. "Iraq, North Korea, and the end of American global hegemony," *Indian Journal of Asian Affairs* 19 (1) (2006), 1–24.
Lee, Jong-seo. "Keynote speech at the UN General Assembly for the first time since President Park Geun-hye took office," October 6, 2014, *Newsmaker*, www.newsmaker.or.kr/news/articleView.html?idxno=5753.
Lee, Min-jeong. "Iraq to store strategic oil in South Korea," *The Wall Street Journal*, September 11, 2013, www.wsj.com/articles/SB10001424127887324549004579069062851115976.
Lee, Shimgi. "Hyundai Corporation exports $15mn power cables to Iraq," *Hankyung*, April 13, 2000.
Marashi, Ibrahim. "Lessons learned: Civil-military relations during the Iran-Iraq War and their influence on the 1991 Gulf War and 2003 Iraq War," in Nigel Ashton and
Marx, Axel and Jadir Soares. "South Korea's transition from recipient to DAC Donor: Assessing Korea's development cooperation policy," *International Development Policy* 4 (2) (2013), 107–142.
MBC. "MB received direct report on Kurdish oilfields," May 20, 2018, 00:46:56, https://imnews.imbc.com/replay/straight/4613231_28993.html.

MBN. "South Korean Ambassador to Iraq: The price of resource diplomacy is rising," April 23, 2008, www.mbn.co.kr/news/politics/340032.

MENA Report London. "Iraq, Republic of Korea: Kurdistan Region and South Korea reiterate broadening relations," December 29, 2012.

Mirhosseini, Seyed Mohsen. "Evolution of dual containment policy in the Persian Gulf," *Sociology and Anthropology* 2 (3) (2014), 106–112.

Myers, Steven Lee. "Clinton proposes a budget increase for the military," *The New York Times*, A1-1.

National Iraqi News Agency. "Defense Minister heads to South Korea to discuss military cooperation and support aspects of Seoul for Iraq." December 13, 2014.

National Iraqi News Agency. "Iraq/South Korea/reconstruction of liberated areas," March 19, 2015.

National Iraqi News Agency. "Iraq calls on South Korea to support inclusion its marshes file on the World Heritage list," June 20, 2016.

National Iraqi News Agency. "South Korea reaffirms its support for Iraq in its war against terrorism," June 28, 2016.

O'Hanlon, Michael. *Defense Strategy for the Post-Saddam Era* (Washington DC: Brookings Institution Press, 2005).

Park, Chan-gi. "The Middle East after the 2003 Iraq War and South Korea's countermeasures [in Korean]," *National Security and Strategy* 4 (3) (2004), 193–200.

Park, Gap-chul. "Quasi-War posture in Kuwait…prohibition of entry of foreigners, disruption of the withdrawal of Koreans from Iraq," *Chosun Ilbo*, October 2, 1980, 1.

Park, Seongtae. "A diplomatic catastrophe of the Lee administration," *JTBC*, October 24, 2014, https://news.jtbc.joins.com/article/article.aspx?news_id=NB10615873.

PBS News Hour. "Statement from Saddam Hussein calls for jihad," April 1, 2003, www.pbs.org/newshour/nation/middle_east-jan-june03-saddam_04-91.

Pressian. "North Korea is not a criminal, but a negotiator <Newsweek Press Conference,> The U.S. should refrain from excessive adventurism," February 24, 2003.

Pressian. "Roh-Bush: Peaceful solution sought for North Korea's nuclear development and in seeking active cooperation in invasion of Iraq," March 14, 2003.

Reuters. "South Korea to get at least 250,000 bpd in emergency crude from Iraq," April 28, 2011, www.reuters.com/article/oil-korea-iraq-idCNL3E7FS0CC20110428.

ROK Ministry of Foreign Affairs. "Republic of Korea diplomatic documents release," 1976.

ROK Ministry of National Defense. "Status of overseas contingent units in the Middle East," 2019.

Salaheddin, Sinan. "Iraq threatens to stop crude exports to South Korea over Kurdish oil deal," *Whitehorse Daily Star*, December 28, 2007, 17.

SBS News. "Al Zawahiri: Attack Korea too," October 2, 2004, *News Clip*, 1:15, https://news.sbs.co.kr/news/endPage.do?news_id=N0311670212&srm=comment.

SIPRI. "SIPRI fact sheet: Trends in international arms transfers, 2019," March 2020, www.sipri.org/sites/default/files/2020-03/fs_2003_at_2019.pdf.

SIPRI. "SIPRI arms transfers database," 2020, http://armstrade.sipri.org/armstrade/html/export_values.php.

SIPRI. "Military expenditure by country as percentage of government spending, 1988–2019," 2020, www.sipri.org/databases/milex.

Starr, Barbara. "North Korea helping with Scuds?" *ABC News*, January 7, 2006, https://abcnews.go.com/International/story?id=82923&page=1.
The Jamestown Foundation. "Al-Qaeda threatens Korea," May 9, 2005, Vol. 1 No.6, https://jamestown.org/program/al-qaeda-threatens-korea/.
The Wall Street Journal. "South Korea estimates Iran-Iraq building orders: Special to the Wall Street Journal," August 11, 1988, 1.
The White House. "Saddam Hussein's support for international terrorism," n.d., https://georgewbush-whitehouse.archives.gov/infocus/iraq/decade/sect5.html.
Toronto Star. "South Korea again delays sending army team to Iraq; protesters oppose helping US with war; many want American soldiers to go home," March 29, 2003, A25.
Trading Economics. "South Korea imports from Iraq," n.d., https://tradingeconomics.com/south-korea/imports/Iraq.
Tucker-Jones, Anthony. *The Gulf War: Operation Desert Storm 1990-1991* (Barnsley: Pen & Sword Military, 2014).
U.S. Department of State. "Patterns of global terrorism 2002," April 2003.
U.S. Energy Information Administration. "South Korea," July 16, 2018, www.eia.gov/international/analysis/country/KOR.
U.S. Government Publishing Office. "Public Law 102-1 102d Congress: Joint resolution," January 14, 1991.
U.S. Government Publishing Office. "Operation Desert Storm: Evaluation of the air campaign," Letter Report, June 12, 1997, GAO/NSIAD-970-134.
"U.S. Policy toward North Korea I: Perry Review," *House Hearing, 106 Congress* (Washington DC.: U.S. Government Printing Office, 2000).
Yonhap News Agency. "One Korean worker detained in Iraq," August 3, 1990.
Yonhap News Agency. "The impact of the Middle East conflict on the domestic economy," August 3, 1990.
Yonhap News Agency. "Korea's Iraq-Kuwait bond issued are $134mn," August 5, 1990.
Yonhap News Agency. "Interview with high-ranking diplomatic, security, and economic officials," August 8, 1990.
Yonhap News Agency. "The U.S. requests military supplies from Korea," August 18, 1990.
Yonhap News Agency. "Exports to eight countries in the region are disrupted by Gulf War," August 21, 1990.
Yonhap News Agency. "U.S. request to South Korea for strengthening support of the Gulf War," August 22, 1990.
Yonhap News Agency. "Formalizing requests for boosting support from allies," August 31, 1990.
Yonhap News Agency. "The 12th Korea-Indonesia Resource Cooperation Committee established," September 7, 1990.
Yonhap News Agency. "Solomon not to consider requesting South Korea to dispatch troops to the Middle East," September 20, 1990.
Yonhap News Agency. "70.7bn won to enter the construction market," October 17, 1990.
Yonhap News Agency. "Iraq-Kuwait owes $120mn to South Korea," November 29, 1990.
Yonhap News Agency. "$1bn in exports disrupted by collapse," January 10, 1991.

Yonhap News Agency. "Government introduces contingency planning in preparation of the Gulf War," January 11, 1991.

Yonhap News Agency. "Solomon thanks the Korean government for their support to the U.S. for the Persian Gulf War," January 18, 1991.

Yonhap News Agency. "High approval rate for additional support to the Gulf," February 4, 1991.

Yonhap News Agency. "Korea shares 78% of world-class defense costs," April 22, 1993.

Yonhap News Agency. "Statement released by the Ministry of Foreign Affairs on Iraq," November 19, 1997.

Yonhap News Agency. "Economic and security impact of Iraqi airstrike," December 17, 1998.

Yonhap News Agency. "Korean NGOs urge the lifting of economic sanctions against North Korea," May 4, 1999.

Yonhap News Agency. "Korea-Kurdish joint working level committee established," June 3, 2004.

Yonhap News Agency. "Baghdad Trade Center opens next month," September 20, 1999.

Yonhap News Agency. "Spying on the activities of a terrorist group, "God's Lion" targeting Koreans," August 3, 2004.

Yonhap News Agency. "Interview with Erbil governor," March 11, 2007.

Yonhap News TV. "The recruitment of a Korean IS member," September 13, 2014, www.ytn.co.kr/_ln/0104_201409131141472143.

YTN. "Indonesian arrested for his involvement in IS: What is South Korea's counterterrorism policy?" November 18, 2015, *News Clip*, 9:07, www.ytn.co.kr/_ln/0101_201511181851380228.

YTN. "North Korea threatens to withdraw delegation over diplomatic relations established between Korea and the Soviet Union," News Clip, 02:15, March 29, 2021, www.ytn.co.kr/_ln/0101_202103291714441271.

6 Conclusion

South Korea's role construction in middle power diplomacy

The ascendance of middle powers has been preceded by recurring economic crises, the rise of intrastate conflicts, and transnational security issues (i.e. terrorism and radicalism). These factors, coupled with the shifting nature of the post-Cold War security architecture, have been followed by the decline of U.S. hegemony while greater emphasis has been accorded to the broadening scope of global security agenda at the intersectionality of domestic and international politics.[1] The three defining principles of middle power diplomacy are based on the respect of international norms and universal principles; building a coalition of like-minded states; serving as an instrumental bridge, catalyst, or facilitator between developed and developing countries.[2] The existing literature on middle power is bifurcated into two conceptual frameworks, one which is *functional* – whereby the middle power uses its resources to address a specific issue, and the other which is *behavioral*, which propagates a norm-based definition of multilateralism and conflict management.[3] This book has addressed the former, specifically as it relates to how South Korea has contributed to post-war reconstruction efforts in Iraq, Iran, and Kuwait and assumed a supportive role in the U.S.-led regional conflicts at the same time as pursuing national interests. Though less prominent relative to the functional and behavioral facets of middle power, *ideational* conceptions of middle power are also featured in the middle powers literature, that is, the ways in which states cultivate a middle power-oriented foreign policy identity and assume a role that is consistent with their identity as a middle power.[4] The ideational factor bears emblematic significance for capturing the modern history of South Korea's commercial, diplomatic, and political engagements with the Middle East.

The ruptures in the global system since the post-1945 world order gave impetus to multiple waves of middle power diplomacy. The first wave of middle power was centered on mediation and peacekeeping in international organizations, including the UN agencies and other intergovernmental organizations. The second wave of middle power was dealt with issue-specific global initiatives linked to human security concerns led by the International

DOI: 10.4324/9781003092100-6

Criminal Court and Responsibility to Protect. The third wave of middle power witnessed the formation of a flurry of informal institutionalizations associated with G20. Therefore, the criteria for the third wave of middle power was loosely defined as clusters of countries that enjoy economic prowess and politico-institutional reputation but are devoid of the great power status.[5] Alternatively, middle powers are also conceptualized as a collective unit, based on structural position and interactions among a network of countries that do not identify as great powers.[6] Seen in this light, middle power is a hybrid concept that considers both individual foreign policy behavior and collective international role on global issues. It focuses on a class of power, which theorizes the significance of national attributes and elements of national power that embodies structuralist-realist assumptions.[7]

As the multifarious definitions of middle power imply, there is lack of consensus on defining middle power. The ambiguity that characterizes middle powers has resulted in identifying a broad array of countries that are better known by what they are not than what they are. The conceptions of middle power are often imbued with fluid constructions by positing that it evolves against the broader structural changes. Robert Cox, for example, suggests that middle power plays a supportive role whether there is a hegemonic order or the absence thereof.[8] In search for a systemic and coherent analytical framework, the focus has been perpetually caught in a core-periphery dichotomy. There are a range of qualitative and quantitative criteria for gauging national attributes such as geography, population and military, economic, technological and diplomacy capacity, and national reputation and political and/or moral clout.[9] As a result, a plethora of countries have been included in the category, including traditional middle powers, such as Canada and Australia, and emerging middle powers, namely South Korea, Brazil, India, and South Africa.[10]

In addition, niche diplomacy, which refers to the functional practice of how middle powers identify positional, ideational, and behavioral needs and attempt to fill those niche issues selectively, is imperative for a successful middle power diplomacy.[11] Evan Potter suggests that in the face of traditional foreign policy issues including nonproliferation, economic diplomacy, alliance politics, and multilateralism, niche diplomacy demands a more selective strategy – a move away from "diffuse internationalism" to an entrepreneurial approach with maximum impact.[12] Seoul has been predisposed to multilateralism since Park Chung-hee inaugurated the now-defunct Asia Pacific Council (ASPAC) in 1966. In a similar vein, successive administrations continued the legacy of promoting regional economic and security cooperation such as through East Asia Vision Group and East Asia Study Group under Kim Dae-jung and Northeast Asia Cooperation Initiative during the Roh Moo-hyun administration. However, in identifying niche issues and concentrating resources in specific areas, South Korea has disproportionately focused its energy on prioritizing regional cooperation and institution-building in East Asia. Previous chapters have shown that there have been signs of deploying social and cultural resources to foster South Korea's multilateral engagement with the Arab world, including through the establishment of Korea–Arab Society in 2008. However, in fostering multilateral engagements, these initiatives are relatively at rudimentary stages of development and will require a more consistent effort in successive administrations.

While middle powers are defined based on structural shifts at the global, regional, and national levels as well as economic, political, and military clout, it is equally based on role conceptions and functional utility in middle power activism, which is premised on peacemaking.[13] The principle of neutrality, however, is only upheld in theory. In practice, middle powers have contradicted themselves in their foreign policy and diplomatic practices by implicitly aligning with major powers based on historical, strategic, and political factors. As John Holmes note, there is a constant dilemma among middle powers over how to be a loyal ally without being a satellite state and how to preserve sovereignty and national identity.[14] Despite the historical affinities between middle powers and their allies, at a closer look, the relationship is complicated. South Korea's foreign policy in the Middle East is inextricably tied to its longstanding alliance with the U.S. However, complying with the unilateral U.S. sanctions and UNSC sanctions regimes against Iran and Iraq have hurt South Korea's commercial interests. Although Roh Moo-hyun had often actively defied the U.S. interests during his presidential term, as Young Jong Choi notes, South Korea's middle power activism has not lived up to its rhetoric and expectations.[15] Military dispatch to the Middle East, as demonstrated through the 2003 Iraq War, has been a product of Seoul's alliance commitment to the U.S. As a result, becoming the third largest contributor of foreign troops in the 2003 Iraq War inevitably reinforced South Korea's national image as a U.S. ally.

With reference to the cases of Korea and Australia, David Hundt points out that these middle powers are facilitators or team players in regional diplomacy but are rarely "leaders" or regional powers; nor do they show a penchant for neutrality as they have shown a clear preference for a U.S.-led regional order in Asia.[16] While the first part of the statement generally rings true, South Korea's support for the U.S.-led East Asian security architecture has degenerated under Trump's America First policy. Moreover, as embodied through Lee Myung-bak's Global Korea policy, perceptions over the U.S.-led regional security architecture have been divided along party lines, with the conservatives showing a stronger preference for American alliance than the progressives. South Korea's status as a middle power was affirmed through the first hosting of the G20 Summit in 2010 by a non-G7 member and the Nuclear Security Summit in 2012 as the first non-Western state. Moreover, it also spearheaded efforts in promoting trade liberalization by having its first bilateral FTA with Chile signed into effect in April 2004. In normative terms, Seoul has also assumed a constructive role in bridging the ties between the developed and developing countries and Western and non-Western countries.[17] At the same time, South Korea's ability to pursue an independent foreign policy the Middle East has effectively been constrained by factors such as North Korea's nuclear weapons development, the evolving nature of ROK–U.S. alliance, declining U.S. hegemony, American foreign policy in the Middle East, and Seoul's resource diplomacy.

Given that the claim to middle power is predicated on "possession and projection of material capabilities to achieve foreign policy goals,"[18] economic and cultural resources served as a leverage for Seoul to overcome strategic and geopolitical hurdles since the 1990s. South Korea joined the APAC Economic Cooperation forum in 1989 and G20 in 1999 as a founding member and the OECD in 1996. In 1997, it joined the Association for Southeast Asian Nations (ASEAN) plus three, alongside China and Japan.[19] In 1991, Roh Tae-woo declared in a speech at the Hoover Institution that South Korea aims to "seek new roles as a middle power – between the advanced and developing countries."[20] Globalization was referenced for the first time during the Kim Young-sam government, and Roh Moo-hyun was the first South Korean president to refer to South Korea as a middle power. Building on these legacies, it was later during the Lee Myung-bak administration that South Korea was debating the implications for the country's multilateral activism. The latter was pursued based on Seoul's membership in G20 and its contributions to global governance initiatives such as climate crisis and nuclear security.[21]

ROK–U.S. alliance, the rise of China, and East Asian security

Strategic implications are important determinants for positioning middle powers in the international system. A neorealist perspective assumes that the structure of the international system and power balances conditions of middle power's foreign and security policies as part of a structuralist narrative that downplays agency.[22] Seoul has also been somewhat constrained by being geographically sandwiched between the two great powers and with relatively little freedom to shape its own strategic environment. The Cold War legacy of the Korean Peninsula and South Korea's alliance with the U.S. have been critical for South Korea's survival. Washington has also been a gateway for negotiating South Korea's policy preferences on the North Korean issue based on the absence of a formal peace treaty which was replaced by an armistice agreement signed by military commanders.[23] Notwithstanding the controversies stemming from the SOFA agreement and asymmetric alliance, and with policy divergences and the gaps in threat perceptions on North Korea, South Korea's Middle East policy has been closely aligned with American foreign policy in the Middle East.[24]

South Korea's dependence on the U.S. alliance has been attributed to the historical legacy of the Korean War coupled with North Korea's nuclear programs and the rise of China. Promoting peace and prosperity on the Korean Peninsula, which has been a primary driver in South Korea's participation of multilateral initiatives, illustrates the extent to which Seoul's middle power diplomacy is functional in nature. However, as previous chapters have demonstrated, Seoul's middle power diplomacy is equally *ideational* in nature considering that it has been employing economic development and public diplomacy as a means for increasing national competitiveness and capacity-building. In parallel with the North Korea factor, South Korea's deployment of troops to the UN peacekeeping operations and the U.S.-led international coalition forces was also partially driven by the desire to facilitate a smooth political transition and promote political stability in the Middle East. The latter has had equally profound implications for South Korea's energy security. The historical and strategic importance ascribed to Korea's alliance with the U.S. has been a dominant factor in having an impinging effect on South Korea's economic and security policy in the Middle East. Though South Korea's foreign policy on the Middle East has been primarily driven by its growing energy demands to support its EOI, South Korea's decision to contribute troops, including noncombatant contingents, to the past conflicts in the 1991 Gulf War and the 2003 Iraq War has directly resulted from America's demands. South Korea's compliance with American pressure is linked to its strategic interests on the Korean Peninsula. Regardless of the perceptions on North Korea as a foe or a friend, Pyongyang's nuclear programs have remained a chief concern for the South Korean government. Nevertheless, as previous chapters have shown, Pyongyang's nuclear technology and ballistic missile cooperation with Tehran and Baghdad has not been a hindrance for South Korea to establish full-fledged diplomatic ties with these countries.

The rise of China has equally been a critical factor in configuring and cementing the networks of alliances in the APAC security theater. The significance of the rise of China lies in the latter being a major trading partner of South Korea. In addition to the economic factor, South Korea's foreign policy and security has been linked to China through geography, the North Korean issue, and ROK–U.S. alliance. China has been able to rein in on North Korea as the largest trading partner and a principal guarantor to North Korea. China has provided food and energy aid to Pyongyang, and accounts for around 70% of North Korea's total trade.[25] As a traditional middle power, Australia has been straddling the strategic and economic alignments between the U.S. and China. Dubbed "the rise of Asia," Australia Department of Defense posited that Asia will account for almost half of the world's output by 2025.[26] As a consequence, the economic growth of these Asian countries was anticipated to have profound strategic ramifications by enabling states to increase their military expenditure, modernize their defense capabilities, and acquire advanced arms and technology.[27] As a middle power in Northeast Asia, South Korea shares Australia's concerns both in the commercial and strategic realms and in employing a hedging strategy against the decline in American hegemony.

Despite the prevalence of the East Asian security literature that pits Washington against Beijing, rather than having a decisive impact on South Korea's foreign policy in the Middle East, the rise of China has fueled competition from the increasing share of Chinese economy in the Middle

Eastern construction market. Notwithstanding the structural connotations of South Korea's response to the rise of China, the latter's influence has been mostly confined to the East Asian security theater; its impact on Seoul's Middle East security and foreign policy has been minimal. Instead, the impact of China has been limited to economic competitions in the construction, shipbuilding, and EPC sectors. As a major global economic powerhouse that is in a confrontational course with the U.S., China's relations with Iran has deepened at the expense of its relations with the U.S., which has strained in recent years. Though China–Iran ties have not had a direct impact on South Korea's relations with Iran, Tehran has often juxtaposed Seoul and Beijing's foreign policy positions when lodging complaints against the former regarding frozen Iranian assets. According to an analyst, "even China has been giving Iran cash to survive but Koreans treated as if they did not care at all which made Iran furious."[28] Though Iran has assets held in South Korean, Japanese, and Iraqi banks as a result of U.S. sanctions, it has denied speculations that it has frozen assets in Chinese banks.[29] While China has signed a 25-year comprehensive strategic partnership agreement with Iran in March 2021, which entails trading $400 bn of Chinese investments on Iran in exchange for a cheap and steady supply of crude oil from Iran and strengthening strategic and defense cooperation. By contrast, South Korea remains aligned to Washington's position in its Middle East economic and security policy. In addition to South Korea's military dispatch to the 1991 Gulf War and the 2003 Iraq War, Seoul had also expanded the scope of its antipiracy naval force, Cheonghae unit, to the Strait of Hormuz since January 2020, which has vexed Iran. In Northeast Asia, however, South Korea has been employing a hedging strategy in maintaining a balancing act between China and the U.S.

American foreign policy in the Middle East and the dusk of Pax Americana

The traditional conceptions of middle power posit that "middle powers are not powerful enough to act alone, yet not small enough to render the pursuit of their national interests futile."[30] According to this logic, South Korea is among the eight states that are archetypes characterized as "positional middle powers." These include South Korea, Australia, Brazil, Indonesia, Malaysia, South Africa, Thailand, and Turkey. The two key criteria that are intimately bound up with this notion are that first, they are first-generation followers of Pax Americana in the post-1945 global order. Second, "niche diplomacy" or mission-oriented diplomacy that underscores the role of entrepreneurial states in drawing functional expertise to act as a manager, peacekeepers, mediators, or a leader on a given global issue.[31] According to Michael Hudson, America's foreign interests in the region have been guided by three pillars: oil, Israel, and anti-communism.[32] Energy security remains a key engine in driving South Korea's pivot to the Middle East. Though there was a spike in South Korea's import of American crude oil between 2018 and the second half of 2019, there was a sharp decline in South Korea's U.S. crude imports in December 2020 which dropped by 67.9% year on year. This was in stark contrast to the surge in Saudi oil imports which increased by 60.3% year on year in the same period.[33] South Korea remains dependent on the Middle East as reliable sources for crude oil, including Saudi Arabia, which is the top crude oil supplier to South Korea, during times of economic uncertainty. While South Korea's foreign policy interests had been compatible with the U.S. position in countering communism in the Cold War era and has also prioritized energy security as national interests, it has been reluctant to be associated with the U.S.-led conflicts in the Middle East amid rising anti-American and anti-war sentiments under the Bush administration, particularly following the 2003 Iraq War.

South Korea's first military contribution to the Middle East was to Saudi Arabia when it sent 154 military medical personnel during the 1991 Gulf War. This was also the first military dispatch to overseas conflict since its deployment of ROK Army Tiger Division to the Vietnam War.[34] In the post-1945 global order, the George H.W. Bush administration has been credited with ushering in the new era of American hegemony through the 1991 Gulf War and the Madrid Conference.[35] Apparently, there was a clear difference that set the 1991 Gulf War apart from the subsequent 2003 Iraq War in that the former enjoyed far more widespread support, legitimacy, and international consensus concerning international coalition-building. Despite the strategic importance accorded to the Middle East as the major source of crude oil to South Korea, given the geographic remoteness, there has been a lack of cultural awareness of the Middle East among the South Korean public. Perception gaps on Pyongyang also widened following George W. Bush's 2002 State of the Union address which designated Iran, Iraq, and North Korea as "Axis of Evil." In the post-9/11 global order, South Korea's perceptions of the Arab and Islamic world have been largely colored through the abductions of South Koreans in Iraq, Afghanistan, Libya, and Yemen since post-2003 Iraq.

Obama's pivot to Asia doctrine was a structural response that sought to deepen its engagement with the APAC while countering the rise of China. The then U.S. Secretary of State Hillary Clinton noted that "harnessing Asia's growth is vital to America's economic and strategic interests and a key priority for President Obama." She then went on to identify six pillars of action which includes strengthening bilateral security alliances; deepening working relationships with emerging powers, including China; engaging with regional multinational institutions; expanding trade and investment; forging a broad-based military presence; and advancing democracy and human rights.[36] However, the Obama administration's decision to rebalance against China came at the expense of maintaining its commitments to the Middle East and elsewhere. Obama's military drawdown was criticized by its Middle Eastern allies and Saudi Arabia as they feared that a scaled-back U.S. military presence would embolden Iran's influence in the region.[37] Though generally welcomed in Asia, Obama's pivot to Asia was not received well by the European and

Middle Eastern counterparts that feared that it would undermine transatlantic relations and security in the Middle East. Fundamentally, skeptics of pivot to Asia have pointed out that rebalancing to Asia is a relative shift, not new.[38] While the economic significance of pivot to Asia was duly noted, the security implications premised on preventing the rise of a regional hegemon and polarization were just as important; this was done by maintaining a hub-and-spoke model of security alliance with the APAC. However, critics have regarded the policy as counterproductive by unnecessarily provoking Beijing by expanding U.S. military presence in East Asia.[39]

Contrary to the popular belief that America's retrenchment in the Middle East would reduce conflicts in the region and promote America's national interests and global order, it is also said that America's retreat did not bring security to the region.[40] Saudi Arabia and the UAE vehemently objected to Obama's conciliatory approach toward Iran, which culminated with the passage of the JCPOA in 2015. From the perspective of Asia's Middle East policy, the American pivot to Asia exhibited the greatest perception gap vis-à-vis JCPOA. In spite of the Pyongyang–Tehran strategic cooperation noted earlier, South Korea has primarily viewed its relations with Iran in pragmatic terms. Commercial interests have trumped political or security considerations in the Middle East. More importantly, as discussed in Chapter 2, the implementation of enabled South Korea to resume and expand its commercial and diplomatic ties as embodied through Park Geun-hye's historic visit to Tehran in May 2016.

The Obama administration's approach of valuing alliances and global engagement and multilateral institutions was reversed under the Trump administration.[41] Nevertheless, Gregory Gause argues that the Obama administration and the Trump administration shared similar policy positions when it comes to favoring military retrenchment.[42] By contrast, they diverged on Iran policy. Trump's maximum pressure campaign and principled realism, which called for a new antiterrorism strategy in containing Iran, received mixed appraisals.[43] Though Trump's maximum pressure campaign on Iran received widespread support from the Gulf states, namely Saudi Arabia, the UAE, and Bahrain, critics have blasted Trump's Middle East policy as reckless and unprincipled. Trump's America First policy had been undergirded by redefining exceptionalism. Whereas Trump's predecessors had taken exceptionalism to be permanent and intrinsic to American identity, Trump's viewed exceptionalism as a conditional state which is predicated upon "throwing themselves into the game of international relations, or international deal-making, and playing to win."[44] According to this line of reasoning, Trump rejects American exceptionalism grounded in liberalism and a positive-sum game-oriented mindset.

While Trump's America First policy caused a great outcry in Korea especially concerning defense burden-sharing, Trump's maximum pressure campaign, which eventually led to South Korea's military dispatch to the Strait of Hormuz in January 2020, equally elicited sharp criticisms from South

Korean civil society organizations. The assassination of Qasem Soleimani in January 2020 drew widespread concerns about irking Iran and jeopardizing South Korea's national security by sending troops to the Strait of Hormuz. The initial euphoria of pushing for North Korea's denuclearization by engaging them through the Trump-Kim summits between 2018 and 2019 was short-lived while the Trump administration's unilateral withdrawal from JCPOA and reimposed sanctions on Iran fueled diplomatic tensions between South Korea and Iran. Iran's capture of the South Korean oil tanker Hankuk Chemi on January 4, 2021 reinforced South Korea's image as a U.S. ally. While South Korea's alliance with the U.S. has been critical for maintaining order and security on the Korean Peninsula, they were on different wavelengths on maximalist or belligerent Middle East policy.

Separate from the question of functional and strategic necessity of the ROK–U.S. alliance, South Korea had been reluctant to support neoconservative American foreign policy in the Middle East during the Bush administration and Obama's pivot to Asia had not lived up to the expectations. To compound things further, America First policy and maximum pressure campaign under the Trump administration have undermined multilateralism and the ROK–U.S. alliance.

The miracle on the Han River and Seoul's resource diplomacy

South Korea's rapid industrialization in the 1960s which is referred to as "the Miracle on the Han River" was a watershed period that transformed South Korea's international standing. By achieving a double-digit growth, South Korea's rapid economic growth led to great strides in economic welfare, democratization, and soft power projection.[45] Korea's industrialization experience which became a model for successful economic development in developing countries not only underlies South Korea's state-building process but equally serves a vital instrument of statecraft and public diplomacy. As quoted during Roh Moo-hyun's visit to the UAE in 2006, "the Miracle on the Han River" narrative has buttressed South Korea's relations with the Middle East and has, to an extent, helped neutralize South Korea's image as an American ally even when the U.S. credibility was at an all-time low in the Middle East following the 2003 Iraq War. While South Korea's ties with the U.S. have not been a hindrance for forging ties with the Gulf monarchies in the region, that has not been the case with Iran. As discussed in Chapter 3, the Miracle on the Han River narrative is at the backbone of Saudi–Korean Vision 2030. Key areas of complementarity as identified through the Saudi–Korean Vision 2030 include energy cooperation, boosting FDI and bilateral trade, manufacture, economic diversification, and nationalization of human capital.[46]

A combination of traditional high-level meetings and cultural exchanges have facilitated South Korea's resource diplomacy in the region. As discussed in the previous chapters, though prioritizing resource diplomacy, which was the hallmark of Lee Myung-bak's energy security, was a step in the right direction, colossal debts incurred from investing in overseas resource development in the Middle East and Central Asia imply that South Korea's resource diplomacy has been devoid of a strategic long-term planning. South Korea's energy security policy has been poorly implemented with no concrete goals and no rational choice of energy mix plan.[47] While South Korea has secured increased amount of oil and mineral resources in a span of time, not all bilateral MOUs signed in energy cooperation with the Middle East have translated into enhanced resource development capacity. Limitations of South Korea's energy security policy include lack of investment efficiency and resource development capacity and insufficient infrastructure for energy development.[48] In 2014, the ROK Ministry of Trade, Industry and Energy has devised a new policy paradigm which stresses participation of private enterprises and showing a strong preference for securing operating licenses in exploration fields over the traditional methods of mergers and acquisition and buying shares in production fields.[49]

The East Asian counterparts have engaged in similar efforts to enhance energy security. China's developmental pathway, much like their East Asian counterparts, which identify as a DS, relies on state guidance as a way of expanding China's commercial interests overseas. Other facets of economic power focus on the utility of soft power and resource security. The latter presumes that aid and overseas development assistance are traded in exchange for gaining access to natural resources. The three major aims in China's economic diplomacy are thus identified as promoting resource security; enhancing political relations and soft power projection; and boosting commercial opportunities for national companies abroad.[50] Although it would be erroneous to axiomatically assume that all overseas Chinese development programs have a strategic intent to boost resource security, and despite the clear differences in economic and institutional capacity and political influence between a middle power and a great power, South Korea shares similar interests in enhancing resource security and have engaged in efforts for employing economic and soft power tools both as a means and an end (i.e. diplomacy for resource security and resource security for diplomacy), albeit in a much smaller scale, and with greater dependency on the Middle East. In a similar vein, the primacy of energy security in Japan's Middle East policy has predated the 1973 oil embargo. By 1962, Japan was the leading oil consumer for Iran, Kuwait, and Saudi Arabia and by 1973, it was the main importer of Middle East oil.[51] Political neutrality has also been imperative for prioritizing energy security. As highlighted across various sections throughout this book, Seoul has attempted to stay out of regional conflicts, as was Japan. However, in practice, this was not always the case, as demonstrated through both Japan and South Korea's response to the 1973 oil embargo.[52]

Considering that resource diplomacy is a priority concern, South Korea has tried to complement, rather than strictly move away from traditional G2G relations through a tripartite economic framework that has been formulated under Saudi–Korean Vision 2030. In partnership with South Korea's major businesses (*chaebol*), SMEs and state-run enterprises such as KNOC, KOGAS, KORES, and KEPCO, and the South Korean government agencies, The Eximbank of Korea, KOTRA, the Ministry of Foreign Affairs, and the Ministry of Trade, Industry and Energy have played a pivotal role in advancing PPP for South Korea's resource diplomacy in the Middle East. As exemplified through the largest number of business delegations headed by Park Geun-hye's visit to Tehran in May 2016, mobilizing resources at the institutional, economic, and social levels have been critical for fostering G2G, B2B, and B2G relations. Furthermore, multilateral G2G relations is an area which South Korea's middle power diplomacy could contribute to going forward.

Though structuralist undertones have been predominant in theorizing middle powers, there are conflictual accounts on defining the relationship between great powers and middle powers. A structuralist perspective suggests that America's decline and the possible vacuum of a global hegemon would improve the prospects for middle powers to elevate their status in the international system.[53] Yet at the same time, the erosion of American hegemony and multilateralism which accelerated under the Trump administration, and heightened regional conflicts have undermined opportunities for middle powers to revitalize multilateral diplomacy with the Middle East.

Recently, however, the invitation for South Korea to attend the G7 summit as a guest nation in January 2021 has renewed hopes for enhancing Korea's engagement in global governance as part of a concerted effort to tackle issues of regional and global significance. The G20 Riyadh Summit Leaders Declaration hosted in Riyadh has also agreed on key initiatives for tackling inequalities and promoting economic resilience and sustainability as part of a broader roadmap for combating Covid-19.[54] There are ongoing efforts for South Korea to engage the Middle East by participating in major global fora, including the UNGA, OECD, World Economic Forum, and G20. Park Geun-hye's keynote speech delivered on creative economy at the OECD ministerial meeting in October 2015, which offered a synchronized framework for reinforcing bilateral cooperation with Saudi Arabia, is a case-in-point. While South Korea continues to actively pursue multilateral activism insofar as the regional and global fora permits, the Biden administration's resolve to restore alliances and recommit to multilateralism and the precise implications of multilateralism and Pax Americana on positional middle powers remain to be seen. In addition to the ideational facet, as a middle power, South Korea should boost multilateral G2G relations and functionally broaden its engagements with Middle Eastern countries on transnational issues that have regional and global significance.

Conclusion

This book has focused on the extent to which Seoul has been able to exploit its economic and cultural capabilities in a traditional hub-and-spoke model of bilateral relations with select Middle Eastern countries. South Korea has cemented its foreign policy identity as a middle power in the region based on its geographic and demographic profile and economic, military, technological and diplomacy capacity, and national reputation. South Korea's industrialization narrative and its status as an emerging market and the world's sixth strongest military, and its policy of non-interference in the Middle East have made it an attractive partner for Middle Eastern countries seeking to diversify their diplomatic relations. South Korea's foreign policy identity as a middle power has bolstered its position in the Middle East. At the same time, it has been challenging for South Korea to pursue its national interests in the region while complying with U.S. demands. There has been a lack of institutional consistency in implementing a coherent Iran and Middle East policy. The post-2003 Iraq War has complicated matters by instigating a proxy war between Tehran and Washington. Therefore, South Korea's middle power diplomacy in the Middle Eastern context is primarily understood not in behavioral or normative terms but in ideational terms. Korea's functional role as a middle power on the other hand has been confined to contributing to post-war reconstruction efforts and providing noncombatant support to regional conflicts (i.e. 1991 Gulf War and 2003 Iraq War) but was not directly party to the conflict.

Notwithstanding that South Korea's multilateral activism lies beyond the scope of this book, South Korea's participation in regional initiatives with ASEAN countries and oil producers and oil importers in the APAC is a promising mechanism for reinvigorating South Korea's energy security strategy. International efforts to bolster multilateralism should be pursued in tandem with proactive foreign policy. At a national level, an exponential increase in initiating high-level meetings during the Roh Moo-hyun government laid the groundwork for promoting commercial diplomacy and Lee Myung-bak's nuclear and security cooperation with the UAE and Park Geun-hye's cultural diplomacy and creative economy initiatives have demonstrated South Korea's resolve for promoting commercial diplomacy. Yet at the same time, institutional constraints, which stem from inconsistent foreign policy under a presidential system and domestic politics, persist. B2B relations and multilateral G2G relations should complement bilateral G2G engagements in the region. As was the case with Iran, interparliamentary meetings and cultural and exchange diplomacy have offered alternative avenues for deepening bilateral relations as well as for resolving political conundrum. Exercising political and diplomatic tact and savviness is crucial for fostering relations with the Middle East. But more importantly, diplomatic engagements should extend beyond the traditional emphasis on economic cooperation and energy security by launching public diplomacy campaigns for engaging the broader Korean public and private entities on raising cultural awareness about the wider Middle East and the Islamic world.

Notes

1 Sook Jong Lee, "South Korea Aiming to be an Innovative Middle Power," in *Transforming Global Governance with Middle Power Diplomacy* (New York, NY: Palgrave Macmillan, 2016), 12.
2 Shin-wha Lee & Chun Young Park, "Korea's middle power diplomacy for human security: A global and regional approach," *Journal of International and Area Studies* 24 (1) (2017), 21.
3 Ralf Emmers & Sarah Teo, "Regional security strategies of middle powers in the Asia-Pacific," *International Relations of the Asia-Pacific* 15 (2) (2015), 189.
4 James Manicom & Jeffrey Reeves, "Locating middle powers in international relations theory and power transitions," in Bruce Gilley & Andrew O'Neil (Eds.) *Middle Powers and the Rise of China* (Washington DC: Georgetown University Press, 2014), 29; Cameron G. Thies & Agnguntari C. Sari, "A role theory approach to middle powers: Making sense of Indonesia's place in the international system," *Contemporary Southeast Asia* 40 (3) (2018), 401.
5 Andrew F. Cooper & Emel Parlar Dal, "Positioning the third wave of middle power diplomacy: Institutional elevation, practice limitations," *International Journal* 71 (4) (2017), 517.
6 David A. Cooper, "Challenging contemporary notions of middle power influence: Implications of the proliferation security initiative for Middle Power Theory," *Foreign Policy Analysis* 7 (3) (2011), 317–336; Lee & Park, "Korea's Middle Power Diplomacy," 25.
7 Cooper, "Challenging contemporary notions of middle power influence," 318.
8 Robert W. Cox, "Middlepowermanship Japan and future world order," *International Journal* XLIV (1989), 825–826.
9 Cooper, "Challenging contemporary notions of middle power influence," 319.
10 Young Jong Choi, "South Korea's regional strategy and middle power activism," *The Journal of East Asian Affairs* 23 (1) (2009), 50.
11 Emel Dalal Par & Ali Murat Kursun, "Assessing Turkey's middle power foreign policy in MIKTA," *International Journal* 71 (4) (2016), 617–624.
12 Evan H. Potter, "Niche diplomacy as Canadian foreign policy," *International Journal* 52 (1) (1996), 25–29.
13 Janis van der Westhuizen, "South Africa's emergence as a middle power," *Third World Quarterly* 19 (3) (1998), 436.
14 John W. Holmes, "Canada as a middle power," *The Centennial Review* 10 (4) (1966), 436.
15 Choi, "South Korea's regional strategy," 54.
16 Michael J. Green, "Korean middle power diplomacy and Asia's emerging multilateral architecture," *Center for Strategic and International Studies*, 2017, 24.
17 Lee & Park, "Korea's middle power diplomacy," 22.
18 Thomas S. Wilkins, "Australia: A traditional middle power faces the Asian century," in Bruce Gilley & Andrew O'Neil (Eds.), *Middle Powers and the Rise of China* (Washington DC, Georgetown University Press, 2014), 151.

188 *Conclusion*

19 TongFi Kim, "South Korea's middle power response to the rise of China," in Bruce Gilley & Andrew O'Neill (Eds.) *Middle Powers and the Rise of China* (Washington DC: Georgetown University Press, 2014), 84–103.
20 Kim, "South Korea's middle power response," 85.
21 Scott A. Snyder, *South Korea at the Crossroads* (New York, NY: Columbia University Press, 2018), 193.
22 Manicom & Reeves, "Locating middle powers in international relations theory," 24.
23 See U.S. Department of State, "Text of the Korean War Armistice Agreement," July 27, 1953.
24 Hyun-Wook Kim & Won K. Paik, "Alliance cohesion in the post-Cold War U.S.-South Korea security relations," *The Journal of East Asian Affairs* 23 (2) (2009), 18; Gi-Wook Shin, Hilary Izatt & Rennie J. Moon, "Asymmetry of power and attention in alliance politics: The U.S.-Republic of Korea case," *Australian Journal of International Affairs* 70 (3) (2016), 12, 17; Chae-Sung Chun, "Theoretical approaches to alliance: Implications on the ROK-U.S. alliance," *Journal of International and Area Studies* 7 (2) (2000), 81–85.
25 Emma Chanlett-Avery, Ian Rinehart & Mary Beth D. Nikitin, "North Korea: U.S. relations, nuclear diplomacy, and internal situation – CRS Report No. R41259, January 15, 2016," in Douglas C. Lovelace (Ed.) *Terrorism: Commentary on Security Documents: The North Korean Threat* Vol. 145 (New York, NY: Oxford University Press, 2017), 35.
26 Australia Department of Defence, "Australia in the Asian Century," October 2012, 6.
27 Ibid., 7.
28 Najmeh Bozorgmehr & Song Jung-a, "Iran's $7bn battle: Tanker seizer 'slap in the face' to South Korea," *Financial Times*, January 10, 2021, www.ft.com/content/3549c3bc-0c7a-4b17-b45d-5acd83aad176.
29 *Financial Tribune*, "Iran has no frozen assets in China," October 19, 2020, https://financialtribune.com/articles/national/105771/iran-has-no-frozen-assets-in-china.
30 Manicom & Reeves, "Locating middle powers in international relations theory," 30.
31 Ibid., 31.
32 Michael C. Hudson, "To play the hegemon: Fifty years of U.S. Policy toward the Middle East," *Middle East Journal* 50 (3) (1996), 229.
33 Charles Lee, "South Korea data: December U.S. crude import mark biggest drop of 67.9%," *S&P Global Platts*, January 18, 2021, www.spglobal.com/platts/en/market-insights/latest-news/oil/011821-south-korea-data-dec-us-crude-imports-mark-biggest-drop-of-679.
34 Brian Bridges, "South Korea and the Gulf crisis," *The Pacific Review* 5 (2) (1992), 141.
35 Hudson, "To play the hegemon," 337.
36 Hillary Clinton, "America's Pacific Century," *Foreign Policy*, October 11, 2011, https://foreignpolicy.com/2011/10/11/americas-pacific-century/.
37 Chris J. Dolan, *Obama and the Emergence of a Multipolar World Order: Redefining U.S. Foreign Policy* (Lanham, MD: Lexington Books, 2018), 143.
38 David Shambaugh, "Assessing the U.S. "Pivot" to Asia," *Strategic Studies Quarterly* 7 (2) (2013), 11.
39 Shambaugh, "Assessing the U.S. "Pivot" to Asia," 16; Robert S. Ross, "The problem with the pivot: Obama's new Asia policy is unnecessary and counterproductive," *Foreign Affairs* 91 (6) (2012), 78–79.

40 Robert J. Lieber, "Saudi Arabia and U.S. Middle East policy: The consequences of retrenchment," in *Saudi Arabia, the Gulf and the New Regional Landscape, Begin-Sadat Center for Strategic Studies* (2017), 47.
41 Janine Davidson, "The U.S. Pivot to Asia," *American Journal of Chinese Studies* 21 (2014), 79.
42 F. Gregory Gause, III "Donald Trump and the Middle East," in Robert Jervis, Francis J. Gavin, Joshua Rovner & Diane Labrosse (Eds.), *Chaos in the Liberal Order: The Trump Presidency and International Politics in the Twenty-First Century* (New York, NY: Columbia University Press, 2018), 273.
43 Gause, "Donald Trump and the Middle East," 7.
44 Stephen Wertheim, "Trump against exceptionalism: The sources of Trumpian conduct," in Robert Jervis, Francis J. Gavin, Joshua Rovner, Diane N. Labrosse & George Fujii (Eds.), *Chaos in the Liberal Order* (New York, NY: Columbia University Press, 2018), 129.
45 Jongryn Mo, "South Korea's middle power diplomacy," *International Journal* 71 (4) (2016), 593.
46 Saudi Ministry of Economy and Planning, "Saudi-Korean Vision 2030," 2017, 5.
47 Se Hyun Ahn, "Republic of Korea's energy security conundrum: The problems of energy mix and energy diplomacy deadlock," *Journal of International and Area Studies* 22 (2) (2015), 67.
48 Ahn, "Republic of Korea's energy security conundrum," 71.
49 Ibid; ROK Ministry of Trade, Industry & Energy, "Korea energy master plan: Outlook and policies to 2030," n.d., 110.
50 Deborah Bräutigam & Tang Xiaoyang, "Economic statecraft in China's new overseas economic zones: Soft power, business or resource security?" *International Affairs* 88 (4) (2012), 800–801.
51 William Nester & Kweku Ampiah, "Japan's oil diplomacy: Tatemae and Honne," *Third World Quarterly* 11 (1) (1989), 75.
52 Nester & Ampiah, "Japan's oil diplomacy," 72; Loftur Thorarinsson, "A review of the evolution of the Japanese oil industry, oil policy and its relationship with the Middle East," *Oxford Institute for Energy Studies*, 2018, 28.
53 Beeson & Higgott, "The changing architecture of politics," 221–225.
54 G20 Research Group, "G20 Saudi Arabia 2020 Riyadh Summit: Leaders' declaration," November 21, 2020.

References

Ahn, Se Hyun. "Republic of Korea's energy security conundrum: The problems of energy mix and energy diplomacy deadlock," *Journal of International and Area Studies* 22 (2) (2015), 67–87.
Australia Department of Defence. "Australia in the Asian century," October 2012.
Bozorgmehr, Najmeh and Song Jung-a. "Iran's $7bn battle: Tanker seizer 'slap in the face' to South Korea," *Financial Times*, January 10, 2021, www.ft.com/content/3549c3bc-0c7a-4b17-b45d-5acd83aad176.
Bräutigam, Deborah and Tang Xiaoyang. "Economic statecraft in China's new overseas economic zones: Soft power, business or resource security?" *International Affairs* 88 (4) (2012), 799–816, https://doi.org/10.1111/j.1468-2346.2012.01102.x.

Bridges, Brian. "South Korea and the Gulf crisis," *The Pacific Review* 5 (2) (1992), 141–48, https://doi.org/10.1080/09512749208718968.
Chanlett-Avery, Emma, Ian Rinehart and Mary Beth D. Nikitin. "North Korea: U.S. relations, nuclear diplomacy, and internal situation – CRS Report No. R41259, January 15, 2016," in Douglas C. Lovelace (Ed.), *Terrorism: Commentary on Security Documents: The North Korean Threat Vol. 145* (New York, NY: Oxford University Press, 2017), 24–56.
Choi, Young Jong. "South Korea's regional strategy and middle power activism," *The Journal of East Asian Affairs* 23 (1) (2009), 47–67.
Chun, Chae-Sung. "Theoretical approaches to alliance: Implications on the ROK-U.S. alliance," *Journal of International and Area Studies* 7 (2) (2000), 71–88.
Clinton, Hillary. "America's Pacific Century," *Foreign Policy*, October 11, 2011, https://foreignpolicy.com/2011/10/11/americas-pacific-century/.
Cooper, David A. "Challenging contemporary notions of middle power influence: Implications of the proliferation security initiative for Middle Power Theory," *Foreign Policy Analysis* 7 (3) (2011), 317–336.
Cooper, Andrew F. and Emel Parlar Dal. "Positioning the third wave of middle power diplomacy: Institutional elevation, practice limitations," *International Journal* 71 (4) (2017), 516–528, https://doi.org/10.1177/0020702016686385.
Cox, Robert W. "Middlepowermanship Japan and future world order," *International Journal* XLIV (1989), 823–862, https://doi.org/10.2307/40202638.
Davidson, Janine. "The U.S. Pivot to Asia," *American Journal of Chinese Studies* 21 (2014), 77–82.
Dolan, Chris J. *Obama and the Emergence of a Multipolar World Order: Redefining U.S. Foreign Policy* (Lanham, MD: Lexington Books, 2018).
Emmers, Ralf and Sarah Teo. "Regional security strategies of middle powers in the Asia-Pacific," *International Relations of the Asia-Pacific* 15 (2) (2015), 185–216, https://doi.org/10.1093/irap/lcu020.
Financial Tribune. "Iran has no frozen assets in China," October 19, 2020, https://financialtribune.com/articles/national/105771/iran-has-no-frozen-assets-in-china.
Gause, III, F. Gregory. "Donald Trump and the Middle East," in Robert Jervis, Francis J. Gavin, Joshua Rovner and Diane Labrosse (Eds.), *Chaos in the Liberal Order: The Trump Presidency and International Politics in the Twenty-First Century* (New York, NY: Columbia University Press, 2018), 273–286.
Green, Michael J. "Korean middle power diplomacy and Asia's emerging multilateral architecture," *Center for Strategic and International Studies*, 2017.
G20 Research Group. "G20 Saudi Arabia 2020 Riyadh Summit: Leaders' declaration," November 21, 2020.
Holmes, John W. "Canada as a middle power," *The Centennial Review* 10 (4) (1966), 430–445.
Hudson, Michael C. "To play the Hegemon: Fifty years of U.S. policy toward the Middle East," *Middle East Journal* 50 (3) (1996), 329–343.
Kim, Hyun-Wook and Won K. Paik. "Alliance cohesion in the post-cold war U.S.-South Korea security relations," *The Journal of East Asian Affairs* 23 (2) (2009), 1–40.
Kim, TongFi. "South Korea's middle power response to the rise of China," in Bruce Gilley and Andrew O'Neill (Eds.), *Middle Powers and the Rise of China* (Washington DC: Georgetown University Press, 2014), 84–103.

Lieber, Robert J. "Saudi Arabia and U.S. Middle East policy: The consequences of retrenchment," in Saudi Arabia, the Gulf and the New Regional Landscape, *Begin-Sadat Center for Strategic Studies* (2017).

Lee, Charles. "South Korea data: December U.S. crude import mark biggest drop of 67.9%," *S&P Global Platts*, January 18, 2021, www.spglobal.com/platts/en/market-insights/latest-news/oil/011821-south-korea-data-dec-us-crude-imports-mark-biggest-drop-of-679.

Lee, Shin-wha and Chun Young Park. "Korea's middle power diplomacy for human security: A global and regional approach," *Journal of International and Area Studies* 24 (1) (2017), 21–44.

Lee, Sook Jong. "South Korea aiming to be an innovative middle power," in *Transforming Global Governance with Middle Power Diplomacy* (New York, NY: Palgrave Macmillan, 2016).

Manicom, James and Jeffrey Reeves. "Locating middle powers in international relations theory and power transitions," in Bruce Gilley and Andrew O'Neil (Eds.), *Middle Powers and the Rise of China* (Washington DC.: Georgetown University Press, 2014), 23–44.

Mo, Jongryn. "South Korea's middle power diplomacy," *International Journal* 71 (4) (2016), 587–607, https://doi.org/10.1177/0020702016686380.

Nester, William and Kweku Ampiah. "Japan's oil diplomacy: Tatemae and Honne," *Third World Quarterly* 11 (1) (1989), 72–88, https://doi.org/10.1080/01436598908420140.

Par, Emel Dalal and Ali Murat Kursun. "Assessing Turkey's middle power foreign policy in MIKTA," *International Journal* 71 (4) (2016), 608–629, https://doi.org/10.1177/0020702016686382.

Potter, Evan H. "Niche diplomacy as Canadian foreign policy," *International Journal* 52 (1) (1996), 25–38, https://doi.org/10.2307/40203170.

ROK Ministry of Trade, Industry & Energy. "Korea energy master plan: Outlook and policies to 2030." n.d.

Ross, Robert S. "The problem with the pivot: Obama's new Asia policy is unnecessary and counterproductive," *Foreign Affairs* 91 (6) (2012), 70–82.

Saudi Ministry of Economy and Planning. "Saudi-Korean Vision 2030," 2017.

Shambaugh, David. "Assessing the U.S. "Pivot" to Asia," *Strategic Studies Quarterly* 7 (2) (2013), 10–19.

Shin, Gi-Wook, Hilary Izatt and Rennie J. Moon. "Asymmetry of power and attention in alliance politics: The U.S.-Republic of Korea Case," *Australian Journal of International Affairs* 70 (3) (2016), 235–255, https://doi.org/10.1080/10357718.2015.1113228.

Snyder, Scott A. *South Korea at the Crossroads* (New York, NY: Columbia University Press, 2018).

Thies, Cameron G. and Agnguntari C. Sari. "A role theory approach to middle powers: Making sense of Indonesia's place in the international system," *Contemporary Southeast Asia* 40 (3) (2018), 397–421.

Thorarinsson, Loftur. "A review of the evolution of the Japanese oil industry, oil policy and its relationship with the Middle East," *Oxford Institute for Energy Studies*, 2018.

US Department of State. "Text of the Korean War Armistice Agreement," July 27, 1953.

Wertheim, Stephen. "Trump against exceptionalism: The sources of Trumpian conduct," in Robert Jervis, Francis J. Gavin, Joshua Rovner, Diane N. Labrosse and George Fujii (Eds.), *Chaos in the Liberal Order* (New York, NY: Columbia University Press, 2018), 125–135.

Westhuizen, Janis van der. "South Africa's emergence as a middle power," *Third World Quarterly* 19 (3) (1998), 435–455.

Wilkins, Thomas S. "Australia: A traditional middle power faces the Asian century," in Bruce Gilley and Andrew O'Neil (Eds.), *Middle Powers and the Rise of China* (Washington DC.: Georgetown University Press, 2014), 149–170.

Index

Abu Dhabi Investment Authority 125
Abu Dhabi National Oil Company 112
Afghanistan 3, 13, 34, 41, 111, 117, 128, 181
Ahmadinejad, Mahmoud 37, 41
Akh unit 118, 124, 125
Algeria 10, 12, 67, 107
Algiers Agreement 32
Al Maliki, Nouri 36, 155, 157, 158
Al Mubarak, Khaldoon 95
Al Nahyan, Khalifa bin Zayed 115
Al Nahyan, Mohammed bin Zayed 125
Al Saud, Abdullah bin Abdulaziz 77, 78, 82
Al Saud, Alwaleed bin Talal bin Abdulaziz 70, 72, 75, 76, 78, 88, 90, 96
Al Saud, Faisal bin Abdulaziz 64, 68
Al Saud, Fahd bin Abdulaziz Al Saud 66, 74, 77, 81
Al Saud, Mohammed bin Salman 85, 91, 93
Anglo-Persian Oil Company 13
APR-1400 95, 121
Arab League 66, 126, 127
Asian Financial Crisis 19, 72, 75, 76
Axis of Evil 34, 35, 147, 181
Ayatollah Khomeini 12, 30, 35, 48

Baath 11, 14, 139, 142, 153
Baghdad Pact 65
balance diplomacy 91
Ban, Ki-moon 39, 42, 79, 162
Bank Mellat 44, 45, 46, 49
Barakah nuclear plant 95, 121, 123, 124
Biden, Joe 4, 185
big deal 112
burden-sharing 72, 110, 143, 182
Burj Khalifa 104, 114
Bush, George H.W. 108, 140, 143, 181

Bush, George W. 34, 35, 40, 42, 145, 148, 150, 181
business diplomacy 35, 63, 68, 75, 76, 81, 82, 89, 92, 97, 112, 113, 118

chaebol 8, 185
cheonghae unit 53, 54, 116, 118, 180
China 1, 3, 4, 17, 19, 36, 38, 41, 47, 49, 50, 73, 80, 82, 84, 85, 91, 93, 96, 107, 110, 117, 122, 143, 146, 178, 179, 180, 181, 184
Choi, Kyu-hah 28, 64, 65, 81, 82
cold war 1, 2, 3, 5, 16, 17, 18, 27, 28, 31, 54, 63, 64, 65, 67, 73, 105, 109, 110, 122, 140, 147, 175, 178, 181
cold war diplomacy 27
collaborative governance 79, 148
communism 63, 65, 66, 122, 180, 181
construction boom 30, 81, 112, 114, 120
core group 153
creative economy 63, 88, 89, 91, 185, 186
cultural diplomacy 54, 126, 186

Daiman unit 79, 118, 148
Davos Forum 87, 89
Daewoo 46, 47, 72, 78, 112, 124, 145
Dayyani, Mohammad Reza 44, 46, 47
denuclearization 34, 38, 48, 88, 183
desalination plant 74, 89, 112
developmental state 5
Dubai boom 113
Dubai Port International 114
Dubai Port World 115
Dubai Techno Park 119, 120

economic diversification 77, 89, 91, 104, 113, 120, 128, 183

Egypt 1, 2, 10, 11, 12, 36, 49, 65, 73, 79, 82, 107, 108, 142, 145, 147, 150, 159
electric vehicles 94, 96
embargo 19, 26, 28, 30, 38, 64, 68, 109, 137, 139, 143, 184
energy security 2, 18, 72, 83, 116, 126, 128, 137, 141, 156, 157, 158, 159, 179, 180, 181, 184, 186
engineering, procurement, and construction 32, 33, 34, 50, 81, 86, 88, 93, 94, 95, 121, 122, 123,124, 180, 185
entekhab industrial group 46, 47
Erbil 148, 150, 151, 152, 153, 156, 159

foreign direct investment 10, 32, 72, 81, 106, 183
fourth industrial revolution 93

G20 16, 86, 91, 176, 177, 178, 185
Geneva Agreement 43, 52
Global Financial Crisis 115, 119, 120, 142
globalization 6, 17, 114, 178
Gulf Cooperation Council 1, 14, 16, 65, 69, 80, 81, 82, 84, 85, 92, 97, 111, 116, 123
Gulf of Aden 53, 116, 117, 118, 128
Gulf of Oman 53, 110, 111
Gulf War vii, 19, 72, 73, 74, 75, 107, 109, 111, 128, 137, 138, 139, 140, 141, 142, 143, 144, 146, 147, 148, 151, 179, 180, 181, 186
GS Energy 126

halal 126, 127, 129
hallyu 27, 42, 126, 127
heavy and chemical industry drive 105, 108, 128
hostage crisis 31, 138
Houthi 117
Hussein, Saddam 14, 79, 85, 139, 142, 143, 144, 148, 149, 150, 157, 159
Hyundai Engineering & Construction 33, 34, 76, 84, 86, 112, 114, 119, 124, 137, 139, 141, 153
Hyundai Motors 34, 76, 78

India 40, 41, 50, 79, 106, 107, 110, 113, 115, 116, 128, 176
Indian Ocean ii, 106, 116, 128
innovation 8, 9, 10, 16, 50, 84, 89, 92, 119, 120, 128

inter-Korean relations 34, 37, 40
International Atomic Energy Agency 39, 40, 41, 51, 122, 146, 147
International Monetary Fund 9, 76, 77
interparliamentary exchanges 29, 43, 44, 54, 187
Israel 1, 7, 11, 12, 36, 38, 40, 43, 64, 65, 66, 67, 73, 113, 180
Iranian Central Bank 44, 46, 52, 54
Iranian revolution 26, 27, 28, 30, 31, 38, 41, 54, 106
Iran-Iraq war 2, 18, 19, 26, 27, 31, 32, 33, 36, 68, 69, 106, 137, 139, 145
2003 Iraq War 3, 19, 111, 128, 137, 148, 149, 150, 152, 153, 163, 164, 177, 179, 180, 181, 183, 186
Iraqi Federal Government 19, 117, 137, 154, 159, 164
Islamic revolution 27, 29, 31, 47
Islamic revolutionary guard corps 38, 44, 51, 52, 54
Islamic State of Iraq and the Levant vii, 137, 142, 149, 154, 160, 162, 163

Japan 1, 3, 4, 5, 7, 8, 18, 38, 45, 47, 49, 50, 53, 64, 67, 68, 69, 72, 75, 80, 82, 84, 85, 93, 95, 107, 111, 114, 120, 123, 125, 140, 145, 147, 151, 153, 178, 180, 184
Jema unit 79, 80, 148
Joint Comprehensive Plan of Action vii, 26, 27, 37, 47, 48, 49, 50, 52, 54, 183
Jordan 1, 2, 10, 11, 12, 34, 65, 73, 77, 79, 80, 82, 93, 108, 119, 122, 141, 142, 159

KhalifaSat 120
Khatami, Mohammad 33, 39
Kingdom Holding Company 76, 88, 96
Kim, Dae-jung 34, 73, 77, 78, 112, 147, 176
Kim, Jong-pil 64, 66, 68, 78
Kim, Sun-il 151, 164
Kim, Young-sam 36, 77, 178
knowledge-based economy 9, 83, 96, 120
King Abdullah City for Atomic and Renewable Energy 88, 94, 96
Korea Advanced Institute of Science and Technology 94, 121
Korea Atomic Energy Research Institute 40, 94, 96
Korea-Arab Society 84, 93, 126, 177
Korea Central Bank 44
Korea Development Institute 71

Korea Electric Power Corporation 94, 95, 121, 122, 123, 124, 185
Korea eximbank 34, 38, 44, 81, 84, 95
Korea Gas Corporation 152, 155, 156, 157, 160, 185
Korea-GCC FTA 81, 82
Korea Heavy Industries 70, 74, 112
Korea Hydro & Nuclear Power 94, 95, 121, 123, 124, 156
Korea International Cooperation Agency 153, 159
Korea National Oil Corporation 125, 126, 154, 156, 157, 185
Korean Peninsula 1, 3, 29, 30, 31, 35, 36, 37, 43, 47, 48, 55, 65, 76, 80, 88, 108, 111, 128, 143, 144, 148, 149, 179, 183
Korea Trade-Investment Promotion Agency 45, 51, 84, 92, 124, 144, 145, 153, 185
Korean Cultural Center 49, 126
Korean Peninsula Energy Development Center 111
Korean War 1, 3, 4, 8, 73, 80, 105, 128, 140, 141, 178
Kurdistan Democratic Party 138
Kurdistan Regional Government 19, 137, 150, 153, 154
Kuwait 1, 2, 11, 13, 30, 35, 42, 67, 72, 75, 82, 88, 107, 108, 109, 113, 114, 118, 137, 139, 140, 141, 142, 143, 148, 155, 161, 175, 184

Lee, Myung-bak 35, 43, 50, 69, 84, 85, 86, 87, 91, 97, 115, 118, 119, 121, 129, 154, 155, 156, 158, 159, 177, 178, 184
Libya 1, 2, 3, 11, 34, 36, 39, 67, 75, 107, 125, 142, 181

maximum pressure campaign 4, 50, 54, 55, 182, 183
medical tourism 126, 127
Middle East Respiratory Syndrome 71
Miracle on the Han River 4, 6, 7, 17, 63, 120, 183
Miracle of the desert 116, 120, 128
Mohammed bin Rashid Space Centre 120
Mohammad Reza Shah 27, 28, 29, 47
Moon, Jae-in 53, 92, 94, 95, 122, 125, 129
Mosul 160, 161, 162

National Iranian Oil Company 30
Nawah Energy Company 124

newly industrialized countries 4
Nasser, Gamal Abdel 2, 11, 12, 54, 93
non-aligned movement 2, 31
non-oil sectors 45, 63, 80, 81, 82, 96, 97
North Korea 1, 2, 3, 8, 18, 26, 28, 31, 34, 35, 36, 37, 38, 39, 40, 41, 42, 48, 53, 54, 55, 64, 65, 66, 108, 110, 111, 116, 117, 144, 145, 146, 147, 148, 149, 150, 151, 162, 178, 179, 181, 183
nuclear energy cooperation 49, 94, 96, 104, 118, 122, 123
nuclear nonproliferation treaty 35, 38, 39, 40
nuclear phase-out 92, 94, 95, 97, 122, 123, 124, 129
nuclear power plant 49, 85, 88, 92, 93, 94, 95, 96, 121, 122, 123, 124

Obama, Barack 3, 4, 34, 37, 42, 45, 152, 161, 162, 181, 182, 183
oil crisis 32, 67, 83
oil shock 28, 50, 73, 107, 143
Operation Desert Storm 74, 146

Palestinian Liberation Organization 66
Pakistan 36, 49, 65, 113, 117
Park, Chung-hee 8, 27, 30, 31, 47, 64, 65, 88, 105, 107, 112, 122, 128, 176
Park, Geun-hye 18, 27, 47, 49, 54, 71, 88, 91, 97, 126, 129, 159, 162, 182, 185, 186
people-to-people connectivity 48, 76, 116, 127, 129
people's diplomacy 35, 63, 81, 96
piracy 17, 53, 116, 117, 118, 125, 128, 138, 180
pivot to Asia 3, 29, 41, 67, 69, 180, 181, 182, 183
Port Rashid 106, 107
post-war reconstruction 19, 32, 33, 108, 109, 138, 148, 149, 152, 153, 155, 158, 164, 175, 186
public-private partnerships 9, 34, 51, 68, 85, 95, 159
Pyongyang 1, 2, 26, 28, 31, 33, 34, 36, 37, 39, 40, 48, 66, 67, 111, 117, 144, 145, 146, 147, 149, 180, 182, 183

Qaddafi, Muammar 39, 40, 142
Qatar 1, 2, 11, 16, 37, 73, 75, 82, 88, 108, 114, 127, 161

rafiq 88, 89, 91
Red Sea 106, 117

renewable energy 49, 88, 92, 94, 96, 120, 122
rentier effect 13, 14, 16
rentier state 13, 14, 15, 16, 18
resource diplomacy 18, 19, 75, 81, 84, 85, 87, 114, 118, 126, 154, 179, 183, 184, 185, 186
Rhee, Syngman 1, 8, 122
Rice, Condoleezza 82
robot diplomacy 93
rogue regime 37, 146, 147, 149
Roh, Moo-hyun 16, 42, 53, 79, 82, 97, 113, 115, 118, 128, 149, 177, 178, 183, 186
Roh, Tae-woo 74, 119
ROKS Cheonan 3, 37, 38
Rouhani, Hassan 38, 42, 43, 47, 48

SABIC 84, 92
sales diplomacy 81, 88, 91, 95, 97, 114
Samsung C&T 104, 114
Samsung Engineering 124
Samsung Electronics 34, 80, 93
sanctions 26, 27, 31, 33, 37, 38, 43, 44, 45, 46, 47, 48, 50, 51, 52, 54, 55, 72, 73, 87, 91, 108, 117, 126, 139, 140, 142, 144, 145, 146, 161, 177, 180, 183
Saudi Aramco 30, 51, 63, 73, 74, 76, 77, 85, 90, 91, 92, 93, 96
saemaeul undong 29, 88
Saudi-Korea Vision 2030 vii, 19, 63, 91, 93, 94, 96
second middle east boom 32, 33, 158, 162
second oil boom 48, 86, 88, 92, 97
security cooperation ii, vii, 4, 104, 113, 115, 118, 125, 126, 128, 160, 176, 186
Seohee unit 79, 80, 148
Seoul park 27, 49
Seoul National University Hospital 70, 71, 127
Sheikh Khalifa Specialty Hospital 71, 127
shipbuilding 34, 88, 91, 180
Shuaiba power and desalination plant 74
SK Energy 76, 154
six-party talks 80, 148, 151
small and medium enterprises 45, 48, 83, 92, 97, 113
S-Oil 30, 76, 77, 85, 90, 97
Soleimani, Qasem 26, 51, 52, 163, 183

south pars gas field 34, 37, 39, 45
sovereign diplomacy 80, 83
sports diplomacy 28, 127
Ssangyong oil company 30, 73, 76
Ssangyong Motors 79
state-business relations 5, 8, 9, 15, 19, 63, 114
Strait of Hormuz 31, 32, 41, 43, 51, 52, 53, 54, 68, 106, 108, 111, 141, 180, 182
sunshine policy 34, 77, 112, 147
System-Integrated Modular Advanced Reactor (SMART) 88, 92, 94, 95, 96

Talabani, Jalal 154, 155
Taliban 41, 42, 117
Team Korea 124
Tehran vii, 18, 26, 27, 28, 29, 30, 31, 33, 34, 35, 36, 37, 39, 41, 43, 46, 47, 48, 49, 50, 51, 52, 53, 54, 91, 179, 180, 182, 185, 186
Tehran street 26, 49
Trump, Donald 2, 3, 4, 18, 27, 50, 52, 54, 55, 110, 163, 177, 182, 183, 185

UAE Centennial 2071 120
UAE Vision 2021 120
UN Security Council 37, 45, 139
universal globalism 77
urbanization 118, 120
uranium enrichment 36, 38, 40, 41, 42, 43
U.S. invasion of Iraq 79, 80, 144, 148, 150, 152

velayat e-faqih 30, 41
Vietnam War 29, 67, 70, 79, 140, 181

Washington 12, 16, 37, 40, 52, 53, 66, 89, 97, 140, 144, 148, 149, 153, 178, 179, 180, 186
Weapons of Mass Destruction 33, 36, 40, 43, 44, 146, 147, 148, 149, 150
Westinghouse 121
White Revolution 12, 29

Yemen 1, 11, 12, 42, 73, 75, 105, 106, 107, 110, 111, 116, 117, 118, 142, 152, 181

Zarif, Mohammad Javad 51, 52
Zaytun unit 80, 118, 148, 150, 151, 152, 153, 155, 156, 159

Printed in the United States
by Baker & Taylor Publisher Services